Risk Intelligence

ALSO BY DYLAN EVANS

Placebo: Mind over Matter in Modern Medicine

Emotion: The Science of Sentiment

Introducing Evolutionary Psychology

Introducing Evolution

An Introductory Dictionary of Lacanian Psychoanalysis

Risk
Intelligence

How to Live with Uncertainty

DYLAN EVANS

Atlantic Books
London

First published in the United States in 2012 by Free Press, a
division of Simon & Schuster Inc., New York.

First published in Great Britain in 2012 by Atlantic Books,
an imprint of Atlantic Books Ltd.

This edition published in Great Britain in 2013 by Atlantic Books.

10 9 8 7 6 5 4 3 2 1

A CIP catalogue record for this book is available from
the British Library.

Paperback ISBN: 978 1 84887 739 9
E-book ISBN: 978 0 85789 926 2

Printed and bound by CPI Group (UK) Ltd, Croydon, CR0 4YY

Atlantic Books
An Imprint of Atlantic Books Ltd
Ormond House
26–27 Boswell Street
London
WC1N 3JZ

www.atlantic-books.co.uk

To Louise, who took the risk of marrying me

CONTENTS

Risk Intelligence

CHAPTER 1

Why Risk Intelligence Matters

He who knows best,
best knows how little he knows.
—THOMAS JEFFERSON

Kathryn, who is a detective, is good at spotting lies. While her colleagues seem to see them everywhere, she is more circumspect. When she's interviewing a suspect, she doesn't jump to conclusions. Instead she patiently looks for the telltale signs that suggest dishonesty. Even so, she is rarely 100 percent sure that she's spotted a lie; it's more often a question of tilting the scales one way or another, she says.

Jamie is viewed as a bit of an oddball at the investment bank where he works. When everyone else is sure that prices will continue to go up, Jamie is often more skeptical. On the other hand, there are times when everyone else is pessimistic but Jamie is feeling quite bullish. Jamie and his colleagues are not always at odds, but when they disagree it tends to be Jamie who is right.

Diane is overjoyed about her new relationship. When she phones her best friend, Evelyn, to tell her all about the new man in her life, Evelyn urges caution. "What's the chance that you'll still be with this guy in twelve months?" she asks, as she has done before. Diane's reply is just as predictable. "Oh, ninety, maybe ninety-five percent," she replies, as she always does. "I'm sure Danny is the one!" Two months later, she's broken up again.

Jeff has just been promoted to the rank of captain in the US Army. Since he is new to the role, he often feels unsure of his decisions and seeks out his colonel for a second opinion. The colonel is beginning to get rather tired of Jeff's pestering him, and has taken to playing a little game. Whenever Jeff asks his opinion, he responds by asking how confident Jeff is of his own hunch. Usually Jeff replies that he's only about 40 or 50 percent sure. But nine times of out ten, the colonel agrees with Jeff's opinion.

These four people display different degrees of risk intelligence. Kathryn and Jamie have high risk intelligence, while Diane and Jeff are at the other end of the spectrum. What exactly do I mean by risk intelligence? Most simply put, it is the ability to estimate probabilities accurately, whether the probabilities of various events occurring in our lives, such as a car accident, or the likelihood that some piece of information we've just come across is actually true, such as a rumor about a takeover bid. Or perhaps we have to judge whether a defendant in a murder trial is guilty, or must decide whether it's safe to take a trip to a country that's been put on a watch list. We often have to make educated guesses about such things, but fifty years of research in the psychology of judgment and decision making show that most people are not very good at doing so. Many people, for example, tend to overestimate their chances of winning the lottery, while they underestimate the probability that they will get divorced.

At the heart of risk intelligence lies the ability to gauge the limits of your own knowledge—to be cautious when you don't know much, and to be confident when, by contrast, you know a lot. People with high risk intelligence tend to be on the button in doing this. Kathryn and Jamie, for example, are relatively risk intelligent because they know pretty well how much they know and have just the right level of confidence in their judgments. Diane and Jeff are much less proficient, though in different ways; while Diane is overconfident, Jeff is underconfident.

This is a book about why so many of us are so bad at estimating probabilities and how we can become better at it. This is a vital skill to develop, as our ability to cope with uncertainty is one of the most important requirements for success in life, yet also one of the most neglected. We may not appreciate just how often we're required to exercise it, and how much impact our ability to do so can have on our lives, and even on the whole of society. Consider these examples, from the relatively mundane to the life-threatening:

- You are buying a new 42-inch HDTV, and a sales assistant asks if you would also like to purchase an extended warranty. He explains that if anything goes wrong with your TV in the next three years, the warranty will entitle you to swap it for a brand-new one, no questions asked. When deciding whether or not to purchase the extended warranty, you should consider the price of the TV, the price of the warranty, and the probability that the TV will indeed go wrong in the next three years. But what's the chance that this will actually happen? Here's where your risk intelligence comes in.

- A bank manager is explaining to you the various options available for investing a windfall that has just come your way. Riskier investment funds pay more interest, but there's also a higher chance of making a loss. How much of your money should you allocate to the high-risk funds and how much to the low-risk ones? It's partly a question of risk appetite, but you also need to know more about *how much* riskier the high-risk funds are. Are they 2 percent or 10 percent riskier? You need, in other words, to put a number on it.

- Doctors have discovered a tumor in your breast. Luckily, it is not malignant. It will not spread to the rest of your body, and there is no need to remove your breast. But there is a chance that it may recur and become malignant at some time in the future, and it might then spread quickly. In order to prevent this possibility, the doctor suggests that you do, after all, consider having your breast removed. It's a terrible dilemma; clearly you don't want the cancer to recur, but it seems a trag-

3

edy to remove a healthy breast. How high would the chance of recurrence have to be before you decided to have the breast removed?

When making evaluations in situations of uncertainty, people often make very poor probability estimates and may even ignore probabilities altogether, with sometimes devastating consequences. The decisions that we face, both individually and as a society, are only becoming more daunting. The following cases further illustrate how important it is that we learn to develop our risk intelligence.

THE *CSI* EFFECT

The television drama *CSI: Crime Scene Investigation* is hugely popular. In 2002, it was the most watched show on American television, and by 2009 the worldwide audience was estimated to be more than 73 million. It isn't, however, such a hit with police officers and district attorneys, who have criticized the series for presenting a highly misleading image of how crimes are solved. Their fears have been echoed by Monica Robbers, a criminologist, who found evidence that jurors have increasingly unrealistic expectations of forensic evidence. Bernard Knight, formerly one of Britain's chief pathologists, agrees. Jurors today, he observes, expect more categorical proof than forensic science is capable of delivering. And he attributes this trend directly to the influence of television crime dramas.

Science rarely proves anything conclusively. Rather, it gradually accumulates evidence that makes it more or less likely that a hypothesis is true. Yet in *CSI* and other shows like it, the evidence is often portrayed as decisive. When those who have watched such shows then serve on juries, the evidence in real-life court cases can appear rather disappointing by contrast. Even when high-quality DNA evidence is available, the expert witnesses who present such evidence in court point out that they are still dealing only in probabilities. When the jurors contrast this with the certainties of television, where a match between a trace of DNA found at a crime scene and that of the suspect may be unequivocal, they can be less willing to convict than in the past.

The phenomenon has even been given a name: "the *CSI* effect." In 2010, a study published in *Forensic Science International* found that prosecutors now have to spend time explaining to juries that investigators often fail to find evidence at a crime scene and hence that its absence in court is not conclusive proof of the defendant's innocence. They have even introduced a new kind of witness to make this point—a so-called negative evidence witness.

Unrealistic expectations about the strength of forensic evidence did not begin with *CSI*, of course. Fingerprints led to the same problem; they have been treated by the courts as conclusive evidence for a hundred years. In 1892, Charles Darwin's cousin Francis Galton calculated that the chance of two different individuals having the same fingerprints was about 1 in 64 billion, and fingerprint evidence has been treated as virtually infallible ever since, which means that a single incriminating fingerprint can still send someone to jail. But, like DNA evidence, even the best fingerprints are imperfect. After a mark is found at a crime scene, it must be compared to a reference fingerprint, or "exemplar," retrieved from police files or taken from a suspect. But no reproduction is perfect; small variations creep in when a finger is inked or scanned to create an exemplar.

More important, fingerprint analysis is a fundamentally subjective process; when identifying distorted prints, examiners must choose which features to highlight, and even highly trained experts can be swayed by outside information. Yet the subjective nature of this process is rarely highlighted during court cases and is badly understood by most jurors. Christophe Champod, an expert in forensic identification at the University of Lausanne in Switzerland, thinks the language of certainty that examiners are forced to use hides the element of subjective judgment from the court. He proposes that fingerprint evidence be presented in probabilistic terms and that examiners should be free to talk about probable or possible matches. In a criminal case, for example, an examiner could testify that there was a 95 percent chance of a match if the defender left the mark but a one-in-a-billion chance of a match if someone else left it. "Once certainty is quantified," says Champod, "it becomes transparent." Certainty may not seem like the kind of thing that *can* be quantified, but this is exactly what numerical probabilities are designed to do. By expressing chance in terms of numbers—by saying, for example, that there is a 95 percent chance that a fingerprint was left by a particular suspect—the strength of the evidence becomes much clearer and easier to comprehend. Even with a probability of 95 percent it is clear that there is still a one-in-twenty chance that the mark came from someone else.

The tendency to consider fingerprint evidence as more conclusive than it is can have tragic consequences. Take the case of Shirley McKie, a successful Scottish policewoman who was accused of leaving her fingerprint at a crime scene and lying about it. In 1997, McKie was part of a police team investigating the vicious murder of Marion Ross in Kilmarnock, Scotland. After the thumbprint of a local builder was found on a gift tag in the victim's home, he was accused of the murder. When the murdered woman's fingerprints were found on a cookie tin stuffed with banknotes, which McKie discovered when searching the builder's bedroom, it looked like an open-and-shut case. At the time, fingerprints were the gold standard of forensic evidence, and even a single print was sufficient to secure a conviction. Moreover, in the ninety-two years since Scotland Yard had first used them to prove a murderer's guilt, their veracity had never been successfully challenged in a Scottish court.

Then the forensic team discovered something else. They identified a thumbprint on the bathroom door frame at the victim's house as belonging to Shirley McKie. This was a serious matter, as McKie had never been granted permission to enter the dead woman's bungalow, which had been sealed off. If she was thought to have crossed the cordon and contaminated vital forensic evidence, she would face disciplinary action. But McKie knew she had never set foot inside the crime scene, so the match between her print and the mark on the bathroom door frame could only be a mistake. Could it have been mislabeled by the fingerprint experts?

The Scottish Criminal Record Office (SCRO) refused even to contemplate the possibility. Not only would it undermine its case against the builder they suspected of murdering Marion Ross, but it might also wreck the Lockerbie trial—conducted in The Hague under Scottish jurisdiction—of two Libyans accused of blowing up a Boeing 747 while en route from London to New York in December 1988. The case against one of the Libyan suspects involved a contentious fingerprint found on a travel document, and several senior figures involved in the Lockerbie trial were also involved in the Marion Ross investigation. If the work of those experts was revealed to be so seriously flawed that they could not even accurately match a blameless policewoman's prints, both cases could fall flat. According to Pan Am's senior Lockerbie investigator, the FBI was so concerned that the case against the two Libyans might be undermined by the McKie debacle that they put pressure on the Scottish team to interfere with the evidence against her.

Since McKie had stated at the murder trial that she had never been in the victim's house, she was charged with perjury. Arrested in an early-morning raid, she was taken to the local police station (where her father had been a commanding officer), marched past colleagues and friends, strip-searched, and thrown in a cell. Luckily, two US fingerprint experts came to McKie's rescue. Pat Wertheim and David Grieve spent hours comparing the fingerprint on the door frame with an imprint of McKie's left thumb and concluded that they belonged to different people. Moreover, they became convinced that the misidentification of the two marks could not have been an honest mistake. "Shirley's thumbprint appears to have been smudged to mask the differences with the mark on the frame," Wertheim noted. That clinched it; the jury acquitted McKie of perjury in May 1999, saving her from a possible eight-year jail sentence. Effectively they saved her life, since McKie later admitted that she could not have faced prison knowing she was innocent.

As she left the court, McKie thought she would receive a formal apology and be invited to return to the job she loved. Instead, she was deemed medically unfit for service and forced into a long legal battle with the police. Although she was eventually awarded £750,000 in compensation, the SCRO never admitted it was wrong, and nobody ever offered her an apology.

HOMELAND SECURITY

Of the many new security measures introduced in the wake of the terrorist attacks of September 11, 2001, few have caused more irritation than those implemented at airports.

Two days after the attacks, the Federal Aviation Administration (FAA) promulgated new rules prohibiting any type of knife in secured airport areas and on airplanes. The hijackers had been able to carry box cutters through security because at the time any knife with a blade up to four inches long was permitted on US domestic flights. In November 2001, all airport screening in the United States was transferred from private companies to the newly created Transportation Security Administration (TSA). Since then, every new terrorist plot adds further checks to the gauntlet that passengers must run.

After the "shoe bomber" Richard Reid failed in his attempt to blow up a commercial aircraft in flight, all airline passengers departing from an airport in the United States were made to walk through airport security in socks or bare feet while their shoes were scanned for bombs. After British police foiled a plot to detonate liquid explosives on board airliners in 2006, passengers at UK airports were not allowed to take liquids on board, and laptop computers were banned. The restrictions were gradually relaxed in the following weeks, but the ability of passengers to carry liquids onto commercial aircraft is still limited. The attempted bombing of Northwest Airlines Flight 253 on Christmas Day 2009, in which a passenger tried to set off plastic explosives sewn to his underwear, led the US government to announce plans to spend about $1 billion on full-body scanners and other security technology such as bomb detectors.

While for many passengers, waiting in line and taking off their shoes are necessary evils (a poll conducted by Rasmussen Reports shortly after the failed bombing attempt on Flight 253 found that 63 percent of Americans felt security precautions put in place since 9/11 were "not too much of a hassle"), many others disagree. Martin Broughton, the chairman of British Airways, probably spoke for many when, at a meeting for airport operators in October 2010, he described the security procedures as "completely redundant" and called for them to be ditched. The security expert Bruce Schneier has dubbed many of the measures "security theater" on the grounds that they serve merely to create an appearance that the authorities are doing something but do nothing to reduce the actual risk of a terrorist attack. Indeed, it is intelligence tip-offs, not airport checkpoints, that have foiled the vast majority of attempted attacks on aircraft.

Schneier may be right that many of the new airport security procedures are purely theatrical, but that begs the question as to *why* they are such good theater. In other words, it is not enough to point out the mismatch between *feeling* safe and *being* safe; if we want to understand this blind spot in our risk intelligence, we need to know *why* things such as taking one's shoes off and walking through a body scanner are so effective in creating such (objectively unreliable) feelings of safety. It probably has something to do with their visibility; intelligence gathering may be more effective at reducing the risk of a terrorist attack, but it is by its very nature invisible to the general public. The illusion of control may be another factor; when we do something active such as taking our shoes off, we tend to feel more in control of the situation, but when we sit back and let others (such as spies gathering intelligence) do all the work, we feel passive and impotent. Maybe there's a ritual aspect here, too, as in the joke "Something must be done. This is something. Therefore, we must do it." The default assumption is that the "something" is good, and we feel better. Psychologists have long known that the illusion of control is a key factor in risk perception; it is probably one of the main reasons why people feel safer driving than when flying, even though driving is more dangerous.

Politicians have an obvious incentive to put on this security theater; they get credit for taking visible action. A little reflection, however, should make clear that not everyone is equally likely to be carrying a bomb. The International Air Transport Association (IATA), the air transport industry's trade body, has argued for a more selective approach by, for example, prescreening passengers before they turn up at the airport and flagging the more suspicious ones for a more thorough pat-down. Better training of airport screeners could also help them improve their ability to spot suspicious behavior.

Now consider the costs. To gauge the true cost of screening passengers at airports in the United States, it is not enough to look at the TSA's operating budget; we should also take into account the extra time passengers have spent waiting in line, taking their shoes off, and so on. Robert Poole, a member of the National Aviation Studies Advisory Panel in the Government Accountability Office, has calculated that the additional time spent waiting at airports since 9/11 has cost the nation about $8 billion a year. It is by no means clear that this was the wisest use of the security budget. Every dollar spent on one security measure is a dollar that can't be spent on an alternative one.

The costs of the new security procedures do not end there. Long lines at airports have prompted more people to drive rather than fly, and that has cost lives because driving is so much more dangerous than flying. The economist Garrick Blalock estimated that from September 2001 to October 2003, enhanced airport security measures led to 2,300 more road fatalities than would otherwise have occurred. Those deaths represent a victory for Al Qaeda.

One of the principal goals of terrorism is to provoke overreactions that damage the target far more than the terrorist acts themselves, but such knee-jerk responses also depend on our unwillingness to think things through carefully. As long as we react fearfully to each new mode of attack, democratic governments are likely to continue to implement security theater to appease our fears. Indeed, this is the Achilles' heel of democracy that terrorists exploit. One thing we could all do to help combat terrorism is to protect this Achilles' heel by developing our risk intelligence.

GLOBAL WARMING AND CLIMATE CHANGE

High levels of risk intelligence will be required to deal not just with the threat of international terrorism but also with other big challenges that humanity faces in the twenty-first century. Climate change is a particularly vexing case in point. Nobody knows precisely how increasing levels of greenhouse gases in the atmosphere will affect the climate in various regions around the globe. The Intergovernmental Panel on Climate Change (IPCC) does not make definite predictions; instead, it sets out a variety of possible scenarios and attaches various probabilities to them to indicate the level of uncertainty associated with each.

Knowing how to make sense of this information is crucial if we are to allocate resources sensibly to the various solutions, from carbon-trading schemes to the development of alternative energy sources or planetary-scale geoengineering. But how can citizens make informed decisions about such matters if they are not equipped to think clearly about risk and uncertainty?

One problem is that too often, the pundits who take opposing views about climate change make exaggerated claims that convey greater certainty than is warranted by the evidence. Rarely do we hear them quote probabilities; rather, critics dismiss the IPCC's claims out of hand, while believers in climate change paint vivid pictures of ecological catastrophes. Both kinds of exaggeration seriously hamper informed debate; the latter also terrifies kids. One survey of five hundred American preteens found that one in three children between the ages of six and eleven feared that the earth would not exist when they reached adulthood because of global warming and other environmental threats. Another survey, this one in the United Kingdom, showed that half of young children between ages seven and eleven are anxious about the effects of global warming, often losing sleep because of their concern. Without the tools to understand the uncertainty surrounding the future of our climate, we are left with a choice between two equally inadequate alternatives: ignorant bliss or fearful overreaction.

Some environmentalists have attempted to dress up the second alternative in fancy theoretical clothing. The so-called precautionary principle states that new policies or technologies should be heavily regulated or even prohibited whenever there is a possible risk to the environment or human health. This principle may appear sensible at first glance, but scratch the surface and it turns out to be terribly misguided. To be fair, it should be noted that there are many alternative versions of the precautionary principle, and some of them are less stupid than others. But the common theme that links all of the versions together is an overemphasis on downside risks and a corresponding neglect of the benefits of new technologies (the "upside risks").

The precautionary principle is most often applied to the impact of human actions on the environment and human health and in the context of new technological developments. According to stronger versions of the principle, risky policies and technologies should be regulated or even prohibited, even if the evidence for such risks is weak and even if the economic costs of regulation are high. In 1982, the UN World Charter for Nature gave the first international recognition to a strong version of the principle, suggesting that when "potential adverse effects are not fully understood, the activities should not proceed."

That sets the bar way too high. The potential adverse effects of any new technology are *never* fully understood. Nor are the potential benefits, for that matter, or the costs of regulation. Advocates of the precautionary principle often make no attempt to estimate the probabilities of the alleged dangers, on the grounds that they are "unknowable." But that just shows a deep misunderstanding of what probabilities are. Probabilities are an *expression* of our ignorance; by quantifying uncertainty, we are already conceding that we don't "know" the relevant facts with 100 percent certainty and admitting that we have to work on the basis of educated guesses. It is much better to reason on the basis of such guesses than to neglect probabilities altogether.

At first blush, the precautionary principle may not seem relevant to climate change, since few people doubt that our planet is getting warmer and that the chief cause of this is the burning of fossil fuels. It is a near certainty that the global climate will change. The polar ice caps will melt, and the sea will rise and flood a great deal of land that is now inhabited. There is, however, much debate about the extent of the danger. The precautionary principle suggests that this uncertainty is in itself good reason to take aggressive action. The planet is at risk, the argument goes, so it would be prudent to take bold steps immediately. Isn't it better to be safe than sorry?

Not necessarily, argues Cass Sunstein, a legal scholar who was appointed to head the Office of Information and Regulatory Affairs in 2009. Sunstein points out that there are always risks on both sides of a decision; inaction can bring danger, but so can action. Precautions themselves, in other words, create risks. No choice is risk free.

A high tax on carbon emissions, for example, would increase the hardship on people who can least afford it and probably lead to greater unemployment and hence poverty. A sensible climate change policy must balance the costs and benefits of emissions reductions. A policy that includes costly precautions should be adopted only if the costs are outweighed by the benefits.

Such rational analyses are often trumped, however, by the strong emotional responses triggered by images of dramatic climate change such as those in films like *The Day After Tomorrow* (2004) and *An Inconvenient Truth* (2006). Sunstein has also argued that "in the face of a fearsome risk, people often exaggerate the benefits of preventive, risk-reducing, or ameliorative measures." When a hazard stirs strong emotions, people also tend to factor in probability less, with the result that they will go to great lengths to avoid risks that are extremely unlikely. Psychologists refer to this phenomenon as "probability neglect" and have investigated it in a variety of experimental settings.

As with the threat of international terrorism, high levels of risk intelligence will be required to face the challenges posed by climate change. If we are to contribute sensibly to the debate, we must learn to deal better in probabilities and to craft policies that are sensitive to the different probabilities of the various possible scenarios.

EXPERTS AND COMPUTERS CAN'T SAVE US FROM OURSELVES

Many of us may be inclined to believe that it's best to defer to experts regarding such tricky assessments or, when possible, to allow computer programs to do the hard work for us, as so many bankers decided to do in assessing the risks of subprime mortgages in the decade preceding the 2007 financial crisis. But it's a big mistake to think we can off-load the responsibility for risk intelligence. Indeed, research suggests that many experts have quite poor risk intelligence, and the financial crisis illustrated all too well the problems of relying too heavily on computer models.

Take the experts first. A famous study by the psychologist Philip Tetlock asked 284 people who made their living "commenting or offering advice on political and economic trends" to estimate the probability of future events in both their areas of specialization and areas in which they claimed no expertise. Over the course of twenty years, Tetlock asked them to make a total of 82,361 forecasts. Would there be a nonviolent end to apartheid in South Africa? Would Mikhail Gorbachev be ousted in a coup? Would the United States go to war in the Persian Gulf? And so on.

Tetlock put most of the forecasting questions into a "three possible futures" form, in which three alternative outcomes were presented: the persistence of the status quo, more of something (political freedom, economic growth), or less of something (repression, recession). The results were embarrassing. The experts performed worse than they would have if they had simply assigned an equal probability to all three outcomes. Dart-throwing monkeys would have done better.

Furthermore, the pundits were not significantly better at forecasting events in their area of expertise than at assessing the likelihood of events outside their field of study. Knowing a little helped a bit, but Tetlock found that knowing a lot can actually make a person less reliable. "We reach the point of diminishing marginal predictive returns for knowledge disconcertingly quickly," he observed. "In this age of academic hyperspecialization, there is no reason for supposing that contributors to top journals—distinguished political scientists, area

14

study specialists, economists, and so on—are any better than journalists or attentive readers of the *New York Times* in 'reading' emerging situations." And the more famous the forecaster, the lower his or her risk intelligence seemed to be. "Experts in demand," Tetlock noted, "were more overconfident than their colleagues who eked out existences far from the limelight."

As far as relying on computer programs to help us assess risks, the story of the 2007 financial crisis reveals the vital importance of more nuanced human risk intelligence in alerting us to risks even when the data tell us not to worry.

During the 1990s, Wall Street was invaded by a new breed of risk assessors. According to Aaron Brown of AQR Capital Management, a hedge fund located in Connecticut, Wall Street used to be full of game players—literally. Many of those in trading and running trading-related businesses in the 1970s were frequent poker players, bridge players, and backgammon players. Those who weren't gamblers in the strict sense of the term were nevertheless used to taking risks in all aspects of their lives. But in the 1990s, the risk lovers were gradually edged out and replaced by a new wave of risk avoiders. Put simply, the banks wanted to stop gambling. That, it turned out, was a mistake.

The most famous invention of the new risk avoiders, who became known as "quants," short for quantitative analysts, was the Black-Scholes formula, which made it possible to put a price on financial instruments that weren't traded very often. Trading is an effective way of determining value, so if an instrument is not traded frequently it can be hard to price it. The formula devised by Fischer Black and Myron Scholes came up with a value for rarely traded instruments by linking them with a comparable security that did trade regularly. Taking things a step further, a team of quants at J.P. Morgan developed a way to sum up the risks of whole portfolios of financial assets in a single number called value at risk, or VaR. The beauty of VaR was that it synthesized the dizzying variety of variables that make up the market risk of an investment portfolio into a single dollar value that risk managers could report to top executives.

At first the nonquants—the traders and executives who had been running Wall Street more on the basis of hunches and educated guesswork than on math—were suspicious of the new methods. But as the equations turned out to be right again and again, the executives came round to the new way of thinking, and by the late 1990s VaR was firmly entrenched in both the practice and regulation of investment banking.

The ironic outcome of this was that during the last decade of the twentieth century, Wall Street hemorrhaged risk intelligence. People who were used to thinking about risk intuitively left the banks for new pastures, and their ranks were filled by people who were more at home in the world of equations and formulae. According to Aaron Brown, that was an important but widely neglected cause of the 2007 crisis.

The problem with any kind of mathematical technology is that you may come to rely on it so much that your capacity to benchmark it against other standards withers away, leaving you unable to spot previously obvious errors. A case in point is the replacement of slide rules by pocket calculators in the 1970s. When people used slide rules to carry out multiplication and division, they would constantly check their intermediate steps against common sense and an understanding of their subject as they performed calculations. In particular, they had to note the order of magnitude at each stage and so were less likely to make wildly wrong errors. With an electronic calculator, the intermediate steps are all taken care of by the machine, so the habit of checking tends to atrophy, leaving people less able to spot, for example, that the decimal point is now in the wrong place.

In the same way, the greater reliance on IT systems has led to a "de-skilling of the risk process," according to Stephen O'Sullivan, formerly of Accenture, a consultancy. A friend of mine who worked in the Foreign Exchange Complex Risk Group at a major international bank told me a story that illustrates the dangers of such uncritical reliance on mathematical technology. One morning he watched the global exchange rate for a pair of currencies, both from G7 economies, get fixed, all around the world, at an obviously stupid price. One bank's automated trading system had developed a problem and was quoting a wildly inaccurate "giveaway" price, well below the true market rate. The rest of the global FX market participants, many of them running their own automated trading systems, rapidly switched to trading with the error-hit system, buying currency at cheap prices. The speed and magnitude of the market's rush to exploit the mistake by one automated trading system meant that the incorrect price became, for a brief while, the global exchange rate for that pair of currencies. It was only when human traders literally pulled the plug on the automated trading system that the bank stopped bleeding money. In the next few minutes the global exchange rate fell back to where everyone knew it was supposed to be, and the blip passed.

Many errors have been caused by computerized trading, at great cost to investors, and they are fixed only when actual people step in and switch off the machine that has screwed up. The only reason this is possible is that some people still have, in their heads, standards against which they can benchmark the performance of the machines.

THE DARKENED ROOM

The unfortunate fact, though, is that most of us simply aren't comfortable with or adept at making judgments in the netherland of uncertainty, and this is largely due to our reluctance to gauge the limits of what we know. Picture your mind as a lightbulb shining in an otherwise dark room. Some nearby objects are fully illuminated; you can see them in every detail, present and identifiable. They are the things you know very well: the names of your friends, what you had for breakfast this morning, how many sides a triangle has, and so on. The objects on the other side of the room are completely shrouded in darkness. They are the things about which you know nothing: the five thousandth digit of *pi*, the composition of dark matter, King Nebuchadnezzar's favorite color. Between the light and the darkness, however, lies a gray area in which the level of illumination gradually shades away.

In this twilight zone, the objects are not fully illuminated, but neither are they completely invisible. You know something about those things, but your knowledge is patchy and incomplete—the law of the land (unless you are a lawyer), the evidence for climate change (unless you are a climatologist), the causes of the credit crunch (even economists are still arguing about this). The question is, *how much* do you know about those things? How good are you at judging the precise level of illumination at different points in the twilight zone?

In 1690, the English philosopher John Locke noted that "in the greatest part of our concernments, [God] has afforded us only the twilight, as I may so say, of probability." Yet we are still remarkably ill equipped to operate in this twilight zone. If we're cautious, we relegate everything beyond the zone of complete illumination to complete obscurity, not daring to venture an opinion on things about which we do, in fact, have some inkling. If we're overconfident, we do the opposite, expressing views about things in the twilight zone with more conviction than is justified. It's hard to steer between the two extremes, daring to speculate but with prudence. This book is a traveler's guide to that twilight zone and a manifesto for what the poet John Keats called "negative capability": "when man is capable of being in uncertainties, Mysteries, doubts without any irritable reaching after fact and reason."

THE LIGHT AT THE END OF THE TUNNEL

It's not all doom and gloom. There is light at the end of the tunnel. Although the general level of risk intelligence is not high, and therefore many of the mechanisms that we invent to help us do a better job of assessing risks (such as color-coded warnings about terrorist threat levels and elaborate mathematical models for measuring financial risks) can lead to perverse results, we are not condemned to repeat our mistakes. There are in fact people, such as the hypothetical Kathryn and Jamie I described at the beginning of this chapter, who have high risk intelligence—at least in certain subject areas—and I have found that by studying them, and the patterns that show up in people's risk judgments more generally, it's possible to discern ways in which we can all boost our risk intelligence.

Philip Tetlock's conclusions about the limited value of expertise, which I introduced earlier, must be qualified. Many self-proclaimed experts are indeed no better than monkeys at forecasting world events. But Tetlock also found that among the hundreds of experts he studied, there were a handful who seemed particularly good at estimating probabilities. If your sample is large enough, of course, you're bound to come across a few outliers by chance alone, but the wise forecasters identified by Tetlock do not seem to be a statistical fluke. Psychologists have also identified other groups with unusually high risk intelligence, which suggests that risk intelligence can be developed significantly under the right conditions. In fact, it was a fascinating study about one such group that first got me thinking about this whole subject. The group in question was a bunch of men who were fanatical about horse racing.

Let me take you to a sunny afternoon in 1984 at Brandywine Raceway, a harness racetrack in North Wilmington, Delaware. A young psychologist is chatting with a sixty-two-year-old man. "Which horse do you think will win the next race?" he asks the older man.

"The four-horse should win easily; he should go off three to five or shorter, or there's something wrong," replies the man, a crane operator who has been coming to the racetrack several times a week for the past eight years.

"What exactly is it about the four-horse that makes him your odds-on favorite?"

"He's the fastest, plain and simple!"

The psychologist looks puzzled. "But it looks to me like other horses are even faster," he interjects, pointing to a page in the Brandywine *Official Form Program*. "For instance, both the two-horse and the six-horse have recorded faster times than the four-horse, haven't they?"

"Yeah," says the crane operator with a smile, "but you can't go by that. The two-horse didn't win that outing, he just sucked up."

"Sucked up?"

"You gotta read between the lines if you want to be good at this. The two-horse just sat on the rail and didn't fight a lick. He just kept on the rail and sucked up lengths when horses in front of him came off the rail to fight with the front runner."

"Why does that make his speed any slower? I don't get it."

"Now, listen. If he came out and fought with other horses, do you think for one minute he'd have run that fast? Let me explain something to you that will help you understand. See the race on June 6?" he asks, pointing to the relevant line of the racing program. "Well, if the two-horse had to do all of this fighting, he'd run three seconds slower. It's that simple. There ain't no comparison between the two-horse and the four-horse. The four is tons better!"

"And the longer you're on the outside, the longer the race you have to run, right?" asks the psychologist, as he begins to understand what the seasoned handicapper is saying. "In other words, the shortest route around the track is along the rail, and the farther off of it you are, the longer the perimeter you have to run."

"Exactly," replies the crane operator. "But there's another horse in this race that you have to watch. I'm talking about the eight-horse. He don't mind the outside post because he lays back early. Christ, he ran a monster of a race on June 20! He worries me because if he repeats here, he's unbeatable."

"Do you like him better than the four-horse?"

"Not for the price. He'll go off even money. He isn't that steady to be even money. If he's geared up, there's no stopping him, but you can't bet on him being geared up. If he were three to one, I'd bet him in a minute because he'll return a profit over the long run. But not at even money."

The psychologist's name was Stephen Ceci. In 1982, not long out of grad school, Ceci and his colleague Jeffrey Liker had approached the owners of Brandywine Raceway to ask permission to conduct a study of their clients. Ceci and Liker identified thirty middle-aged and older men who were avid racetrack patrons and studied them over a four-year period. None of the men earned their living by gambling, though all of them attended the races nearly every day of their adult lives.

As part of their study, Ceci and Liker asked all thirty men to handicap ten actual horse races—that is, to estimate the chances of each horse winning—as well as fifty imaginary ones they concocted. As it happened, the men fell into two distinct groups, one of which was significantly better than the other at handicapping. Moreover, the experts seemed to be unconsciously using a highly sophisticated mental model. For example, to predict the speed with which a horse could run the final quarter mile of the race, the experts took as many as seven different variables into account, including the speed at which the horse had run in its last race, the quality of the jockey, and the current condition of the racetrack. And they didn't just consider each of these factors independently. Rather, they considered them all in context. For example, coming third in one race may actually be more impressive than coming first in another race if the quality of the competition was higher in the former.

Ceci and Liker also tested the men's IQs. And that was when they got their biggest surprise—as did I, when I read their paper some twenty years later. For Ceci and Liker found that handicapping expertise had zero correlation with IQ. IQ is the best single measure of intelligence that psychologists have, because it correlates with so many cognitive capacities. It's that very correlation that underpins the concept of "general intelligence." The discovery that expertise in handicapping doesn't correlate at all with IQ means that whatever cognitive capacities are involved in estimating the odds of a horse winning a race, they are not a part of general intelligence. Or, to put it the other way around, IQ is unrelated to some forms of cognitive calculation that are, nonetheless, clear-cut cases of intelligence.

Not everyone is happy with the concept of general intelligence. The psychologist Howard Gardner argues that, rather than thinking in terms of one unitary measure, we should instead conceive of the mind as possessing multiple types of intelligence. Gardner identifies eight different kinds of intelligence: bodily-kinesthetic, interpersonal, verbal-linguistic, logical-mathematical, naturalistic, intrapersonal, visual-spatial, and musical. None of these involves an ability to estimate probabilities accurately, yet the study by Ceci and Liker shows that this is a cognitive skill that some people are very good at, which suggests that it might constitute a ninth kind of intelligence to add to Gardner's list.

In a similar vein, the psychologist Daniel Goleman argues that IQ tests fail to capture a set of social and emotional skills that he refers to collectively as "emotional intelligence." Goleman claims that proficiency with these skills—which include impulse control, self-awareness, social awareness, and relationship management—is a much stronger indicator of success than high IQ. But measures of EQ are no better than IQ tests at capturing our capacity for judging risks and weighing probabilities. This suggests that we should also test people for risk intelligence (RQ) when selecting candidates for jobs that involve estimating probabilities and making decisions under uncertainty.

This book is a manifesto for this specific kind of intelligence, for coming to appreciate how risk intelligence operates and then working to build up your own skills. I'm going to demonstrate why, when we get it wrong—when banks fail, doctors misdiagnose, and weapons of mass destruction turn out not to exist—we're in such a bad position to understand the reasons. I'll reveal the primary reasons why we tend to be so bad at estimating probabilities and then provide a powerful set of methods whereby we can hone our skills. Expert handicappers are not the only group of people with unusually high levels of risk intelligence; bridge players and weather forecasters are also pretty good in their areas of expertise. By studying what those groups have in common, as well as a fascinating set of findings about how our brains lead us astray in making risk assessments, we can discover ways to improve our own risk intelligence and thereby make better decisions in all aspects of our lives.

CHAPTER 2

Discovering Your Risk Quotient

When you can measure what you are speaking about,
and express it in numbers, you know something about it;
but when you cannot express it in numbers, your knowledge
is of a meagre and unsatisfactory kind; it may be the
beginning of knowledge, but you have scarcely in
your thoughts advanced to the state of science.

—LORD KELVIN

I define risk intelligence, in the simplest terms, as the ability to estimate probabilities accurately. This may seem like a rarefied skill,
but in fact, as we've seen, we're called on to exercise it every day.
Think about this for a little while, and I'm sure you'll recall a host of
instances when you've had to make such assessments, maybe about
your chances of getting the job you've just applied for, or how likely
it is that the stories about the Loch Ness monster are true. Making
educated guesses about probabilities, and being as precise as you can
in doing so, is a powerful way of expressing the strength of your convictions. Beliefs are rarely black or white, and usually come in shades
of gray, covering the whole spectrum from unequivocal assurance to
complete uncertainty. Probabilities permit you to express your degree
of belief in relatively precise numerical terms, and being able to do so
is a key component of risk intelligence.

The notion of risk is inextricably linked in many people's minds with danger, but for those who study risk professionally, danger is only one side of the risk coin, the other being opportunity. In other words, there are upside risks as well downside risks, and the ability to estimate the likelihood of some future possibility applies equally to possibilities that are dangerous and those that are not. Risk intelligence is not, therefore, confined to assessing danger; it should be considered a much more general kind of cognitive skill.

In essence, risk intelligence is all about having the right amount of certainty. It can be seen as a kind of cognitive virtue, since, according to Aristotle, virtue lies halfway between a dangerous excess and an equally problematic deficiency. Just as courage is equidistant from the opposite extremes of recklessness and cowardice, risk intelligence is a golden mean lying halfway between overconfidence and underconfidence. When I use the term "overconfidence," I'm not referring to overly high self-esteem but rather to an *unwarranted* belief in the correctness of one's statements. As used in the study of decision making, it means believing in something more strongly than is justified by the evidence, and thinking you know more than you really do. Underconfidence means thinking you know less than you really do and not having the courage of your convictions. Both are highly problematic for risk intelligence, but overconfidence is much more common than underconfidence. Indeed, according to the psychologist Scott Plous, "No problem in judgment and decision making is more prevalent and more potentially catastrophic than overconfidence."

OTHER APPROACHES TO RISK INTELLIGENCE

It's important to note that the study of risk intelligence is still in its infancy, and not everyone uses the term the way I do or conceives of risk intelligence in the same way. For one thing, some people use the term to refer to objective data about various threats, such as maritime security threats like piracy, or threats of terrorism (as in the phrase "We specialize in gathering risk intelligence"). But even when researchers use the term to indicate a psychological capacity or skill, as I do, they do not all agree with my view that it refers specifically to the ability to estimate probabilities.

David Apgar, for example, defines risk intelligence as "the ability to reach accurate judgments about a specific new risk." According to this view, one's level of risk intelligence varies according to the kind of risk in question. A real estate agent in Los Angeles who deals mainly with large commercial properties, for example, might be good at assessing the risk of moving into one kind of new market, such as smaller commercial properties, but bad at gauging the risk of moving into another market, such as residential properties. Apgar's test for measuring risk intelligence involves asking people to assess themselves on the frequency, relevance, impact, unexpectedness, and diversity of their experiences, and on the extent to which they are methodical about tracking what they learn.

Apgar is an experienced consultant with a strong background in economics. He spent three years at McKinsey and held a senior position at Lehman Brothers in the early 1990s, and his definition of risk intelligence reflects his focus on business. Yet there are some similarities between his approach and my own. For one thing, the fifth element in Apgar's measure—keeping track of what one learns, in a methodical way—turns out to be a crucial characteristic shared by all the groups of people with high risk intelligence that I discuss in this book. Also, I agree with Apgar that those people who seek out diverse sources of information are likely to have higher risk intelligence than those with a narrower cognitive horizon.

A third approach to risk intelligence has been pioneered by Frederick Funston, a principal at Deloitte & Touche and the coauthor of *Surviving and Thriving in Uncertainty: Creating the Risk Intelligent Enterprise*. According to Funston, risk intelligence is "the ability to effectively distinguish between two types of risks: the risks that must be avoided to survive by preventing loss or harm; and the risks that must be taken to thrive by gaining competitive advantage." This approach to risk intelligence highlights a common tendency among business managers to think of risk in a purely negative light, as something that must always be avoided or at least reduced. Funston is right to point out the problems with this view and to encourage executives to consider the upside risks as well as the downside ones.

But, as the title of Funston's book makes clear, he thinks of risk intelligence as an attribute of a company rather than of an individual. My approach views risk intelligence as a cognitive capacity of individual brains. To create a risk intelligent organization, it is not enough to have well-designed risk management policies and procedures; the people who implement those policies must also be individually risk intelligent.

HOW TO MEASURE YOUR RISK INTELLIGENCE

In order to delve into the nature of risk intelligence and to explore ways that it might be strengthened, my colleague Benjamin Jakobus and I created an online risk intelligence test, which you can take for free at www.projectionpoint.com. There's also a pen-and-paper version of the test at the end of this book for those who prefer to take it that way (see Appendix 1).

The test consists of fifty statements—some true, some false—and your task is to say how likely you think it is that each statement is true. It's a simple process; if you are absolutely sure that a statement is true, you assign a probability of 100 percent to it. If you are convinced that a statement is false, you should assign it a probability of 0 percent. If you have no idea at all whether it is true or false, you should rate it as 50 percent probable. If you are fairly sure that it is true but you aren't completely sure, you would give it 60 percent, 70 percent, 80 percent, or 90 percent, depending on how sure you are. Conversely, if you are reasonably confident that it is false but you aren't completely sure, you would give it 40 percent, 30 percent, 20 percent, or 10 percent. When you have estimated the likelihood of all fifty statements in the test, the website will calculate your risk intelligence quotient, or RQ, a number between 0 and 100.

The statements that you're asked to judge in this test don't require you to assess the probability of an event happening, so it may seem an odd way to evaluate risk intelligence. But, as said before, the key to risk intelligence is knowing how much you know about something, and judging the truth or falsehood of a statement is an excellent way to evaluate how good a person is at assessing how much he or she knows.

There are four mental steps that should be followed both when estimating a probability and when assessing the truth or falsehood of a statement:

1. First, take stock of what you know about the issue. Identify the bits of information you already possess that may have a bearing on the statement, no matter how indirectly.
2. Next, for each of those bits of information, decide (a) whether it makes the statement more or less likely, and (b) by how much it affects the probability that you are correct.
3. The outcome of this process should be a hunch or feeling, the strength of which varies according to your degree of belief.
4. Finally, translate this feeling into a number that expresses that degree of certainty.

So how did the people who took my risk intelligence test do? In the first thirteen months after launching www.projectionpoint .com on January 1, 2010, more than 50,000 people visited the site, of which 38,000 took the risk intelligence test. After eliminating those who didn't complete the whole test or who failed to specify their gender or profession, we were left with a total of 14,294 test results. The average RQ score in this group was 64, and the complete breakdown is shown in Figure 1. (The data are discussed in more detail in Appendix 4.)

FIGURE 1: DISTRIBUTION OF RQ SCORES IN THE RESEARCH SAMPLE.

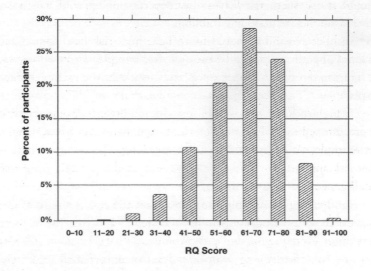

One objection that some people have made about the test is that they think it should ask people to distinguish the risks they would be prepared to take from those they wouldn't. Simply estimating the truth of statements strikes those critics as too narrow and too removed from the real action of risk intelligence. But I think the criticism confuses risk *intelligence* with risk *appetite* (or, as it is also known, risk *attitude*), and that distinction is vital. Risk intelligence is a cognitive capacity, a purely intellectual ability. Risk *appetite*, on the other hand, is an emotional trait. It has to do with how comfortable people are with taking risks—that is, with exposing themselves to greater danger in order to reap a greater reward.

Some people enjoy taking on risk, while others avoid it like the plague. Unlike risk intelligence, there's no right or wrong about risk appetite; it's just a matter of taste. Risk appetite governs how much risk you *want to take*, while risk intelligence involves being aware of how much you actually *are taking*. Some of the expert gamblers I've interviewed have high risk intelligence and a great appetite for risk, but most are risk neutral; they neither love risk nor hate it. Surprising though it may seem, risk leaves most expert gamblers cold, which is a key reason they're good at gambling.

Another possibility would be to have high risk intelligence and low risk appetite, as would be the case, for example, if you were good at figuring out which horses were likely to win at the races yet loath to place a bet. The most dangerous combination would be, of course, to have a high appetite for risk but low risk intelligence. Someone who overestimated his ability to climb high mountains, yet loved danger, for example, would probably not live very long. The key point here is that risk appetite can, and should, be measured separately from risk intelligence.

Another important thing to note about the test is that it is not concerned with measuring people's knowledge. It is possible to score very high even if you don't know much. That's because the test rewards you for gauging your own level of uncertainty accurately, rather than for knowing a bunch of facts. If you don't know much but can do a good job of identifying the nuggets of information you have that may be relevant to judging the likelihood of the various statements on the test, you'll do much better than someone who knows a lot but is no good at reasoning that way. The test also punishes overconfidence; if you think you know more than you really do, your probability estimates will be systematically biased in the direction of greater certainty than is warranted. That may be why some of my brightest students find risk intelligence tests more difficult than their more average peers do. The brightest students are used to being rewarded for knowing facts and are often quite cocky. They also tend to be uncomfortable with uncertainty; they lack Keats's "negative capability."

Of course, some people realize fairly quickly that there is an easy way to game the test. If you assign a probability of 50 percent to every statement, and if the test contains equal numbers of true and false statements, you will score a perfect 100. Such a score would not, of course, reflect high risk intelligence, because you will never have ventured into the gray area of intermediate uncertainty. To address this potential pitfall, I created a second indicator that I call "the K factor"—for John Keats and John Maynard Keynes, both of whom were fascinated by uncertainty, though in different ways.

It works like this: each time a person uses the categories 10 percent, 20 percent, 30 percent, 40 percent, 60 percent, 70 percent, 80 percent, or 90 percent, he or she scores one point. When he or she uses 0 percent, 50 percent, or 100 percent, he or she scores zero. The maximum K factor is therefore 50 for a fifty-question test. The K factor gives an indication of how carefully a person has attempted to evaluate the truth of the statements and is therefore a good gauge of how reliable his or her RQ score is.

CALIBRATION CURVES

RQ is just a number. It provides a "headline figure" summary of your risk intelligence. People like having such headline figures, and they can be useful when conducting research. But a single number is limited in the information it provides; a low RQ score could be due to overconfidence or underconfidence, for example, but it won't be clear from the RQ score alone which of them is to blame. That's where calibration curves come in.

Calibration curves provide a graphical way of visualizing the results of risk intelligence tests, and in doing so they provide a lot more information than the RQ score alone. Besides giving you a visual impression of your overall level of risk intelligence, your calibration curve also provides details about your risk intelligence profile—that is, whether you are underconfident or overconfident and at which points along the calibration curve you display these errors. Risk intelligence tests were, in fact, originally dubbed calibration tests, and many of the scientists whose research I cite in this book still prefer to talk about calibration rather than risk intelligence. In order to calculate a calibration curve, we start by counting all the times you gave statements a 0 percent chance of being true and then count how many of those statements were actually true. If you have perfect risk intelligence, none of the statements should be true; they are the statements that you were absolutely convinced were false. If any of them is actually true, it means that you were being overconfident.

For example, suppose that every evening for a year, just before you go to bed, you record whether it rained or not that day and estimate the chance that it will rain the following day. At the end of the year you would have a list of 365 probability estimates and a record of which days it actually rained. Suppose there were thirty-two occasions when you thought there was absolutely no chance it would rain the next day. If it did, in fact, rain on any of those days, you were being overconfident. The more of those days it rained, the more overconfident you were.

We proceed in the same way for each of the other likelihoods. Let's say there were thirty days when you thought there was a 10 percent chance of rainfall the following day. If you have perfect risk intelligence, it would have rained on exactly three of those days (i.e., 10 percent of thirty days). If it rained on more than three of those days, you were being overconfident. If it rained on fewer than three, you were being underconfident.

Once we have done this for each probability category, we can plot the results on a graph like that in Figure 2. The x-axis represents the probability estimates you assigned to the various statements in the test (0 percent, 10 percent, 20 percent, etc.). The y-axis represents the proportion of statements in each category that were in fact true. In Figure 2 the point marked *a* indicates that, of all the statements to which this person assigned a probability estimate of 10 percent, around 30 percent were in fact true. Even worse, the point marked *b* indicates that, of all the statements to which this person assigned a probability estimate of 70 percent, only around 30 percent were in fact true. The line connecting all the points is called the calibration curve.

A perfect calibration curve lies on the diagonal line where $x = y$ (mathematicians call this the "identity line"). This indicates perfect risk intelligence, where 0 percent of the statements that were assigned a probability of 0 percent turned out to be true, 10 percent of the statements assigned a probability of 10 percent were true, and so on. The further away from that diagonal line the calibration curve lies, the lower your risk intelligence is. If we shade the area between the calibration curve and the diagonal line, as in Figure 3, the size of the area is inversely proportional to your risk intelligence. In other words, the smaller the area, the greater your risk intelligence. With a perfect calibration curve, the shaded area shrinks to nothing.

FIGURE 2: AN ANNOTATED CALIBRATION CURVE.

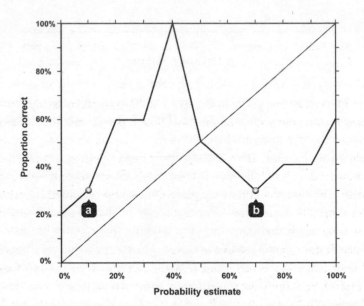

FIGURE 3: A SHADED CALIBRATION CURVE.

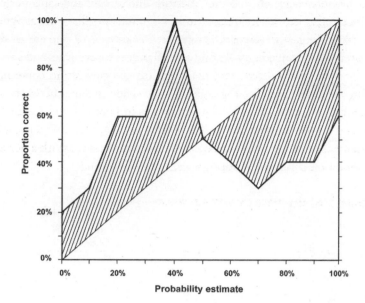

The calibration curve in Figures 2 and 3 is typical of many I have seen. It starts out above the diagonal line of perfect risk intelligence, crosses the line at around the 50 percent region, and then remains below the diagonal. If your calibration curve looks something like this, what does it say about you? It means that you tend to be overconfident. You may sometimes say that you are sure of something when you should be expressing more doubt. But it's important to qualify just how much this test can really tell you about your risk intelligence. It does a good job of assessing how well you judge your degree of knowledge in a broad range of areas and how certain you should therefore be about your probability estimates regarding a wide range of general information. But that doesn't mean that you might not be much more risk intelligent in areas where you have a good deal of experience in judging probabilities.

Indeed, one of the most interesting—and hopeful—findings in the study of risk intelligence is that it seems it can be greatly improved by practicing assessment in a particular domain of expertise. This is dramatically revealed in the remarkable difference between the risk intelligence scores of weather forecasters and those of doctors.

Nobody has perfect risk intelligence, but, as you can see from Figure 4, when making assessments in their field, weather forecasters are pretty close. Meanwhile, as the same figure shows, doctors seem to have very low risk intelligence when evaluating medical risks.

FIGURE 4: CALIBRATION CURVES FOR WEATHER FORECASTERS AND DOCTORS.
Dashes = medical diagonosis; solid line = weather forecasts.

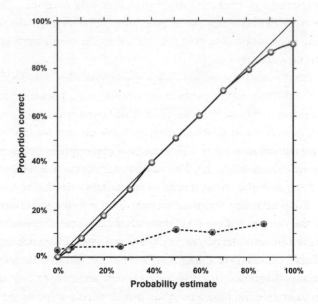

Figure 4 displays data from two different studies. When the weather forecasters in the first study said there was a 90 percent chance of rain the following day, it rained almost 90 percent of the time. But when the doctors in the second study estimated that there was a 90 percent chance that their patients had pneumonia, only about 15 percent of the patients turned out to have the disease. In other words, the doctors had much more faith in the accuracy of their diagnoses than was justified by the evidence. That meant they were likely to recommend more tests than were strictly necessary, prescribe more treatments than warranted, and cause their patients needless worry.

Better safe than sorry, you may say. Perhaps the physicians in this study were more worried by the possibility of a false-negative diagnosis (failing to spot a disease that is there) than of a false-positive one (seeing a disease where there is none). In the former case the patient would not be treated and might die as a result, and the doctor might face a lawsuit. In the latter case, the patient merely undergoes unnecessary tests and worries a bit more than is strictly necessary. Perhaps the doctors in this study were practicing "defensive medicine" by allowing their probability estimates to reflect the asymmetric costs of the two kinds of errors.

The authors of this study ruled out that possibility, however. They asked the doctors to assign a value rating to each possible outcome for the pneumonia diagnosis decision (diagnose a patient who has the disease, diagnose a patient who does not have the disease, fail to diagnose to a patient who has it, and assign a nonpneumonia diagnosis to a patient who doesn't have it). The value rating for each outcome could range from -50 (the worst thing I could do) to +50 (the best thing I could do). The result was that there was no difference between the values the doctors assigned to a correct pneumonia diagnosis and a correct nonpneumonia diagnosis. Nor was there a difference between the values for an incorrect pneumonia diagnosis and an incorrect nonpneumonia diagnosis. By implication, their overestimation bias was due to poor risk intelligence rather than low risk appetite. In other words, the doctors were not deliberately erring on the side of caution; they were simply mistaken.

The dramatic difference in scores between the weather forecasters and doctors raises a number of interesting questions. What is it about the work of the two professions that has taught the one to be adept at estimating probabilities and the other to be so bad at it? Can we identify the factors that favor the weather forecasters, and can we use the information to design ways to increase risk intelligence?

IMPROVING RISK INTELLIGENCE

Sarah Lichtenstein, an expert in the field of risk intelligence testing, speculates that several factors favor the weather forecasters. First, they have been expressing their forecasts in terms of probability estimates for many years; since 1965, National Weather Service forecasters have been required to say not just whether or not it will rain the next day but *how likely* they think it is to rain in percentage terms. They have gotten used to putting numbers on such things and as a result are better at it. Doctors, on the other hand, are under no such obligation. They remain free to be as vague as they like.

Second, the task for weather forecasters is repetitive. The question to be answered ("Will it rain?") is always the same. Doctors, however, must consider all sorts of different questions every day: "Does he have a broken rib?" "Is this growth malignant?" "How will she respond to a different type of antidepressant?" And so on.

Finally, the feedback for weather forecasters is well defined and promptly received. This is not always true for doctors. Patients may not come back, or they may be referred elsewhere. Diagnoses may remain uncertain. Most theories of learning emphasize the need for rapid feedback; the longer the delay between an action (or in this case a prediction) and a corrective signal, the lower the chance that the later information will enable the recipient to profit from it.

Interestingly, some leading medical schools are beginning to wake up to the problem of low risk intelligence among doctors. Something called "confidence-based assessment" or "certainty-based marking" is increasingly being used in those schools. In this form of assessment, students must not only give the right answer but also assess the confidence with which they give each answer. If students give the wrong answer confidently, they receive the worst possible grade. If they give the wrong answer but are not confident, they get a better grade. Giving the right answer without confidence is okay but not ideal, as in real life it could end up with their wasting time having to consult others. The best answer is that which is correct and made with confidence. This form of assessment is a very effective way both to highlight the need to assess one's degree of confidence in an analysis of the available information and to provide feedback. It's intended to help students know when to consult others (or textbooks, etc.) and when to act independently.

If providing prompt feedback is vital when training people in risk intelligence, it also helps to focus on a narrow set of questions. That is another reason weather forecasters tend to have higher risk intelligence than doctors; there is a small range of questions they must answer over and over again, while doctors have to consider a much wider range. The narrower focus means that weather forecasters receive more feedback per question and as a result can build up a much richer mental model of the factors that must be considered when answering them. Interestingly, when the weather forecasters were asked to estimate the probability of general-knowledge statements (such as those listed in Appendix 1), their risk intelligence was much lower.

A 1987 study by the Israeli psychologist Gideon Keren provides further support for the view that estimating probabilities for the same kind of event over and over again boosts risk intelligence. Keren organized two evening bridge tournaments for expert and amateur players. At the end of the bidding in each game and before the play started (and before the dummy cards were laid down), each player had to estimate in private the probability that the final contract would be made. The game of bridge provides an excellent setting for the study of risk intelligence because estimating probabilities is an integral part of the game. During the auction, each player must evaluate the hand he or she has been dealt and, on the basis of this evaluation, estimate the probability that his or her side will make a higher number of tricks than the previous bid. If the player judges this to be likely, he or she will make a bid; otherwise, he or she will pass. A fair amount of risk intelligence is therefore crucial to success at bridge.

Figure 5 shows the calibration curves for the expert and amateur players. As you can see, the expert players (shown by the dotted line) displayed higher risk intelligence than the amateur players (solid line). According to my calculations, the average RQ of the experts was 89, but even the amateurs were pretty good, with an average RQ of 74. That is probably because the amateurs were also fairly experienced; they were members of a sports club that organized regular bridge tournaments, and all of them had been playing the game for years. Although none of them had ever taken part in a national competition (all the experts had), they were far from being novices. Like the experts, they had evaluated thousands of hands, and it was probably the repetitive nature of the task that had allowed them to hone their risk intelligence in this domain.

The calibration curves in Figure 5 highlight an importance difference between the risk intelligence profiles of the amateurs and experts. The higher RQ of the experts is accounted for mostly by their better ability to estimate extreme probabilities—that is, their use of the categories 0 to 20 percent and 80 to 100 percent. The amateurs didn't seem to be much worse than the experts when using the other categories, but when estimating very low or very high probabilities, they were overconfident. In later chapters we'll examine some of the reasons why this is the case, but for now it is enough to note that the ability to discriminate more finely between extreme probabilities is often what sets the most risk intelligent people apart from those who are less proficient.

FIGURE 5: CALIBRATION CURVES FOR EXPERT AND AMATEUR BRIDGE PLAYERS.
Dashes = experts; solid line = amateurs.

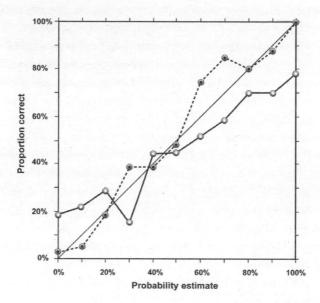

The fact that risk intelligence becomes higher when evaluating probabilities in quite specific areas in which we have lots of experience doing so provides a possible explanation for why Philip Tetlock failed to detect high levels of risk intelligence in the experts he surveyed in the study we looked at in chapter 1. To recap, Tetlock recruited hundreds of pundits who made their living "commenting or offering advice on political and economic trends" and asked them to estimate the probability of future events. When he analyzed their performance, Tetlock found that the experts performed worse than they would have if they had simply tossed a coin. However, the events that Tetlock asked the pundits to forecast covered a wide range of political and geographical areas. Although he did try to distinguish between forecasts that related to each pundit's area of expertise and those that related to events outside his or her field of study (the pundits were equally bad at both), this distinction might still have been too coarse-grained. It might have been that an expert was good at estimating the probabilities of political appointments in the current US administration, for example, but not at forecasting US politics in general.

When we consider what this means for the prospects of developing stronger risk intelligence, the news is actually good. If risk intelligence is increased by repeatedly estimating the probability of a narrow range of events, it suggests a clear direction for research and practice. Training programs could be developed that are tailored to the needs of particular professions.

In the 1970s, Royal Dutch Shell introduced just such a program. Senior executives had noticed that newly hired geologists were far too confident when estimating the chances of finding oil. The geologists might estimate the likelihood of an oil strike in a given region at 40 percent, but when ten wells were actually drilled there, only one or two produced. This overconfidence cost Royal Dutch Shell millions of dry-well dollars.

These judgment flaws puzzled the senior executives, since the geologists had excellent qualifications. As we've already seen, however, a high degree of primary knowledge (knowing about things) does not always go hand in hand with a high level of metacognition (knowing how much you know about things). Experts often think they know more than they really do.

Royal Dutch Shell tackled the problem by implementing an innovative training program. It gave the geologists details of previous explorations and asked them to provide numerical estimates of the chances of finding oil in each case. Then it provided feedback about the number of actual oil strikes. The training worked; by the end of the program, the geologists had much higher risk intelligence. Now when they estimated that there was a 40 percent chance of finding the black stuff in a given region, four out of ten wells drilled would strike oil.

I often wonder why other multinationals have not implemented similar training programs. An engineer at a large IT firm, for example, emailed me the following thoughts:

My department deals with reliability of the running systems and is responsible for dealing with breakages and crises that can impact the entire network. That means risk evaluation skills are particularly important for us. Our engineers also do a lot of interviewing, but at the end of the day only a small percentage of people who get a first interview are hired. I would love to see how candidates' performance on the RQ test compared to their success in the hiring process.

My correspondent did express some caution about using risk intelligence tests as a criterion for hiring without a better understanding of what they actually measure and how cultural and language issues affect performance on a given set of questions. But the fundamental point is well taken: if it worked for Royal Dutch Shell, why don't other large organizations do something similar? For example:

- Banks could require loan officers to estimate the probability of each loan they issue being repaid according to schedule. Over the course of the following months, as some loans went bad, this information could be used to calculate calibration curves for each loan officer, who could use this feedback to improve his or her performance. The calibration curves could be continuously updated as more information about default rates flowed in, allowing the loan officers to monitor improvements in their risk intelligence.

- Intelligence agencies could require analysts to provide numerical probability estimates when forecasting world events and predicting emerging security threats. Over a predefined time frame, information could be collected about whether or not those events came to pass. Finally, RQ scores could be calculated and the performance of the analysts evaluated.

- Publishers could require commissioning editors to provide numerical probability estimates when issuing new contracts.

They could, for example, estimate the probability that the author will earn out his or her advance within a specified time period. As sales figures came in, it would gradually become apparent which editors were shrewd judges and which were overconfident.

- Lawyers could tell their clients how likely they were to win prospective lawsuits. Gradually it would become clearer which lawyers were overconfident, and which were more realistic.

- Armed forces could require battlefield commanders to estimate the probability of destroying various targets or achieving other specified objectives when planning tactical operations. Then, as the battle developed, the accuracy of those estimates could be quantified by means of calibration tests and the results fed back to the commanders in real time.

- Risk intelligence testing could also be used when recruiting and selecting personnel. Many organizations make extensive use of personality testing, and it would be easy to incorporate a simple test of risk intelligence. In the absence of direct measures, existing data on personality profiles could be used as a proxy, since high risk intelligence is favored by some personality traits and hindered by others.

OUT OF THE IVORY TOWER

In March 2010, I got a chance to put some of these ideas into practice. I received an email from an executive at a medium-sized company in the United Kingdom who was concerned that the risk management processes at his firm weren't up to scratch. He had heard of my research on risk intelligence and wondered if I might give him some advice. I was honest with him and told him that, though my research had a solid theoretical foundation and I was beginning to gather some interesting data, I hadn't yet tested my methods in a real business setting. Eventually we struck a deal; I would visit the company and carry out an initial risk intelligence audit for a rather low fee. The company wouldn't have to pay too much for a service whose credentials were not yet established, and I would get a chance to try out my ideas in the context of a real business setting.

A few weeks later, I was in the company's head office, meeting with the risk management team. It turned out that they had been using a popular risk management method that involved first estimating the likelihood and impact of each risk on a simple three-point scale (low, medium, and high). Next, the likelihood and impact of each risk were plotted on a so-called risk matrix in which different regions were defined as high, medium, or low risk.

Such scoring methods are relatively easy to create and teach. Consequently, they have become very popular in a wide variety of business sectors. Respected organizations have designed such methods and represent them as best practices for thousands of users. For example, the US Army has developed a weighted scoring–based method for evaluating the risks of missions. The US Department of Health and Human Services uses a weighted scoring method to determine vaccine allocations in the event of a pandemic outbreak, and NASA uses a scoring method for assessments of risks in manned and unmanned space missions.

I believe that these scoring methods are deeply flawed for many reasons. The first and most fundamental problem is that they are only as good as the initial estimates that serve as input; if you put garbage in, you get garbage out. The initial estimates are usually provided by experts, but even experts suffer from systematic errors and biases when estimating probabilities. Furthermore, these methods fudge matters by using verbal scales in which risks are characterized as "low," "medium," and "high," instead of asking users to state numerical probabilities.

I persuaded the risk management team to try out an alternative method: expressing probability estimates in percentage terms and estimating potential losses in quantitative terms. In other words, instead of rating the likelihood of a given risk as "high" and its impact as "medium," team members would have to state, for example, that there was a "10 percent chance of a loss of inventory worth £2M." In order to prepare them for this new approach, I first asked each member of the team to take a risk intelligence test. We then reviewed their scores and examined some ways in which they could improve their risk intelligence.

The company also installed a customized version of my risk intelligence test on some of their computers. The general-knowledge statements were replaced by statements about specific risks that the company might face over the following few months, such as "The price of electricity will increase by more than 5 percent this month" and "Hackers will access confidential client data this month." Over the next four months, each member of the risk management team provided probability estimates for each of these predictions, just as in the original risk intelligence test. In that way, I was able to measure the risk intelligence of the team members in the context of their day-to-day work and help them identify the risks they tended to underestimate and those that they overestimated.

The biggest surprise concerned the risk of project delays. Most of the systematic biases I identified in the risk management team involved *overestimating* the probability of potential dangers and threats, but when it came to the possibility of projects taking longer than planned, most team members dramatically underestimated the chances. By gathering quantitative data about their mistakes, I was able to help the company devise a set of "bias uplifts" to correct them. This idea was first developed by the Danish academic Bent Flyvbjerg, who recommended that the UK Department for Transport could produce more realistic forecasts of individual project capital expenditures by correcting for "optimism bias" among planners. For example, since the total cost of building a motorway is typically 44 percent higher than estimates suggest when the decision is first made regarding the preferred route, the Department for Transport increases the original estimates by this amount to compensate for the planners' predictable optimism.

That was the first time I took my risk intelligence ideas out of the ivory tower and put them to work in a real business setting. The initial results were promising. The RQ scores of the members of the risk management team all increased during the first few months of the project, and the company now uses quantitative risk estimates instead of fuzzy verbal labels. The proof of the pudding really lies, of course, in the effectiveness of the new program. Many people believe that it is not possible to measure the effectiveness of risk management, because you can't tell what would have happened if a risk had not been managed. What you *can* do, however, is to compare the performance of a company after implementing a new risk management program with its performance beforehand. When I sat down with the risk management team to review the program six months later, we found that less time was now wasted in dealing with low-probability risks, and the budgets set aside for contingency plans were leaner.

Of course, we can't possibly practice assessing probabilities in a vast swath of areas of life in order to bring our risk intelligence to an equally high level in all of them. But by becoming aware of our general tendency to be either overconfident or underconfident in our risk assessments and learning about a key set of underlying reasons why our brains so often lead us astray, we can go a long way toward correcting for the most common errors. Even just taking the risk intelligence test has proven quite enlightening for many people. To judge from the emails I have received, it is not unusual to find the whole business of providing numerical probability estimates quite disconcerting at first, but nevertheless thought-provoking. With further reflection it can lead to profound changes. The psychologist Susan Blackmore, for example, emailed me to say:

> I have, to my surprise, found that learning about risk intelligence has changed my life! I did appallingly badly on the test and that made me realise how often I am unjustifiably confident about things and angry when I am wrong, instead

of judging my own reasons for confidence as I go along. Since doing the test I have, I believe, been less dogmatic and more flexible.

Taking even one risk intelligence test can, it seems, have big effects, providing one reflects on the experience.

But this rapid raising of awareness is the low-hanging fruit. In order to make more substantial and enduring gains, a deeper understanding of why we are so prone to make mistakes when estimating probabilities, and also the ways in which we can correct the errors we make, is required. Providing this deeper understanding is the mission of the rest of this book.

CHAPTER 3

Into the Twilight Zone

On the road from the City of Skepticism,
I had to pass through the Valley of Ambiguity.

—ADAM SMITH

As we've discussed, risk intelligence operates mostly in the gray area between certain knowledge and complete ignorance. Imagine a continuum that stretches between those two extremes. This is represented by the vertical axis in Figure 6. If you locate your degree of belief on this axis and read across to the U-shaped curve, the corresponding point on the horizontal axis shows how that degree of belief is translated into a probability estimate. Complete uncertainty is therefore indicated by a probability of 50 percent. If you say that there's a 50 percent chance it will rain tomorrow, you are effectively admitting that you have no idea whether it will rain or not. You might as well flip a coin.

I like to think of this graph as a valley with a hill on either side. If you are completely uncertain as to whether something is true or false, you are right at the bottom of the valley. If you are completely certain that it is true or that it is false, you are on top of one of the hills. None of these three locations requires much risk intelligence, however. Risk intelligence hangs out on the slopes of the valley, in the regions where you are neither completely certain nor completely uncertain.

FIGURE 6: THE RELATIONSHIP BETWEEN PROBABILITY ESTIMATES AND SUBJECTIVE CERTAINTY. The horizontal axis shows the range of probability estimates from 0 to 100 percent, and the vertical axis shows the spectrum of subjective certainty from complete uncertainty ("I have no idea") to complete certainty ("I'm absolutely sure").

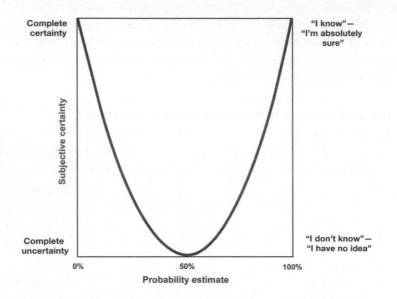

Some people are quite happy wandering around on those slopes; they are comfortable with the whole range of probabilities. Others prefer the safety of the valley and the hilltops; when estimating probabilities, they tend to think only in terms of 0 percent, 50 percent, and 100 percent. The idea of assigning other values seems to produce an emotional reaction in them that can at times be quite visceral. "I hate this test," one person told me after taking the online risk intelligence test, "because I can't see the point of using categories like 10 percent or 20 percent for statements which I either know or don't know." Such an objection supports the view that emotional reactions to ambiguity and uncertainty can have a great impact on one's risk intelligence.

The tendency to think only in terms of complete certainty (0 percent and 100 percent) or complete uncertainty (50 percent) is clear from Figure 7, which shows how often each probability estimate was used by the people who took my online risk intelligence test in 2010. You can see that the three categories of 0 percent, 50 percent, and 100 percent together account for almost half of all the estimates provided. That would be fine if it were an accurate reflection of what these people really knew—if, for example, half of the statements in the test were either completely familiar or totally unknown. But the fact that the average RQ score in this group was only 64 strongly suggests that they were using the categories of 0 percent, 50 percent, and 100 percent more than they should have.

FIGURE 7: DISTRIBUTION OF PROBABILITY ESTIMATES IN THE ONLINE RISK INTELLIGENCE TEST.

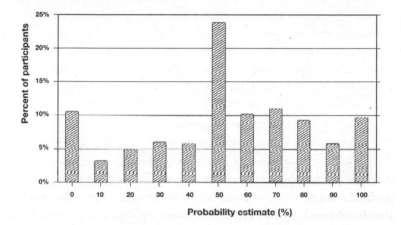

It's also interesting to note that people tended to think that the statements in the test were more likely to be true than false: 46 percent of the estimates were above 50 percent, while only 31 percent were below. Since only half of the statements were, in fact, true, we should expect Figure 7 to be symmetrical. The fact that it is not suggests that there is a "guessing effect" in which, when people are unsure, they are more likely to guess that a statement is true than to guess that it is false. Maybe simply seeing a statement in print bestows on it some degree of spurious authority.

AMBIGUITY INTOLERANCE

The psychological trait known as ambiguity intolerance leads people to respond to novelty, complexity, and uncertainty in a number of ways that undermine risk intelligence, such as seeing things too starkly as either black or white, and reacting to ambiguity with feelings of uneasiness, discomfort, dislike, anger, and anxiety that intrude on rational assessment. For that reason, people who can't tolerate ambiguity are unlikely to develop a high level of risk intelligence. Getting a fix on your own degree of ambiguity tolerance is, therefore, an important step in improving your risk intelligence.

There are various tests for measuring ambiguity intolerance. Some of them require the user to perform a cognitive task, such as the dog-cat test developed by the Polish psychologist Else Frenkel-Brunswik in 1949. Users are shown a picture of a dog followed by a number of pictures representing a gradual transformation of the dog into a cat and asked to say when the animal ceases being a dog. Those who insist the beast is still a dog for longer are considered to be less tolerant of ambiguity. These days, ambiguity intolerance is usually measured by self-report questionnaires, of which the most cited and used is that developed by the psychologist Stanley Budner for his 1960 PhD dissertation. This is a sixteen-item scale that covers three types of ambiguous situations: novel (I would like to live in a foreign country for a while), complex (a good job is one where what is to be done and how it is to be done are not always clear), and insoluble (some problems cannot be solved).

Four decades after the concept of ambiguity intolerance was first proposed by Frenkel-Brunswik, psychologists began developing a similar construct that they called "uncertainty intolerance." The two concepts overlap; this has led to some confusion in the scientific literature, and some researchers seem to use the terms interchangeably. Others have proposed that the concepts should be distinguished according to their different time orientations. Uncertainty intolerance, they suggest, should be taken to refer to an apprehension of future negative events, while ambiguity intolerance is a reaction to "here-and-now" stimuli. In both cases, however, the reactions have a similar emotional nature; the ambiguity or uncertainty is perceived as a threat or a source of discomfort and anxiety.

Journalists and business executives often blame rising prices—or falling prices—on intolerance of uncertainty. In March 2011, for example, AsiaOne News blamed a one-day 0.15 percent fall in the Nikkei 225 index on "uncertainty over Japan's postearthquake nuclear crisis," while BP and Caltex cited uncertainty about supplies from Libya, and the recovery of Japan, when they increased gasoline prices in New Zealand. But that is not strictly correct. If the markets really were uncertain about the prospects in Japan or Libya, prices wouldn't move up or down. Prices change only when information accumulates that tips the balance one way or the other—in other words, when uncertainty *decreases* and the balance of probabilities shifts in a particular direction. The Nikkei 225 index didn't really fall in March 2011 because investors were less certain about the likely course of the nuclear crisis in Japan; it fell because markets became *more* certain that the crisis was going to get worse. And when BP and Caltex decided to increase gasoline prices in New Zealand, it wasn't because they had no idea about what was going to happen to supplies from Libya; it was because they were increasingly convinced that supplies would be disrupted.

Likewise, it is misleading to blame economic malaise on regulatory uncertainty. In 2011, for example, US conservatives argued that a wave of new regulations proposed by the Obama administration was the primary hindrance to business confidence and hiring. But, as one commentator pointed out, it is not "uncertainty" per se that bothers business:

> Whether uncertainty is unwelcome depends entirely on what's at stake. What would you prefer: 100% probability of dying next year, or 50%? Most of us would choose the latter. Similarly,

business would prefer zero probability of a burdensome new rule, but if that's not possible, would certainly take 50% probability over 100%. The administration's decision to delay implementation of a new ozone standard perpetuates uncertainty. Business welcomed it nonetheless because now they do not have to spend money to meet it for at least two years, and perhaps forever if in the interim a new president chooses never to implement it.

It's inaccurate and confusing when the media use "uncertainty" as a euphemism for "increasing certainty that things are going to get worse." A much better example of uncertainty intolerance is a phenomenon that psychologists call catastrophizing. Catastrophizing occurs when we look to the future and anticipate all the things that can go wrong. By dwelling exclusively on the negative possibilities and ignoring the positive ones, we become convinced that bad things will definitely occur ("It's bound to all go wrong . . ."). This can become a self-fulfilling prophecy of failure, disappointment, and underachievement; when we believe something will go wrong, we may act in ways that make it go wrong.

Imagine that you are going for a job interview, for example. Let's suppose that you are well qualified for the job and that you know there's only one other candidate who is a serious contender. If you are comfortable with uncertainty, you will rate your chances of getting the job at around 50 percent. But if you are prone to uncertainty intolerance, you may either convince yourself that you are bound to get it or decide that you don't have a hope in hell (catastrophizing). Which of the alternatives you choose will depend on a variety of factors, including your general level of optimism and the mood you happen to be in at the time, but either one—even the pessimistic alternative—will be preferable to remaining in a state of uncertainty. Some people would rather be certain that they're miserable than risk being happy.

The intolerance of ambiguity and uncertainty is closely related to another psychological phenomenon known as the need for closure. This also tends to lead people to avoid the twilight zone and to make more extreme probability estimates as a result.

WANTING AN ANSWER *NOW*

Imagine the two poles of complete certainty and complete uncertainty as exerting opposing forces upon the mind. The gravitational force exerted by the pole of certainty is what psychologists call "the need for closure." It is the desire for an answer to a question. When this desire becomes overwhelming, any answer, even a wrong one, is preferable to remaining in a state of confusion and ambiguity. Acting in the opposite direction is the gravitational pull of the pole of uncertainty, which is sometimes called "the need to *avoid* closure." When that force becomes overwhelming, no answer is found satisfactory, and the person remains so open-minded that he or she cannot form any opinion at all.

People differ considerably in the extent to which they are swayed by these opposing forces, and the differences can be measured by means of a test that asks how strongly you agree or disagree with statements such as these:

- I feel irritable when one person disagrees with what everyone else in a group believes.
- I hate to change my plans at the last minute.
- It's annoying to listen to someone who cannot seem to make up his or her mind.
- I'd rather know bad news than stay in a state of uncertainty.

Agreement with these statements indicates a greater need for closure, whereas agreement with the following statements suggests a greater need to avoid closure:

- Even after I've made up my mind about something, I am always eager to consider a different opinion.
- I like to have friends who are unpredictable.
- When I go shopping, I have difficulty deciding exactly what it is that I want.
- My personal space is usually messy and disorganized.

In a person with high risk intelligence, these two opposing forces are so evenly matched as to cancel each other out, leaving the work of judgment to proceed entirely on the basis of rational calculation. For most people, however, one force will typically be stronger than the other, and as a result their probability estimates will be systematically biased in one direction or another. If the need for closure is dominant, the probability estimates will be pulled toward the extremes of 0 percent and 100 percent, as in Figure 8*a*. This gives rise to the calibration curve shown in Figure 9*a*, which indicates overconfidence. So if your curve looks like that, this suggests that your mind harbors a strong need for closure. If, on the other hand, the need to avoid closure gains the upper hand, the probability estimates will be pulled toward the midpoint of 50 percent, as in Figure 8*b*. This gives rise to the calibration curve shown in Figure 9*b*, which indicates underconfidence. If your curve looks like this, you may tend to be swayed by the need to avoid closure.

FIGURE 8: TWO FORCES THAT DISTORT RISK INTELLIGENCE. The horizontal axes show the range of probability estimates from 0 to 100 percent, and the vertical axes show the spectrum of subjective certainty from complete uncertainty ("I have no idea") to complete certainty ("I'm absolutely sure"). The U-shaped curve shows the relationship between probability estimates and subjective certainty. The dotted arrows indicate the need for closure (*a*) and the need to avoid closure (*b*).

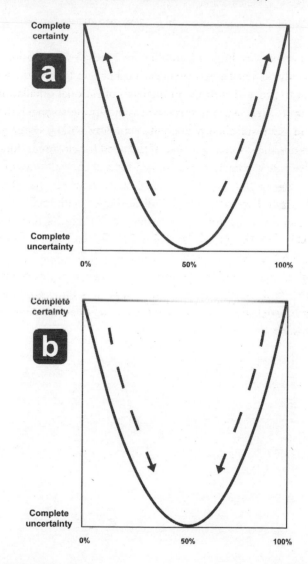

FIGURE 9: CALIBRATION CURVES INDICATING OVERCONFIDENCE (*a*) AND UNDERCONFIDENCE (*b*).

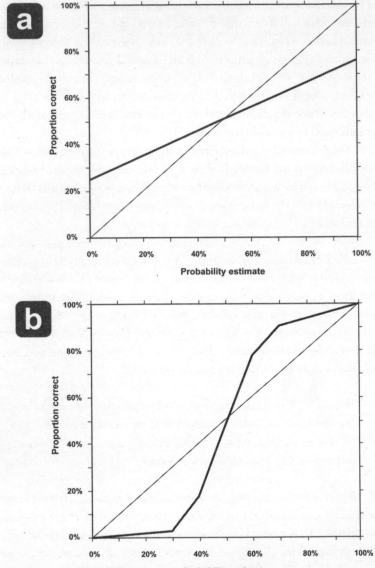

THE FALLACY OF WORST-CASE THINKING

The need to avoid closure can be particularly intense when we grapple with extreme dangers, such as terrorist attacks or ecological catastrophes. As we saw in chapter 1, many people react to the threat of climate change by either blocking it out altogether or becoming desperately concerned about it. It is hard to occupy the middle ground, treating global warming as a serious threat but without freaking out about it. Once we allow ourselves to start contemplating it at all, our minds quickly become overwhelmed.

There's something mesmerizing about apocalyptic scenarios. Like an alluring femme fatale, they exert an uncanny pull on the imagination. That is why what the security expert Bruce Schneier calls "worst-case thinking" is so dangerous. It substitutes imagination for thinking, speculation for risk analysis, and fear for reason.

One of the clearest examples of worst-case thinking was the so-called one percent doctrine, which Dick Cheney is said to have advocated while he was vice president in the George W. Bush administration. According to the journalist Ron Suskind, Cheney first proposed the doctrine at a meeting with CIA Director George Tenet and National Security Advisor Condoleezza Rice in November 2001. Responding to the thought that Al Qaeda might want to acquire a nuclear weapon, Cheney apparently remarked:

> If there's a 1 percent chance that Pakistani scientists are helping al-Qaeda build or develop a nuclear weapon, we have to treat it as a certainty in terms of our response. It's not about our analysis. . . . It's about our response.

By transforming low-probability events into complete certainties whenever the events are particularly scary, worst-case thinking leads to terrible decision making. For one thing, it's only half of the cost-benefit equation. "Every decision has costs and benefits, risks and rewards," Schneier points out. "By speculating about what can possibly go wrong, and then acting as if that is likely to happen, worst-case thinking focuses only on the extreme but improbable risks and does a poor job at assessing outcomes."

An epidemic of worst-case thinking broke out in the United States in the aftermath of the Three Mile Island accident in 1979. A core meltdown in the nuclear power station there led to the release of radioactive gases. The Kemeny Commission Report, created by presidential order, concluded that "there will either be no case of cancer or the number of cases will be so small that it will never be possible to detect them," but the public was not convinced. As a result of the furor, no new nuclear power plants were built in the United States for thirty years. The coal- and oil-fueled plants that were built instead, however, surely caused far more harm than the meltdown at Three Mile Island, both directly via air pollution and indirectly by contributing to global warming.

The impact of the Three Mile Island accident was probably reinforced by the release, twelve days before the meltdown, of *The China Syndrome*, a movie in which a catastrophic accident at a nuclear power plant is averted by the courageous actions of the protagonists. The movie's title is a direct reference to a worst-case scenario—the most dangerous kind of nuclear meltdown, where reactor components melt through their containment structures and into the underlying earth, "all the way to China."

The question of whether environmental impact statements should include discussion of worst-case scenarios is still the subject of intense debate. Environmentalist groups tend to advocate such discussion, in part to grab the attention of the general public. The US government originally required discussion of worst-case scenarios but later changed its mind, apparently on the ground that such discussions tend to provoke overreactions. This is a move in the right direction; if the chance that the worst case will happen is extremely low, the benefits of considering it will be far outweighed by the unnecessary fear that such consideration would provoke. Like radiation, fear damages health and is costly to clear up.

As Bruce Schneier observes, "Any fear that would make a good movie plot is amenable to worst-case thinking." With that in mind, he runs an annual "Movie-Plot Threat Contest." Entrants are invited to submit the most unlikely, yet still plausible, terrorist attack scenarios they can come up with. The purpose of this contest is "absurd humor," but Schneier hopes that it also makes a point. He is critical of many homeland security measures, which seem designed to defend against specific "movie plots" instead of against the broad threats of terrorism. "We all do it," admits Schneier. "Our imaginations run wild with detailed and specific threats. We imagine anthrax spread from crop dusters. Or a contaminated milk supply. Or terrorist scuba divers armed with almanacs. Before long, we're envisioning an entire movie plot, without Bruce Willis saving the day. And we're scared."

Psychologically, this all makes a certain basic sense. Worst-case scenarios are compelling because they evoke vivid mental images that overwhelm rational thinking. Box cutters and shoe bombs conjure up vivid mental images. "We must protect the Super Bowl" packs more emotional punch than the vague "We should defend ourselves against terrorism."

Fear alone is, however, not a sound basis on which to make policy. As we saw in chapter 1, the long lines at airports caused by the introduction of new airport security procedures have led more people to drive rather than fly, and that in turn has led to thousands more road fatalities than would otherwise have occurred, because driving is so much more dangerous than flying. Fear of "stranger danger" has also led to huge changes in parental behavior over the past few decades, which may have a net cost for child welfare. That, at least, is what the sociologist Frank Furedi argues in his challenging book *Paranoid Parenting*. Parents have always been worried about their kids, of course, but Furedi argues that their concerns have intensified in a historically unprecedented way since the late 1970s, to the extent that these days virtually every childhood experience comes with a health warning. The result is that parents look at each experience from the point of view of a worst-case scenario and so place increasing restrictions on what their kids can do; in the past few decades, for example, there has been a steep decline in the number of children who are allowed to bicycle to school and in the distance from home that kids are allowed to go to play unsupervised. There has also been an increase in the amount of time that parents spend on child rearing; contrary to the common wisdom that parents have less time for their children these days, a working mom today actually spends more time with her kids than a nonworking mom did in the 1970s.

I am not aware of any studies that have attempted to measure the psychological changes that have driven this cultural shift. It would be interesting to measure the risk intelligence of parents by, for example, comparing their estimates of certain risks with objective data about the frequency of those risks. Anecdotal evidence, however, suggests that it might be hard to gather such data.

The problem with paranoid parenting is that, like other cases of worst-case thinking, it ignores half of the cost-benefit equation. In worrying about stranger danger, for example, parents focus on the extreme but improbable risk of a child molester attacking or abducting their children and fail to weigh it against the more mundane but far more likely benefits of exercise, socialization, and independence that children gain from being allowed greater freedom. To put it another way, worried parents tend to focus on the risks of giving their children greater leeway and fail to consider the risks of *not* doing so. The long-term developmental consequences of paranoid parenting include isolation from peers, infantilism, and loss of autonomy. Unlike the chance of abduction, though, those risks are highly probable.

Paranoid parenting is also evident in popular attitudes to fever in children. Fever is one of the most common reasons that parents seek medical attention for their children, a habit that is almost certainly due to the widespread belief that fever is a disease rather than the body's way of fighting infection. In 1980, the physician Barton Schmitt coined the term "fever phobia" to designate the numerous misconceptions parents had about fever. Schmitt found that 63 percent of caregivers were worried a great deal that serious harm could result from fever, and 18 percent believed that brain damage could be caused by a mild fever of 38.9 degrees Celsius (102 degrees Fahrenheit)—both of which views were, even then, wildly exaggerated by the standards of proper medical evidence. Two decades later, a team of pediatricians from Johns Hopkins Bayview Medical Center in Baltimore found that attitudes had not changed much. Concern about fever and its potential harmful effects was still leading parents to monitor their children excessively and give them inappropriate treatments, including sponging them with cool water (which can cause significant shivering as a result of the body attempting to stay warm) or even alcohol (which can cause dehydration and hypoglycemia, particularly in young children). Parents were even more dangerously liberal with fever-reducing drugs than they had been two decades before, giving high doses of acetaminophen and ibuprofen, which placed their children at undue risk of toxicity. Interestingly, 29 percent of the people surveyed said that they followed the recommendations of the American Academy of Pediatrics, despite the fact that no such policy existed.

Bruce Schneier tells a story about a security conference he attended where the moderator asked a panel of distinguished cyber-security leaders what their nightmare scenario was. The answers were the predictable array of large-scale attacks: against our communications infrastructure, against the power grid, against the financial system, in combination with a physical attack, and so on. Schneier didn't get to give his answer until the afternoon. Finally, he stood up and said, "My nightmare scenario is that people keep talking about their nightmare scenarios."

THE ALL-OR-NOTHING FALLACY

Another reason that probability estimates are often skewed toward the extremes of 0 and 100 is the widespread influence of what I call "the all-or-nothing fallacy." This is the tendency to think of proof, knowledge, belief, and other related concepts in binary terms; either you prove/know/believe something or you don't, and there are no shades of gray in between. The all-or-nothing fallacy manifests itself in phrases such as these:

- You can't *prove* that.
- You don't really *know* that.
- He thinks there is probably a god, but he isn't a true believer.
- We cannot predict what will happen to oil prices.

What all these phrases have in common is that they set the threshold (for proof, knowledge, belief, predictions, and so on) as high as possible, at the level of absolute certainty. Certainty, of course, is very difficult to achieve, and that's the whole point of this rhetorical move. By setting the bar so high, people who utter such phrases make it very hard for their interlocutor to leap over it. At this point in the argument, the other person usually concedes, rather weakly, "No, of course I can't *prove* it, but . . ."

They should not be so quick to do so. Instead of making the caveat, they should challenge the all-or-nothing fallacy itself. Why *should* proof or knowledge or belief require absolute certainty? Why should predictions have to be categorical, rather than probabilistic? Surely, if we adopt such an impossibly high standard, we would have to conclude that we can't prove or know anything at all, except perhaps the truths of pure mathematics. Nor could we be said to believe anything unless we are fundamentalists or predict anything unless we are clairvoyant. The all-or-nothing fallacy renders notions such as proof, belief, and knowledge unusable for everyday purposes.

One example of the all-or-nothing fallacy that has had serious consequences in the United Kingdom is the refusal of some worried parents to believe that the measles, mumps, and rubella (MMR) vaccine is safe. Doubts about the safety of the vaccine gained prominence in 1998 when Andrew Wakefield, a British doctor, suggested that it might cause autism, and called for administration of the vaccine to be suspended until more research could be done. Immunization rates in Britain subsequently dropped from 92 percent to 73 percent and were as low as 50 percent in some parts of London, as worried parents shunned the vaccine. In the following decade, however, as other researchers tried and failed to confirm or reproduce

Wakefield's research, his claims looked increasingly tenuous. Despite this, immunization rates were slow to recover. Many parents continued to believe that the vaccine might cause autism, and no amount of evidence seemed enough to convince them otherwise.

Of course, you can never prove with 100 percent certainty that something is safe. It is always possible that if you do enough research, you might discover someone who gets ill whenever he or she drinks a cup of pure water. But to refuse to drink water because of this remote possibility would be foolish in the extreme. Millions of people drink water every day without getting sick, and the huge amount of evidence should be enough to convince anyone that water is safe.

Despite the old saw that "absence of evidence is not evidence of absence," in many cases it is. It can often be safely assumed that if a certain event had occurred or a particular thing existed, evidence of it would probably have been discovered. In such circumstances it is perfectly reasonable to take the absence of evidence as positive proof of its nonoccurrence or nonexistence. The fact that no mermaids have ever been discovered is strong evidence that, unfortunately, mermaids do not exist.

It is fair to ask for evidence before believing some new claim, but a stubborn refusal to believe something unless the evidence is overwhelming is a different matter. Such stubbornness suggests that the demand for evidence is merely a smoke screen and that no amount of evidence will ever really suffice. I often suspect that this is the case when I talk to people who believe in conspiracy theories, such as the idea that the events of 9/11 were orchestrated by members of the Bush administration or that the world is run by a secret cabal of Jews. I can't disprove either of those theories with 100 percent certainty, but I can disprove them to my own satisfaction. If I can't disprove them to *your* satisfaction, either you know something I don't or you have set the bar way too high.

In addition to fostering the idea that something is false just because it can't be proven with 100 percent certainty, the all-or-nothing fallacy also engenders the opposite mistake: assuming that something is true just because it is possible. This strategy, which I call "the argument from possibility," usually exploits the ambiguity of words such as "may" and "might."

For example, I recently heard someone state gravely, "There may be forces at work in the world of which we have no understanding." The other listeners nodded in solemn agreement, as if the speaker had just uttered some profound words of wisdom, but I was appalled by the shoddy piece of intellectual chicanery. Strictly speaking, those weasel words simply mean that the probability that mysterious forces are at work is nonzero. That is true as far as it goes, but it doesn't tell us very much, since it is consistent with the whole range of probability from less than 1 percent to greater than 99 percent. Words such as "may" and "might" are extreme examples of the ambiguity that attaches to other verbal labels such as "likely" and "improbable." Nevertheless, it is not uncommon to find people exploiting this vagueness by first getting someone to concede the mere possibility of something and then expanding the beachhead by assuming that a high degree of probability has thereby been established.

One way to counter this trick is to ask for a probability estimate. That is what I did while everyone else was nodding sagely. After establishing that the forces the speaker was referring to were indeed the kind of spooky supernatural stuff I had guessed he believed in, I simply asked, "How likely do you think it is that these forces do, in fact, exist? Would you say five percent, ten percent, or what?"

After the usual protests that such demands for greater clarity usually elicit, the speaker was finally forced to show his hand. "More than ninety-five percent," he stated confidently. That time the general reaction was one of surprise, and a heated debate ensued about how likely it was that physicists could have missed the alleged spooky forces.

The argument from possibility is often used by journalists to trick interviewees into giving an appearance of assent. By asking whether something is possible, the journalist confronts the interviewee with a dilemma: say "no" and look ridiculously overconfident; or say "yes" and allow the journalist to construe you as admitting that it is probable. It can be hard to challenge the question without appearing evasive, but Julian Assange, the founder of WikiLeaks, managed to do this in an interview with John Humphrys of BBC Radio 4's *Today* program, which was broadcast on December 21, 2010. At the time, Assange was wanted for questioning in Sweden over alleged sex crimes, and some had suggested that the women who had made the allegations were part of a broader US conspiracy.

> *Humphrys*: So you're not suggesting that this was a honey-trap? That you were somehow set up by the Americans, by the CIA? You don't buy into that idea because your lawyer's suggested that that's the case.
>
> *Assange*: He says that he was misquoted. I have never said that this is a honey-trap.
>
> *Humphrys*: You don't believe it?
>
> *Assange*: I have never said that this is not a honey-trap. I'm not accusing anyone until I have proof.
>
> *Humphrys*: Do you believe it is possible?
>
> *Assange*: That's not how I operate as a journalist because almost everything is possible. I talk about what is probable.
>
> *Humphrys*: All right, what do you think is probable here?
>
> *Assange*: What is probable? It is less probable that there was that type of involvement at the very beginning. That kind of classic Russian-Moscow thing. That is not probable.

Not everyone is as adept as Assange at parrying the argument from possibility. Poor Othello is undone by it in Shakespeare's eponymous play when the vengeful Brabantio sows the first seeds of doubt in his mind by warning "Look to her Moor, if thou hast eyes to see, she has deceived her father, and may thee!" Note the word "may" in this remark; once Othello has entertained the *possibility* of Desdemona's infidelity, the way is open for Iago to turn a mere suspicion into overwhelming conviction by means of skillful goading, with ultimately tragic consequences.

In combating the all-or-nothing fallacy, there is a rich tradition of thinking that we can turn to for help: jurisprudence. The law has long recognized that proof does not require complete certainty. Radical doubt may be sufficient to block an argument in the philosophical debating club, but it is not appropriate in the courtroom. The Nebraska Standard, for example, specifically excludes "fanciful conjecture" in its definition of reasonable doubt:

> You may be convinced of the truth of a fact beyond a reasonable doubt and yet be fully aware that possibly you may be mistaken. You may find an accused guilty upon the strong probabilities of the case, provided such probabilities are strong enough to exclude any doubt of his guilt that is reasonable. A reasonable doubt is an actual and substantial doubt reasonably arising from the evidence, from the facts or circumstances shown by the evidence, or from the lack of evidence on the part of the State, as distinguished from a doubt arising from mere possibility, from bare imagination, or from fanciful conjecture.

It is clear from these instructions that "beyond a reasonable doubt" does not mean 100 percent certainty. Indeed, this degree of certainty is to be found only in mathematics and pure logic, so if the standard of proof were set at this level nobody could ever be convicted of a crime. Beyond a reasonable doubt does not mean *mathematical* certainty but, to use that quaint phrase, "moral certainty."

The idea that there may be different standards of *proof* opens up the path to a less dichotomous view of related concepts such as *knowledge* and *belief*. If it is possible to prove something without removing all possible doubt, might it not also be possible to know something without being completely certain and even to believe something without complete conviction?

"Lord, I believe; help thou mine unbelief!" says the father of a boy possessed by spirits when Jesus tells him that a cure is possible if the father believes it is (Mark 9:24). The mere existence of some doubt does not make the man an unbeliever. It's all a question of degree. But how much doubt is allowed before the man no longer qualifies as one of the faithful? And how much more doubt can an agnostic entertain before she becomes a *de facto* atheist?

Richard Dawkins is perhaps the most famous contemporary atheist and is often criticized for taking a particularly strident and dogmatic approach. Indeed, I used to regard him as a kind of secular fundamentalist. I changed my mind, however, when I came across his suggestion, in chapter 2 of *The God Delusion*, that we think of theistic belief in terms of a spectrum of probabilities. At one end of the spectrum is complete certainty that God exists. At the other end is complete certainty that God does not exist. In between there is a continuum, which Dawkins punctuates with several milestones:

- Very high probability but short of 100 percent. *De facto* theist. "I cannot know for certain, but I strongly believe in God and live my life on the assumption that he is there."
- Higher than 50 percent but not very high. Technically agnostic but leaning toward theism. "I am very uncertain, but I am inclined to believe in God."
- Exactly 50 percent. Completely impartial agnostic. "God's existence and nonexistence are exactly equiprobable."
- Lower than 50 percent but not very low. Technically agnostic but leaning toward atheism. "I do not know whether God exists, but I'm inclined to be skeptical."
- Very low probability but short of zero. *De facto* atheist. "I cannot know for certain, but I think God is very improbable, and I live my life on the assumption that he is not there."

Much to my surprise, I discovered that Dawkins places himself in the last category—not a "strong atheist" who believes with complete certainty that God does not exist but a *de facto* atheist who merely thinks that God is very improbable. I eat my words. That is *not* the way a fundamentalist describes himself.

The important thing about Dawkins's spectrum of theistic probability is that the threshold for belief is not 100 percent but somewhat less. Conversely, it is quite possible to be an atheist yet admit that there is some small probability that a god may exist. As the Australian philosopher Jack Smart has noted, a failure to realize this may lead a person who is really an atheist to "describe herself, even passionately, as an agnostic." Smart's point is that it would be misleading for someone who believes that there is no more than a 5 percent chance that God exists to describe herself as an agnostic. Such a pedantic insistence on applying the all-or-nothing fallacy in this context would also, he notes, "preclude us from saying that we know anything whatever except perhaps the truths of mathematics and formal logic."

Learning to feel comfortable in the twilight zone—developing negative capability—is crucial in many areas of life, where certainty is rarely justified. When weighing the risks and benefits of elective surgery, for example, or deciding which college to go to, there are always uncertainties, but you still have to make a decision. Demanding unreasonably large amounts of evidence carries risks of its own, including the risk of inaction. People who spend too long making up their minds may end up like Buridan's ass, locked in a state of analysis paralysis. Alternatively, if the need for closure is too strong, one may jump to conclusions too quickly and act with undue haste. Developing risk intelligence requires getting the balance right, steering between the extremes of uncertainty intolerance and endless calculation.

Practice with risk intelligence tests can help in this regard, providing that one reflects on the experience. One person who took the test commented:

> I just took it and on many occasions was thinking, well that sounds right, and hitting either 100 percent or 0 percent, which isn't actually an accurate statement about what I was thinking. Going through a second time more carefully and rating questions where I was thinking "that sounds right" differently from "I'm certain of that" gave much better results. At least for me, there's a tendency to express myself with more certainty than I actually feel and it was necessary to run through the test more than once to realize I was doing this.

Ambiguity intolerance and the all-or-nothing fallacy are not the only ways in which our minds lead us astray when estimating probabilities. Psychologists have also identified a bag of mental tricks that evolution has endowed us with, cognitive shortcuts—often called heuristics—many of which were once advantageous but don't work so well in our contemporary high-tech world. The ways in which these heuristics undermine our risk intelligence are the subject of the next chapter.

CHAPTER 4

Tricks of the Mind

> So numerous indeed and so powerful are the causes which serve
> to give a false bias to the judgment, that we, upon many occa-
> sions, see wise and good men on the wrong as well as on the
> right side of questions of the first magnitude to society. This
> circumstance, if duly attended to, would furnish a lesson of
> moderation to those who are ever so much persuaded of their
> being in the right in any controversy.
>
> —ALEXANDER HAMILTON

For thousands of years, people have noticed that the moon appears much larger when it is near the horizon than it does when higher up in the sky. Aristotle thought the effect was caused by the earth's atmosphere acting as a magnifying glass, but we now know that it is a purely psychological illusion, since cameras do not see it. A time-lapse sequence of photographs does not show any change in the moon's size as it rises in the sky. Writing at the dawn of the second millennium A.D., the Iraqi scientist Ibn al-Haytham was the first to argue that the illusion was a trick of the mind, not the atmosphere. Scientists today agree about that much but still debate the precise nature of the psychological mechanisms involved.

One theory is that when the moon is very low in the sky, we tend to see it in the context of other objects on the horizon, such as tall buildings or hilltops, while the zenith moon is surrounded by large expanses of empty sky. When the visual system estimates the size of an object, it does not simply consider the size of the image on the retina but also takes other information into account, such as the size of other objects in the immediate visual environment. This explains the Ebbinghaus illusion (see Figure 10). Although both central circles are actually the same size, to many people the lower one looks larger. Perhaps the lower central circle surrounded by small circles is like the horizon moon seen in the context of smaller things such as hills and skyscrapers, while the upper central circle represents the zenith moon surrounded by larger expanses of sky.

FIGURE 10: THE EBBINGHAUS ILLUSION.

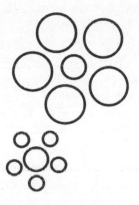

Whatever the precise psychological mechanism involved, one thing is clear; the moon illusion occurs because the visual system relies on a variety of rules of thumb when estimating the size of objects. Most of the time, these heuristics work pretty well, but under certain circumstances they lead to optical illusions.

According to the psychologists Daniel Kahneman and Amos Tversky, something similar can happen when we estimate probabilities. Just as the visual system relies on various heuristics to estimate size, the risk system has its own bag of tricks it uses to estimate probabilities. And just as the heuristics of the visual system sometimes lead to optical illusions, the cognitive shortcuts we use to estimate probabilities can lead us to make systematic errors. In this chapter, we'll look at some of these cognitive shortcuts and see how we can make use of them without being led astray.

Kahneman and Tversky are among the most influential psychologists in history. Born in the 1930s in what was then British-administered Palestine, the two men both received their undergraduate education at the Hebrew University of Jerusalem and did their doctoral research in the United States. In the late 1960s, they began collaborating on the studies that would later give rise to the "heuristics and biases" research program, to which hundreds of other psychologists have since contributed. In 2002, Kahneman was awarded the Nobel Prize in Economics, even though he had never taken a single course in the subject. Sadly, Tversky died in 1996 and so was unable to share in the prize.

Thanks to the many popular accounts of their work, the heuristics and biases discovered by Kahneman and Tversky are now understood and debated far beyond the groves of academe. To some readers, therefore, the material covered in this chapter may already be familiar. To keep these readers interested, I have tried to avoid using the same old examples, and the focus here is also specific to the ways those shortcuts limit risk intelligence.

Before discussing some of the heuristics and biases in detail, however, it is worth becoming clear about the distinction between these two concepts. A *heuristic* is a rule of thumb, or cognitive shortcut, which the mind relies on to help it perform a task more easily. A *bias* is a tendency to make mistakes of a particular kind—not random errors, but ones that are systematically skewed in one direction. In the case of the moon illusion, the heuristic at work is one of the rules that the visual system uses to estimate the size of an object: consider the relative size of other nearby objects. The bias is the tendency to overestimate the size of objects when they are surrounded by smaller ones and underestimate the size of things that are surrounded by larger ones.

Heuristics don't always lead to biases; they often work pretty well and lead us astray only under certain conditions. And not all biases are caused by heuristics misfiring; some are "brute biases" that are always on, regardless of what conditions obtain in the environment.

One such bias in the risk system is the tendency to overestimate the probability of pleasant events. Optimism bias, as it is known, is not caused by the application of any heuristic; it is a fundamental feature of our psychology that operates regardless of the environment. This chapter will look at how both sorts of biases get in the way of developing high risk intelligence.

THE AVAILABILITY HEURISTIC

One well-documented rule of thumb that we tend to rely on when estimating probabilities is the availability heuristic. It works like this: when estimating the likelihood of a future event, we scan our memory for something similar, and base our estimate on the ease of recall. If recall is easy, we assume that the event is likely; if it is hard to think of anything like it, we assume that the event is improbable. The availability heuristic is a good trick because, on the whole, the two variables correlate. Or at least they probably did when our ancestors were evolving on the African plains.

Today, there are novel features in the environment that mess things up. The mass media in particular degrade the correlation between the frequency of certain dangers and the ease with which we can remember them. A telling review of media reporting in Scotland found that the likelihood of a newspaper reporting a death from paracetamol (i.e., acetaminophen), a widely used over-the-counter painkiller, was 1 in 250 deaths, whereas for the drug ecstasy *every* associated death was reported. If people use the ease with which they recall something as a guide to how likely it is, this reporting bias will tend to make people overestimate the risks of taking ecstasy and underestimate the risks of taking paracetamol.

Or suppose you are trying to estimate the probability of some terrible ecological catastrophe happening in your lifetime. If you have recently seen *The Day After Tomorrow*, a 2004 disaster movie that depicts Manhattan being covered with ice in a matter of days, the ease with which the vivid images come to mind may fool you into thinking that something similar is highly likely. Or suppose you are trying to gauge the risk of your child being abducted; dramatic media accounts of other abductions may be fresh in your memory, with the result that you overestimate the risk of something similar happening to your own child. Conversely, you may underestimate the chances of falling off a horse because the media rarely report equine accidents and it is therefore hard to think of any examples.

The availability heuristic works well enough when we have to estimate the probability of things that are entirely within the realm of our personal experience, such as missing the bus or finding a ten-dollar bill. But when we're gauging the likelihood of things that are reported in the media, the correlation between ease of recall and likelihood breaks down, and the availability heuristic leads to biased estimates. TV news presents us with rare and dramatic disasters that we might never otherwise see: plane crashes, tsunamis, terrorist attacks, and so on. The images sear themselves into our memories and are recalled rather too easily. If we rely on the availability heuristic when estimating the probability of such dangers, we will tend to think they are more common than they really are.

But reporting bias in the media is not the only reason why the availability heuristic sometimes leads us astray. Merely imagining an event can also make it easier to picture and thereby cause us to overestimate the likelihood of something similar. Psychologists refer to this phenomenon as imagination inflation and have documented it in dozens of studies. Most of these experiments show that when people are asked to imagine various scenarios, they rate the events depicted in the scenarios as more likely. For example, before the US presidential election of 1976 the psychologist John Carroll asked people to imagine either Jimmy Carter or Gerald Ford winning the election. He then asked them to predict the outcome of the election on a scale from 0 (Carter will definitely win) to 100 (Ford will definitely win). Those who had been asked to imagine that Carter had won were more certain that he eventually would; likewise, those who imagined that Ford had won were more certain that he would be the victor.

Imagination inflation can lead to false memories as well as inflating our predictions. It's worth pausing here to note that our assessments of past events can be just as much the object of risk intelligence as can be our predictions. Conviction comes in degrees, whether thinking about the past or the future, and the standard risk intelligence question ("How sure are you that . . . ?") can and should be asked as much of someone recounting a memory as of someone making a prediction.

In one study, for example, researchers first asked the participants how likely they thought it was that various events had happened to them before the age of ten. The researchers chose events that they had previously established were unlikely (had a probability of less than 50 percent), such as winning a stuffed animal at a carnival game or breaking a window with one's hand. The participants had to rate each event on an eight-point scale, where 1 meant that they thought it definitely had not happened and 8 meant that they were sure it had.

Two weeks later, the participants were given descriptions of a variety of events and asked to picture them as clearly and completely as they could. After that, they were given the same list of events from the first session, and asked to rate each of them again on the same eight-point scale. When the researchers compared the two sets of ratings, they found that participants who had imagined events that they had initially thought to be unlikely were now much more confident that the events had, in fact, occurred. Increased confidence was found in some of the participants who had not been asked to imagine a given event but was much more common among those who had been asked to picture it. For example, among those who were *not* asked to imagine winning a stuffed animal at a carnival game, almost 20 percent became more confident that this had in fact occurred, but of those who were asked to picture this event, 30 percent became more convinced that it had really happened.

The role of imagination inflation in creating false memories should give detectives and psychotherapists pause for thought. When law enforcement officers ask a suspect to imagine his possible role in a murder he does not remember, the activity may unknowingly lead the suspect to believe that he was really involved. Likewise, when a clinical psychologist repeatedly encourages a client to imagine being sexually abused as a child, she may inadvertently foster a memory of something that did not really happen.

What can we do to avoid being led astray by the availability heuristic and imagination inflation? The most obvious remedy is simply to be cautious when estimating the probability of dramatic events. If images of such events come easily to mind, ask yourself if it is because you have personally experienced many of them or because you have read about them on the Web or seen them on TV. Likewise, ask yourself if such events loom large because they have occurred in your life or because you have previously allowed your imagination to give them full rein.

This strategy addresses a basic problem that underlies imagination inflation: source confusion. Source confusion is a type of memory error in which one misremembers where a bit of information was learned or where a particular stimulus was last encountered. We picture ourselves as having lost a toy when young and then assume that the greater availability of this image in our minds is due to having experienced it rather than having imagined it. It may not always be possible to distinguish sources that have become confused in one's mind, but the attempt to do so may itself be useful.

The availability heuristic leads us both to overestimate the probability of dramatic events and to underestimate the likelihood of situations that are not so easy to picture. If we are to avoid being led astray by the heuristic, therefore, we must not only be cautious when estimating the probability of dramatic events, we must also be proactive when estimating the likelihood of situations when images do not come easily to mind. If it is hard to picture an event, ask yourself if it is because it is genuinely rare or simply due to a failure of imagination. Some politicians and security experts, for example, are concerned that not enough is being done to harden the private networks and server farms that make up the critical infrastructure of the internet. They worry that hackers could figure out how to knock out electricity to a northern city in the dead of winter, leaving the elderly and frail vulnerable to freezing to death. However, in the absence of Hollywood films about such possibilities or the equivalent of ships aflame in Pearl

Harbor, the nation may not muster the energy to prepare itself properly for a serious cyberattack.

WISHFUL THINKING

A different kind of confusion lies at the heart of wishful thinking. Here it is a matter of allowing one's beliefs to be influenced by one's desires. Do you wish that people always got their just desserts? Then believe in karma! Do you want your favorite football team to win the championship? Then bet that it will! This is superstitious nonsense, of course, and an enemy of risk intelligence. People with high risk intelligence see the world as it is, not the way they would like it to be. No matter how strongly they want something, they don't allow their hopes and fears to influence their probability estimates. They abide by one of the key principles of decision theory: probability-outcome independence. That is, the probability of an event should be estimated without regard to whether the event would be pleasant or not.

This principle is honored more in the breach than the observance. Psychologists have frequently demonstrated a systematic tendency for people to overestimate the likelihood of positive things happening to them and underestimate the likelihood of negative ones. This is optimism bias that—as I mentioned at the start of this chapter—might be called a "brute bias," since it does not seem to be a by-product of any heuristic, but is a fundamental feature of our psychology that operates regardless of the environment.

Researchers have found examples of optimism bias in a wide range of contexts. MBA students have been shown to overestimate the number of job offers they would receive and their starting salary. Students in general overestimate the scores they will achieve on exams. Almost all newlyweds expect their marriage to last a lifetime, even though they are aware of the divorce statistics. Professional financial analysts consistently overestimate corporate earnings. Most smokers believe they are less at risk of developing smoking-related diseases than others who smoke.

Some research suggests that these biases disappear when people are depressed (a phenomenon that psychologists refer to as "depressive realism"), so unbiased judgments may be possible. According to this view, if we're not depressed, we tend to think we'll be luckier than everyone else. Other research suggests that even depressed people are prone to wishful thinking. Even though the predictions made by depressed people are more pessimistic than average, they are in fact "not pessimistic enough" because they fail to take into account the extent to which they themselves will make things even worse by virtue of their depression. For example, depressed people are less likely to go out and make new friends, and therefore make themselves even lonelier and more isolated, but they do not seem to make enough allowance for their own self-defeating behavior when anticipating their future. Thus, although their predictions are slightly gloomier than those of nondepressed people, there is an even greater gap between their predictions and reality, because *their* reality is so much worse. Paradoxically, then, depressed people may be *more* prone to wishful thinking than others.

Optimism bias undoubtedly played a big part in fueling the asset bubble that burst in 2007, leading to the financial crisis that unfolded over the following year. Lenders and borrowers alike believed that property prices would go on rising indefinitely with a conviction bordering on the delusional. The few naysayers were derided as dour party poopers. When the stock market crashed in 2008, short sellers—those who borrow shares and sell them in the hope of buying them back later at a lower price, thereby profiting from the fall in their value—were cast as the villains of the piece.

As the hedge fund manager Robert Sloan noted in his excellent book *Don't Blame the Shorts*, dislike of shorting has a long history. The Dutch East India Company complained about short sellers to the Amsterdam Stock Exchange in 1609. Napoleon called them "enemies of the state," and Jeffrey Skilling, then the chief executive of Enron, called one notorious short seller an "asshole" for questioning the company's accounts just before the company collapsed. But, as the Enron example shows, short sellers provide a useful corrective to epidemics of optimism bias. During the dot-com bubble, brokers rated forty-nine stocks as buys for every one they rated a sell; it was only the short sellers who couldn't believe the hype and focused on the negative earnings of so many high-tech start-ups. Likewise, short sellers were lone voices crying in the wilderness during the subprime mortgage boom. Subprime securities were indeed overvalued, and short sellers simply accelerated the alignment of prices with reality. It was the "long buying" of previous years that was the problem. The markets were unreasonably optimistic and badly in need of a dose of depressive realism.

What can we do to overcome optimism bias? One solution is to develop corrective procedures that compensate for the bias after the event. For example, the UK government explicitly acknowledges that optimism bias is a problem in planning and budgeting infrastructure projects, which results in systematic underestimation of costs and completion time. *The Green Book*, which sets out the government framework for the appraisal and evaluation of all policies, programs, and projects, states that "appraisers should adjust for optimism bias in the estimates of capital costs." As a result, the UK Department for Transport now requires project planners to use so-called optimism bias uplifts for large transport projects in order to arrive at accurate budgets. These specify different percentage amounts by which initial estimates of costs should be increased in order to compensate for optimism bias, depending on the kind of project and the desired degree of certainty that cost overruns will not occur.

We can apply our own optimism bias uplifts in a rough and ready way. For example, students who have to write an essay could double their first estimate of the time it will take them. Likewise, many people underestimate costs and overestimate revenues when writing business plans, so they should probably halve their plans for revenues and double their estimates of costs to make their startups more robust. Such corrections must not be so excessive that we fall into the opposite error of pessimism, but given the overabundance of wishful thinking, this is not a common danger. When it comes to making plans for the future, most of us need a dose of cold water, not a shot of self-esteem.

SOURCE CREDIBILITY

"You never know how good the intel is," says federal agent Tony Almeida in an episode of *24*, a TV series about the maverick Jack Bauer, who regularly uses torture to extract information from terrorists. The caveat doesn't seem to bother Bauer, who never tortures the wrong person and whose victims never lie. But in the real world, where evidence gained from torture is notoriously unreliable and spies often make mistakes, Almeida's dictum holds true. By coincidence, this particular episode was first broadcast in late 2002, while US and British intelligence operatives were coming under increasing pressure from their respective political masters to downplay similar worries about the reliability of the intelligence they were getting about weapons of mass destruction (WMD) in Iraq.

Those worries were exposed three years later, when *The Sunday Times* published the "Downing Street memo," a note of a secret meeting held on July 23, 2002. On that day, a group of senior British government, defense, and intelligence figures met at 10 Downing Street, the residence of the British prime minister, to discuss the buildup to the invasion of Iraq. The memo records the head of MI6, the British secret intelligence service, as expressing the view that the intelligence was "being fixed around the policy." It also quotes the UK foreign secretary, Jack Straw, as saying that it was clear that President George W. Bush had already "made up his mind" to take military action but that "the case was thin."

Despite the various official inquiries into the intelligence failures surrounding the Iraq War, many details remain murky. It would appear that British intelligence analysts were concerned that there was not enough evidence to support the claim that Iraqi forces could deploy WMD within forty-five minutes of Saddam Hussein's giving an order to use them, but came under pressure to tone down the caveats. As a result, the "September Dossier," which summarized the evidence behind the UK government's assessment of the threat posed by Saddam, was probably more categorical than the spooks would have liked.

The political motives for this are understandable. Government ministers may have worried that a more nuanced account of the uncertainties that bedevil all intelligence would have confused the public and thereby weakened the support for war. That fear is not unreasonable; given how bad most people are at reasoning on the basis of uncertain information, the politicians were probably right to assume that giving the public more details about the fog of war would only make them more hesitant to support military action against Iraq. But that only begs the question as to why any intelligence information at all was published. Historically, intelligence has been a profoundly secret matter, and the decision to use it as part of a campaign of public persuasion was unprecedented. If it is hard for politicians to evaluate intelligence reports, with all their inevitable uncertainties, it would seem unreasonable to expect the general public to do so. Critics who accused the UK government of lying and of "sexing up" the intelligence were badly off the mark: as the British commentator Douglas Murray argued, "the real fault lay in telling the people too much, revealing information that no previous government would have revealed, and, through this process, seriously compromising and embarrassing their security services."

With hindsight, it appears that there were only a few sources who told Western intelligence operatives that Saddam Hussein had WMD, but they were particularly vociferous. The most convincing, it seems, was an Iraqi defector code-named Curveball by the German and US intelligence officers who dealt with him. In a series of meetings during 2000, Curveball told a German agent identified as "Dr. Paul" that Saddam Hussein possessed mobile biological weapons labs.

A decade later, Curveball confessed that his tales of WMD had all been lies. His real name, the US TV show *60 Minutes* revealed in 2007, was Rafid Alwan al-Janabi. After fleeing to Germany in 1995 to seek asylum, Janabi had been identified by the BND, the German secret service, as a Baghdad-trained chemical engineer. When the BND approached him to see if he had inside information about Saddam's weapons program, Janabi told them what they wanted to hear. "They gave me this chance," he later told *The Guardian*. "I had the chance to fabricate something to topple the regime."

The Germans passed the intel on to US intelligence officials, and Secretary of State Colin Powell relied heavily on Janabi's tales in his speech to the United Nations on February 5, 2003, which paved the way for the invasion of Iraq the following month. Later, Powell's chief of staff, Lawrence Wilkerson, would wonder why the director of the CIA, George Tenet, and his deputy, John McLaughlin, had believed Janabi's claims so readily and why they had conveyed them to Powell "with a degree of conviction bordering on passionate, soul-felt certainty."

One reason for their mistaken confidence in Janabi may have been a common error in judgment that was first documented by Dale Griffin and Amos Tversky. They discovered that people tend to put more emphasis than they should on the *strength* of the evidence and not enough on its *credibility*, so when the evidence points strongly to one conclusion but the source credibility is low, overconfidence is likely to result.

The strength of the evidence refers to the relative support that the evidence gives to *one hypothesis as opposed to another*. Credibility, on the other hand, refers to the ability of the evidence to lend support to *any hypothesis at all*. When evaluating a job reference for a potential employee, for example, managers may consider both how positive the reference is and how well the referee knows the candidate. The first question refers to the strength or extremeness of the evidence, whereas the second refers to its weight or credibility. Griffin and Tversky suggest that people attend first to the strength of the evidence and then make some adjustments in accordance with its weight. Crucially, however, the adjustment is generally insufficient. In the case of a positive job reference, for example, employers might be overly impressed by the warmth of the recommendation and not make enough allowance for the fact that the writer has known the candidate for only a few months.

The case of Curveball exhibits the same pattern. Janabi's tales gave strong support to the hypothesis that Saddam possessed WMD, but the credibility of Janabi as a source was already in doubt well before Powell made his famous speech to the United Nations. Toward the end of 2000, British and German intelligence officers had flown to Dubai to interview Janabi's former boss in Iraq, Dr. Basil Latif, who had cast doubt on a number of Janabi's claims, including his tales of bioweapons trucks. US intelligence officials knew about those doubts and may have taken them into account, but not enough. Their evaluation of Janabi's evidence had been overly influenced by its extreme nature.

You might think that one way to prevent people from being overly impressed by the strength of the evidence, and make them pay more attention to the credibility of the source, might be to label the evidence with a discounting cue. For example, when passing on evidence from a low-credibility source, intelligence analysts could tag it with a disclaimer that would arouse a recipient's suspicion of the validity of the evidence. Unfortunately, however, the effects of such disclaimers seem to be short-lived; some research suggests that people heed such warnings at the time of exposure and discount material from untrustworthy sources accordingly, but as time goes on the original skepticism fades and the untrustworthy material comes to be accepted. For example, in political campaigns during important elections, undecided voters may see negative advertisements about a party or candidate running for office. At the end of the advertisement, they might also notice that the opposing candidate paid for the advertisement. Presumably, that would make voters question the truthfulness of the advertisement, and consequently they might not be initially persuaded. However, doubts about the credibility of the source of the advertisement tend to fade over time, with the result that some weeks later voters tend to remember only the content of the advertisement, and ultimately vote against the target of negative campaigning. This pattern of attitude change is referred to as the sleeper effect, and it has puzzled social psychologists for more than half a century. The sleeper effect may be another reason why the initial doubts about Janabi's credibility gradually evaporated, leading his claims about WMDs in Iraq to become more persuasive in the months leading up to the Iraq War.

CONFIRMATION BIAS

Another reason why politicians and senior intelligence officials were too easily persuaded by the shaky evidence regarding the existence of WMDs in Iraq may have been confirmation bias. This is the tendency to pay more attention to information that confirms what we already believe and to ignore contradictory data. Instead of carefully considering the evidence for and against something *before* they make up their minds, many people jump to conclusions and then justify themselves post hoc by looking for reasons why they might be right. They leap first and look later. This is one of the biggest enemies of risk intelligence. As the English philosopher and scientist Francis Bacon noted in 1620:

> The human understanding when it has once adopted an opinion . . . draws all things else to support and agree with it. And though there be a greater number and weight of instances to be found on the other side, yet these it either neglects or despises, or else by some distinction sets aside or rejects; in order that by this great and pernicious predetermination the authority of its former conclusions may remain inviolate.

One of the most famous demonstrations of confirmation bias was provided by the British psychologist Peter Wason. He presented students with a series of three numbers (2, 4, 6) and asked them to guess the rule that he had used to devise the sequence. The students were invited to test their hunches by generating their own three-number sequences, and Wason would tell them whether they conformed to his rule or not. Only when the students had proposed enough of their own sequences to feel certain that they understood the rule would they announce their conclusion. As it happened, only one in five of the students correctly guessed the rule, even though all were confident that they had discovered it.

Typically, Wason's students would form an initial hypothesis (e.g., counting by twos) and then propose sequences that conformed to this rule (e.g., 6, 8, 10). That is, they sought only evidence that would confirm their hypothesis and neglected to seek any evidence that might show they were wrong. They did not, for example, propose sequences such as 5, 6, 7 or 2, 8, 9. If they had, they might have been surprised to discover that those sequences also obeyed Wason's rule. For the rule was, in fact, that the sequence should merely consist of three ascending numbers.

The importance of searching for contradictory evidence was demonstrated by the Israeli psychologist Asher Koriat and his colleagues in a revealing study of confirmation bias published in 1980. Koriat asked participants to take two risk intelligence tests consisting of questions in a "binary-alternative" format like this:

The Sabines were part of
    (a) ancient India or (b) ancient Rome.

Participants selected the alternative they thought was correct and then indicated how confident they were in choosing that alternative by means of a probability estimate between 0.5 and 1 (it couldn't be less than 0.5, since in that case they would have chosen the other alternative). They then did another, similar test, but this time, before choosing an answer and providing a probability estimate, they were asked to spell out all the possible reasons they could think of for and against each of the answers. They were told to write the reasons down in the appropriate boxes in a chart like that in Table 1.

TABLE 1: KORIAT'S CHART.

	Answer (a)	Answer (b)
Reasons for		
Reasons against		

The participants were urged to provide reasons in all four boxes of the table and to formulate each statement in a manner that conveyed their degree of certainty in it, such as "I know for sure that . . ." or "I vaguely remember that . . ." Finally, they were asked to rate each reason on a seven-point scale according to how strong it was (1 was labeled "weakest possible" and 7 "strongest possible"). Figure 11 shows the calibration curves for the two tests.

FIGURE 11: CALIBRATION CURVES FROM KORIAT'S FIRST EXPERIMENT.
Solid line = first test (no reasons). Dashes = second test (reasons for and against provided). Note that the scale goes only from 50 percent to 100 percent, and not from 0 percent to 100 percent, because the tests consisted of questions in a binary alternative format.

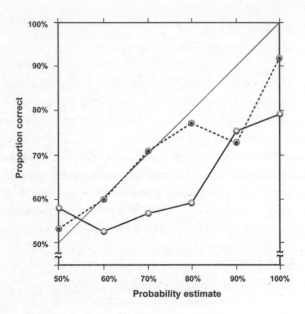

As is clear from Figure 11, risk intelligence improved in the second test. The calibration curve from the first test departs significantly from the diagonal, which indicates perfect risk intelligence. It lies mostly underneath the diagonal, which indicates overconfidence. The second calibration curve lies much closer to the diagonal line. Some overconfidence is still evident but is confined mostly to very-high-probability estimates.

Koriat and his colleagues were intrigued. The second calibration curve was one of the best that they had ever seen. But they began to wonder whether the improvement in risk intelligence was due to brainstorming reasons for and against each of the answers or whether one set of reasons might be more important to focus on than the other. They had a hunch that the key lay in looking for reasons *against* rather than in reasons *for*.

Two aspects of the data led them to this conclusion. First, the participants gave more reasons *for* than reasons *against*. Second, reasons *for* were assigned higher strength than reasons *against*. This pattern is evidence of confirmation bias.

Koriat speculated that the requirement to produce reasons *against* as well as reasons *for* might have counteracted the natural tendency to focus only on the latter. Was it this, he wondered, that explained the amazing increase in risk intelligence?

To find out, he conducted a second experiment. This time, he divided the participants into three groups. As in the first experiment, all three groups first took a test in which they merely provided probability estimates, and then took a second test in which they had to provide reasons for their answers. This time, however, the three groups provided different types of reasons. Those in the first group were asked to write down one reason in favor of their chosen answer and one reason against it. The second group was asked to provide the best reason they could think of that supported their chosen answer but no reasons against. The third group only specified the best reason they could think of why they might be wrong.

The calibration curves for the three groups are shown in Figures 12*a*, 12*b*, and 12*c*.

FIGURE 12*A*: CALIBRATION CURVES FOR GROUP 1 FROM KORIAT'S SECOND EXPERIMENT.
Solid line = no reasons. Dashes = one reason for and one *against* provided.

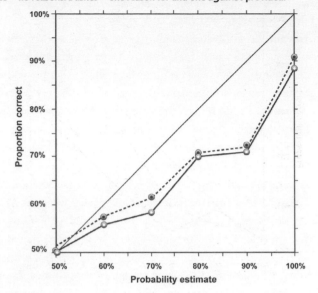

FIGURE 12*B*: CALIBRATION CURVES FOR GROUP 2 FROM KORIAT'S SECOND EXPERIMENT. Solid line = no reasons. Dashes = one reason *for* provided.

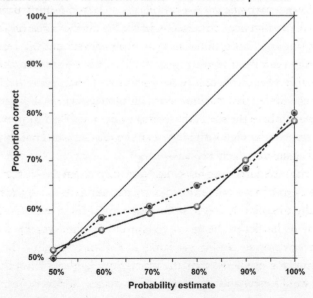

FIGURE 12C: CALIBRATION CURVES FOR GROUP 3 FROM KORIAT'S SECOND EXPERIMENT. Solid line = no reasons. Dashes = one reason *against* provided.

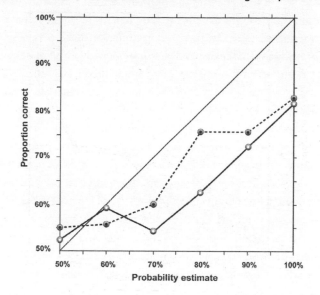

As you can see from the three graphs, only those who were asked to write down a *contradicting* reason (Figure 12*c*) significantly improved their risk intelligence in the second test. Producing a reason for and against (Figure 12*a*) resulted in a slight improvement, whereas simply noting reasons in favor (Figure 12*b*) had almost no effect at all—presumably because people were thinking of such reasons already. Koriat concluded that the improvement shown in the first experiment was due mainly to the search for reasons why one might be wrong and not to an even-handed weighing of all the reasons one could think of for and against one's chosen answer.

Koriat's research suggests that one way to improve risk intelligence is to expose ourselves to a greater diversity of opinion, and especially to seek out views that are opposed to our own. Curiously, this may be harder in the age of the internet than it was when information was not so readily available. In the early days of the Web, cyberutopians predicted that the greater availability of information online would inevitably expand people's mental horizons. Yet, as the activist Eli Pariser argues in his thoughtful book *The Filter Bubble*, the Web now seems to be having the opposite effect. Search engines such as Google increasingly use algorithms to tailor results to each individual's personal tastes, with the consequence that no two searches are exactly alike. Pariser noticed that people with a liberal orientation would get one set of responses when using a search engine, while conservatives might get an entirely different set of responses. For example, a liberal typing "BP" might get information about the oil spill in the Gulf of Mexico, while a conservative entering the same search string might get investment information about the oil company. And this algorithmic editing is invisible, so unless you sit down with a friend and try googling the same phrase side by side, it's hard to know how your searches differ from those of others. You don't see what has been edited out, and you can't choose what gets in. And it's not just search engines that are using these filters; news sites are experimenting with personalization too. Take all those filters together, argues Pariser, and the result is a uniquely personal universe of information that you live in online—a filter bubble—from which dissenting voices and different perspectives are silently excluded. We encounter less information that could challenge or broaden our worldview, and as a result our opinions may harden into dogma.

While I was writing this book, it occurred to me that I had inadvertently created a filter bubble of my own when forming my views on the 2003 Iraq War: everything I had read about it had come from one section of the political spectrum (the liberal Left), and from sources in one country (the United Kingdom). As a result, I firmly subscribed to all the shibboleths of the liberal consensus: that the Bush administration had done very little planning for the postwar occupation of Iraq, for example, and that the only reason for invading Iraq was to stop Saddam from using WMD. In the course of writing this chapter, and in particular this section about confirmation bias, I began to feel like a hypocrite, so I decided to start practicing what I was preaching. I began to seek out conservative accounts of the war, such as Donald Rumsfeld's autobiography, and gradually my views became more nuanced. I realized that there was much I didn't know about the decision to invade Iraq and that some of the press reports on which I had based my earlier views were very one-sided.

Naturally, this caused some alarm among my liberal friends. One friend in particular became particularly heated when, in the course of arguing about the intelligence failures that had led up to the invasion of Iraq, I cited an extract from Rumsfeld's memoir. "You can't take everything that man says at face value!" exclaimed my friend with great indignation. "Of course not," I replied, "but nor should *you* discount it entirely."

Likewise, I realized that the only times I ever listened to conservative talk radio was when clips were played on liberal radio programs, which of course picked the most embarrassing sound bites and provided damning commentaries on them. When I started listening to conservative talk radio in unedited form, however, I was forced to abandon my sneering liberal bias and admit that some of the shows were actually pretty smart and many of them highly entertaining.

I am not saying we should abandon all our critical faculties in some sort of postmodern free-for-all. Far from it. "Keep your mind open," the saying goes, "but not so open that your brain falls out." It is essential to retain a healthy degree of skepticism, but such skepticism should be applied impartially to those from all sections of the political spectrum and not reserved exclusively for those we disagree with. When estimating probabilities, or deciding how credible an argument is, we should act like a wise and fair judge, who listens equally attentively to the lawyers representing both parties. When confirmation bias gets the better of us, we start to act instead like one of the lawyers, marshaling all the evidence we can muster in support of our case and downplaying any contrary evidence. Whenever we notice that happening, we should do our best to play devil's advocate to ourselves— or find someone else who can argue against us.

THE DANGERS OF HINDSIGHT

If, despite the effects of confirmation bias, we eventually encounter information that causes us to change our minds, another problem often emerges: we then say that we really knew it all along and deny ever having held the beliefs we have abandoned. This phenomenon is known as hindsight bias, and it is one of my pet hates.

Hindsight bias undermines risk intelligence because it prevents us from learning from our mistakes. How can we learn from them if we don't admit we have made them in the first place? But perhaps the saddest consequence of hindsight bias is a diminished capacity for surprise. In order to be surprised, you have to be aware of the mismatch between the evidence in front of you and your previous expectations. If you deceive yourself into thinking that the evidence is, in fact, just what you had expected all along, you won't experience that curious mental jolt, that sense of wonderment at the unforeseen, which is both pleasurable in itself and absolutely crucial if learning is to take place.

A friend of mine told me about a particularly annoying case of hindsight bias he came across when attending a baseball game in Boston. The guy standing behind him would say after every play, like clockwork, "I knew that was going to happen." If the batter struck out, "I knew he was going to do that by the way he approached the plate." If he got a hit, "I knew the pitcher was trying too hard to get a strike." Then came one of the rarest plays in baseball, an unassisted triple play. Sure enough came the familiar cry, "I knew that was going to happen." At that point, my friend decided he had had enough. He turned around and told the self-professed clairvoyant, "Tell me what's going to happen on the next play—and if you're wrong, please shut up for the rest of the game."

The first people to study hindsight bias systematically were the Israeli psychologists Baruch Fischhoff and Ruth Beyth. In 1972, as Richard Nixon was preparing to make his historic visit to China, they asked volunteers to estimate the probabilities of various possible outcomes, such as whether Nixon would meet Mao Zedong and whether the United States would establish a permanent diplomatic mission in Beijing. When Nixon returned to the United States, Fischhoff and Beyth asked the participants to recall their predictions. They found that if an event had actually occurred, the participants tended to err on the side of recalling higher estimates than the ones they had originally provided. Conversely, if the event had *not* occurred, they made the opposite mistake, reporting that they had assigned it a lower probability than they actually had.

More recently, Gavin Cassar and Justin Craig carried out a study of 705 people in the early stages of starting new business ventures. They asked the budding entrepreneurs to estimate the chances that their start-ups would become operating businesses. Later, 198 of those whose businesses had failed were asked to recall their original estimates. Hindsight bias was clearly at work; the entrepreneurs had originally estimated their chances of success at 80 percent on average, but after their start-ups had gone to the wall they claimed that they had anticipated only a 50 percent success rate. Interestingly, previous experience of starting a business made no difference; the old hands had failed to draw any lessons from the past.

We're all guilty of hindsight bias to some extent. Some commentators now talk as if the financial crisis of 2007–2008 was almost inevitable, even though it caught most of us by surprise. Some of those who confidently predicted that the US invasion of Iraq would rapidly usher in democracy now say it was obvious that things would turn out badly. But rewriting the past in this way makes it impossible to learn from our mistakes. And, as Baruch Fischhoff wondered when he first started thinking about hindsight bias in the early 1970s, "If we're so prescient, why aren't we running the world?"

While she was writing her book *Being Wrong*, Kathryn Schulz found yet more evidence of how difficult it can be to remember our mistakes. When she told people what she was writing about, many would respond by saying "You should interview me, I'm wrong all the time." Schulz would then ask for an example, at which point the other person would fall silent and, after scratching his head awhile, admit to drawing a blank. One person told her:

> It's funny; I can sort of picture many times where I've said, "oh, no, I'm so wrong, this is so bad or so embarrassing," and I can even sort of recall losing sleep and missing dinners and being all uptight, but I can't actually remember a single specific instance of being wrong.

Even when we do remember our mistakes, we may still reduce our chances of learning from them by making excuses. Schulz notes two particularly common examples. The first involves inserting the crucial word "but," as in "I was wrong, *but* . . ." The second involves using the passive rather than the active voice, as in "mistakes were made." By minimizing our errors or distancing ourselves from them, we rob them of their teaching potential.

One of the hardest questions to answer at a job interview is "What was the biggest mistake you made in your last job?" If you can't remember making any mistakes at all, the interviewers will rightly infer that you lack insight. If, on the other hand, you own up to a massive blunder, they might doubt your competence. President George W. Bush was caught on the horns of this dilemma when he was asked, at a press conference in April 2004, what his biggest mistake had been and what lessons he had learned from it. His reply was embarrassing to listen to:

> I wish you'd have given me this written question ahead of time so I could plan for it. . . . Er, John, I'm sure historians will look back and say, gosh, he could've done it better this way or that way. . . . Er . . . You know, I just, er . . . I'm sure something will pop into my head here in the midst of this press conference, with all the pressure of trying to come up with an answer, but it hasn't yet . . . I hope . . . I don't want to sound like I have made no mistakes. I'm confident I have. You just put me under the spot here, and maybe I'm not as quick on my feet as I should be in coming up with one.

If you don't want to sound as dumb as Bush did on that occasion when you go for your next job interview, make sure you've got a good answer to this question up your sleeve.

Is there anything we can do to reduce hindsight bias? Simply warning people about its dangers seems to have almost no effect. The best remedy is to record predictions as one makes them and review the notes regularly. The personal prediction test in Appendix 2 provides a structured format for doing just that. By keeping track of which predictions come true and which do not, and checking them against our original probability estimates, it becomes harder to rewrite the past and therefore easier to learn from our mistakes.

THE MIND-READING ILLUSION

Another cognitive bias that hinders the development and exercise of risk intelligence is the mind-reading illusion. This is the tendency to think we are better at reading other people than we really are. One of its most common manifestations is the completely unjustified faith many of us have in our ability to spot lies.

When I was seventeen I fell victim to the effects of the mind-reading illusion in one of my teachers. I had been accused of some bad behavior at school and was hauled into the teacher's office and subjected to a lengthy interview. At one point, when asked a particularly critical question, I hesitated and looked down before replying. That, it turned out, was a bad move. At the end of the meeting, the teacher pointed to my "shifty gaze" as decisive evidence that I had been lying.

As a matter of fact, I hadn't been lying, but no amount of protesting on my part could change the teacher's mind. And on the basis of that faulty verdict, I was expelled from school.

Many people share that teacher's confidence in their ability to spot lies. Research has consistently shown, however, that such confidence is usually misplaced. The signs that most people look for when attempting to distinguish truth from deception are not reliable.

Contrary to popular opinion, liars do not have trouble making eye contact. Nor do they fidget or sweat more than usual. As a matter of fact, research indicates that innocent people tend to be more nervous than guilty folk when being questioned, because they are so intent on proving that they didn't do it.

"A lot of different signs of anxiety are mistaken for signs of deception," says Kevin Colwell, a forensic scientist at Southern Connecticut State University in New Haven. As Baltimore *Sun* reporter David Simon noted in his book *Homicide: A Year on the Killing Streets*:

> Nervousness, fear, confusion, hostility, a story that changes or contradicts itself—all are signs that the man in the interrogation room is lying, particularly in the eyes of someone as naturally suspicious as a detective. Unfortunately, these are also signs of a human being in a state of high stress.

When people rely on misleading or irrelevant cues, they may become more confident that they have spotted a lie even though they are mistaken.

It is rarely the case that such judgments are clear-cut; more typically, we have some index of suspicion that lies somewhere in between complete confidence and absolute distrust. In other words, the question of whether someone is lying usually demands a probability estimate rather than a simple yes or no. As with all probability estimates, their accuracy may be measured by a risk intelligence test.

Psychologists have carried out dozens of studies asking people to spot lies and measuring how confident they feel about their judgments. A 1997 review of this research, based on studies with a combined total of almost three thousand people, found that people's confidence in their judgments bears no significant relationship to their accuracy. The mismatch is one of overconfidence; not one study found any evidence of people having *less* confidence than was justified.

One of the studies included in this review compared the detection skills of undergraduates with those of new recruits to federal law enforcement jobs and experienced federal law enforcement officers.

Both groups of officers were more confident than the students but no better at spotting lies. The new recruits, who had been on the job an average of only five months, were just as overconfident as the older officers, who had more than seven years of experience. This would seem to imply serious consequences for the criminal justice system.

The psychologist Mark Frank has argued that much of this research is flawed because it tends to focus on low-stakes lies told by students in laboratory conditions. Everyone is bad at spotting such lies, he claims, but police officers may be better than chance (and better than others) at spotting high-stakes lies told by suspects in criminal investigations. When lying successfully can let you literally get away with murder, and getting caught can land you in jail for life, emotions run high and lies may therefore be easier to detect. This is an interesting theory, but it has yet to be properly tested. Until then, the evidence we have points overwhelmingly to the same conclusion: although we are often convinced that we can spot deception, our real ability to sift fact from fiction is scarcely better than flipping a coin.

Training can actually make matters worse. In one study, half the participants were trained in the Reid technique of interrogation, which purports to enhance people's ability to distinguish between truth and lies. The participants were then shown videos of eight suspects being questioned by a detective about their possible involvement in various crimes. The participants had to decide whether they thought each suspect was lying or telling the truth and rate their confidence in that judgment on a scale of 1 to 10. Training had a small *negative* effect; those who had received the training were slightly *worse* at sifting fact from fiction. But even though their judgments were less accurate than those of the naive observers, the trained observers were more confident that they were right. They could also cite more reasons to support their incorrect judgments than the naive observers could—reasons that mostly reflected the training they had been given.

It is worrysome, then, that the Reid technique has been immensely influential among law enforcement officers, since it actually *decreases* their risk intelligence. It seems to achieve this perverse effect by promulgating a false theory about the signs of deception. It repeats, for example, the same old saw that my teacher subscribed to—namely, that liars tend to avoid eye contact. As already noted, nonverbal behaviors such as averting one's gaze may well betray a state of anxiety or distress, but there is no solid evidence for the view that they indicate someone is lying. Conversely, vocal cues that do correlate with deception, such as elevated pitch and hesitations, are generally ignored even by experienced detectives and secret service agents.

Training methods that rely on more accurate theories about behavioral cues for deception may be helpful. But if they increase one's confidence in one's ability to spot lies more than they increase the ability itself, they too will actually *reduce* one's risk intelligence—at least in this particular domain. When considering which kind of training to give to those charged with interviewing suspects, training in risk intelligence may be an important complement to training in lie detection.

Friends and lovers are no better at detecting deception than are law enforcement officers and students. Moreover, as relationships develop and partners become closer, they become more confident in their judgments of each other's honesty without becoming more accurate. They trust each other more and so become more likely to believe each other's statements, regardless of their actual truthfulness. Along with a growing confidence in each other's honesty, people in long-term relationships also become more confident that they know what the other person is thinking, even though this is equally unjustified. Both of these tendencies suggest that it is easier to deceive someone you've been married to for years than to fool a new romantic partner. In the first weeks and months of a relationship, people tend to put more cognitive work into finding out what their partner is thinking, but as the years go by their theories about each other become fossilized, and they score lower on measures of empathic accuracy.

These conclusions tally with a raft of other studies of impression formation, which suggest that people are generally not very good at forming accurate images of one another. A 1995 study by William Swann and his colleagues at the University of Texas at Austin found that after watching just a one-minute video of someone discussing innocuous information about her background and interests, participants significantly reduced their estimates that she was HIV-positive. Swann concluded that many practitioners of risky sex believe that they have considerable insight into the character of their prospective partners even though they have not known them very long. Convinced that the prospective partner is not HIV-positive, they are happy to have unprotected sex.

The possibility that people's faith in their ability to "know their partner" may sometimes be terribly—and tragically—misplaced is graphically illustrated by Stephen King in his 2010 novella "A Good Marriage." After twenty-seven years of marriage, Darcy thinks she knows Bob pretty well:

> Did she know everything about him? Of course not. . . . There was no knowing everything, but she felt that after twenty-seven years, they knew all the important things. It was a good marriage, one of the fifty percent or so that kept working over the long haul. She believed that in the same unquestioning way she believed that gravity would hold her to the earth when she walked down the sidewalk.
>
> Until that night in the garage . . .

While poking around in the garage one evening, Darcy discovers something that shows how misplaced her confidence has been; there is a side of her husband she knew nothing about. This being a Stephen King novella, it is of course a *dark* side:

> All these years she'd been living with a madman, but how could she have known? His insanity was like an underground sea. There was a layer of rock over it, and a layer of soil over the rock; flowers grew there. You could stroll through them

and never know the madwater was there . . . but it was. It always had been.

The gap between what we *think* we know about our partner and what we *really* know is rarely as large and terrifying as this, but it is nonetheless pervasive—and unsettling.

THE ILLUSION OF TRANSPARENCY

It's not just that we think we are better at reading other people than we really are; we also assume that others can read us more accurately than is in fact the case. We suffer, in other words, not just from a mind-reading illusion, but also from an "illusion of transparency," mistakenly believing that our thoughts and feelings "leak out" more often than they really do.

Fyodor Dostoyevsky captured this illusion brilliantly in *Crime and Punishment*, in the scene where Raskolnikov is quizzed by Porfiry Petrovitch, the detective investigating the murders of Lizaveta and Alyona Ivanovna. Dostoyevsky is careful not to reveal whether Petrovitch really does suspect Raskolnikov at this point, so the reader is better able to identify with the doubts in Raskolnikov's own mind:

Did Porfiry wink at me just now? Of course it's nonsense! What could he wink for? Are they trying to upset my nerves or are they teasing me? Either it's ill fancy or they know! Even Zametov is rude. . . . Is Zametov rude? Zametov has changed his mind. I foresaw he would change his mind! He is at home here, while it's my first visit. Porfiry does not consider him a visitor; sits with his back to him. They're as thick as thieves, no doubt, over me! Not a doubt they were talking about me before we came. Do they know about the flat? If only they'd make haste! When I said that I ran away to take a flat he let

it pass. . . . I put that in cleverly about a flat, it may be of use
afterwards. . . . Delirious, indeed . . . ha-ha-ha! He knows all
about last night!

Raskolnikov's exaggerated view of Petrovitch's ability to read his
internal reactions is actually quite common. A dinner guest may be
sure her host can see that she dislikes the undercooked ham that has
just been served, when in fact the host is blithely unaware of the fact.
A secret admirer may cringe in the belief that his crush has been discovered, when in fact his classmate has no idea that she is the object
of his affections. A liar may overestimate the ability of others to detect
his lies and grow nervous as a result, thereby converting his mistake
into a self-fulfilling prophecy.

A study published in 1998 subjected people's lie detection abilities
to scientific scrutiny. Thomas Gilovich and his colleagues had groups
of participants play a round-robin lie detection game in which each
of them told lies and truths to the rest of the group. Participants were
given cards with personal information questions such as "Name a foreign country you have visited" and "What brand of shampoo do you
typically use?" Additionally, each card was either labeled "Truth" or
"Lie." Each participant would then either answer the question truth-
fully or falsely, according to the instruction on the card, while the
other members of the group tried to guess whether they were lying.
Liars were also asked to estimate the number of people in the group
who spotted the lie.

The results provide strong evidence for the illusion of transparency. Liars estimated that around half of the participants would detect
their deception, when in fact only a quarter did so—a success rate
indistinguishable from pure chance. Liars presumably felt as if their
feelings of nervousness leaked out or that others could "see right
through them." To double-check, truth tellers were asked to estimate
how many group members would mistake them for a liar. It turned
out that they expected significantly fewer people to think they were
lying when they were, in fact, telling the truth. In reality, there was no

difference; participants were equally likely to suspect truth tellers and liars of deception.

How can we avoid being led astray by the mind-reading illusion and the illusion of transparency? The first and most basic remedy is simply to treat all your hunches about the thoughts and feelings of other people with a pinch of salt, and to be similarly skeptical about their ability to read your mind. It can be hard to resist the feeling that someone is lying to you, or that your own honesty will shine through, but with practice it can be done. In particular, you should never talk to the police if they suspect you of committing a crime. If you are innocent, you would be a fool to think that your innocence will be obvious to all, or that the police officers are unbiased and objective. If you are guilty, the police won't necessarily be able to tell, but why risk it?

As if it weren't enough that there are so many internal, unconscious forces affecting our ability to make good, rational judgments under conditions of uncertainty, there are also a number of social factors that make matters even worse. They are the subject of the next chapter.

CHAPTER 5

The Madness of Crowds

Men, it has been well said, think in herds; it will be seen
that they go mad in herds, while they only recover
their senses slowly, and one by one.

—CHARLES MACKAY

I n previous chapters we have explored several of the problems
caused by overconfidence. Yet there is a flip side to this story; there
are certain social benefits of overconfidence, and they may explain
why overconfidence persists despite its dangers. Though it's true that
those who overestimate the extent of their knowledge will make more
mistakes in judgment than people with greater risk intelligence, they
will also project more charisma and authority. Since onlookers often
mistake confidence for competence, it may be better to err on the side
of overconfidence. How many of us would trust a leader who said,
"I'm not sure"?

A recently promoted senior executive came to me for advice after
being told by his boss that he needed to be more confident. In the
course of our conversation it became clear that the executive had
high risk intelligence and was happy to admit when he didn't know
the answer. It also became clear that it was precisely this that his
boss objected to. The boss was strong-willed and charismatic and
believed that senior executives should be clear and unambiguous
at all times and hide any doubts they might have. In circumstances
such as these, when social forces militate against the exercise of risk

intelligence, it is not hard to see why overconfidence is so widespread.

In fact, the social forces that promote overconfidence may well have existed for thousands of years, leading natural selection to favor bold leaders over thoughtful ones. Our ancestors' need for reassurance may have led them to place more trust in those who sounded confident than in those who spoke in more measured tones.

Natural selection may also have favored overconfidence for the advantages it conveys in combat. In species where males regularly fight one another, most engage in ritual forms of display before locking horns, so they can size up one another first. The fact that the displays are often enough to settle the disputes on their own supports the idea that males can accurately estimate their chances of winning on the basis of such displays. By signaling submission when it doubts it can win, a less powerful animal can avoid a costly fight. Even when combat does ensue, the fight normally ends with one male surrendering; fights to the death are mainly the province of chimpanzees and humans. These two species have taken killing to a whole new level by developing the special kind of organized group combat called warfare.

Why are we so different? In the context of international relations, this is known as the war puzzle: states led by rational decision makers should never fight because both sides could avoid the costs and risks of war by negotiating a prewar bargain reflecting their relative power. That is, both sides could obtain the same result they would have obtained by going to war without incurring the high costs that war entails, just as males in many other species settle their disputes without actually fighting. But the puzzle isn't restricted to wars between modern nation-states; it also applies to the earliest forms of warfare, from skirmishes between bands of hunter-gatherers to clashes between roving groups of chimpanzees. In all those battles, the bloodshed could be avoided if both sides were able to estimate their chances of winning accurately beforehand and negotiate a precombat bargain reflecting their relative strengths.

One explanation of the war puzzle may be that human groups, whether bands of hunter-gatherers or modern nation-states, tend to overestimate their relative power. That is not strictly necessary; a country that knows itself to be weaker may nevertheless choose to fight in an attempt to force a better negotiated settlement or because it prefers to die on its feet rather than live on its knees. But I suspect that is the exception rather than the rule; when two states go to war, it is typically the case that both think they have a good chance of winning. As Winston Churchill once observed, "However sure you are that you can easily win, . . . there would not be a war if the other man did not also think he had a chance."

Poor risk intelligence may therefore be an important cause of many wars. But that simply begs the question of why humans are not as good as other animals at estimating the chances of winning fights. The British political scientist Dominic Johnson thinks our tendency to overestimate our chances of winning evolved because it was actually beneficial to our ancestors. Natural selection, he argues, favored a certain amount of overconfidence in early humans, as it would have been adaptive in the small-scale, low-tech skirmishes that characterized human combat for most of our evolutionary history. It probably made fighters more tenacious and aggressive, for example. The same overconfidence is probably maladaptive in today's large-scale, high-tech conflicts, but modern warfare is far too recent in evolutionary terms for natural selection to have scaled back our confidence accordingly. Like our preference for sweet foods, which was useful when it motivated our ancestors to seek out nutritious fruit but leads to obesity in today's world of fast-food restaurants and convenience stores, overconfidence may be an evolutionary leftover that no longer serves us well.

There may also be aspects of modern warfare that make the problem worse. When bands of hunter-gatherers meet to do battle, the warriors of each side often first engage in ritual displays, much like other animals. Such displays allow each side to assess its relative power and to flee if the other side looks too intimidating. In modern warfare, Johnson points out, such visual cues are almost completely absent; the scale of operations and the long-distance nature of much modern weaponry "make combat, command and planning much more abstract and isolated from direct feedback." In such conditions, the natural tendency to overconfidence can flourish unchecked.

Unlike bands of hunter-gatherers, modern armies are characterized by long chains of command, and Johnson suggests that the pros and cons of overconfidence may vary at different levels in this chain. For soldiers at the sharp end, overconfidence may still be as advantageous today as it was for our hunter-gatherer ancestors, but for high-ranking officers in charge of strategic planning far from the battlefield, overconfidence may lead to misallocation of resources without any compensating benefit. At the highest levels of political power, the situation may be more akin to that of the grunts than that of the officer corps; shows of resolve and bluffing between national leaders, Johnson notes, are quintessential elements of international politics:

> Genuine conviction and confidence, over and above conscious strategizing, are signalled in public speeches, negotiations, political bargaining, diplomacy, alliance seeking, seeking treaties, development and deployment of military power, and even parliamentary infighting. And such signalling may carry crucial messages not only to rival nations but to one's own domestic audience as well.

A certain amount of overconfidence may therefore be as useful for political leaders as it is for soldiers on the battlefield. But this cuts both ways; resolves and bluffs may at times bolster national security but at other times may drive countries into wars they would have been better off without.

High risk intelligence may be much more important at the intermediate levels in the chain of command, therefore, than at the front line or among political leaders. For high-ranking officers in charge of strategic planning far from the battlefield, overconfidence has no advantages and will merely create havoc. Luckily, the environment in which they work is probably more conducive to careful reasoning, so we might expect to find reservoirs of high risk intelligence among the officer corps. This hunch finds some support in an interesting observation by the Lebanese-American trader Nassim Nicholas Taleb in his book *The Black Swan*:

> My first surprise was to discover that the military people [at a symposium on risk] thought, behaved, and acted like philosophers. . . . When I expressed my surprise to Laurence, another finance person who was sitting next to me, he told me that the military collected more genuine intellects and risk thinkers than most if not all other professions. Defense people wanted to understand the epistemology of risk.

As Taleb notes, this does not show in war movies, where generals are often portrayed as gung ho autocrats. If Johnson's analysis of the pros and cons of overconfidence at different levels in the chain of command is right, we should expect generals to have much higher levels of risk intelligence than both the grunts at the sharp end and their political paymasters. It is the politicians, not the generals, who are more likely to be enthusiastic about going to war.

DON'T BE SO BLIRTATIOUS

There are some other intriguing ways in which the need to project confidence can inhibit risk intelligence. For example, the social pressure to appear confident may lead us to cut short the process of carefully weighing the evidence in any given situation. Indeed, there is a common tendency for us to use the time that someone takes to reply as a proxy measure of their intelligence. As phrases such as "quick-witted" attest, people who reply quickly are often taken to be smart, while people who pause for thought may be regarded as a bit dumb.

Two psychologists at the University of Texas, William Swann and Peter Rentfrow, have developed a Brief Loquaciousness and Interpersonal Responsiveness Test (BLIRT) to measure how quickly and effusively people respond to others verbally. The test asks people to say how strongly they agree or disagree with statements such as the following:

- If I have something to say, I don't hesitate to say it.
- It often takes me a while to figure out how to express myself.
- If I disagree with someone, I tend to wait until later to say something.
- I always say what's on my mind.

By scoring the answers, Swann and Rentfrow come up with a number that indicates how "blirtatious" people are. The most interesting aspect of their research concerns the different ways in which people respond to high and low blirters. In one study, they found that classmates of high blirters were impressed with them early in the semester, but that their favorable opinions waned as the course progressed. "Early in the semester, while impressions are first being formed, high blirters may have the advantage because they seem more engaged, intelligent and competent than their low blirter classmates," says Swann. "But that advantage fades for two reasons. First, as low blirters become more comfortable in the classroom they may say more than at the outset, and second, because blirtatiousness is not associated with intelligence, their classmates come to realize that the exuberance of some high blirters can exceed their insightfulness."

This study suggests that people can see through blirtatiousness eventually, but it takes time. The default assumption, on first meeting a bunch of new people, is that the high blirters are smarter. This provides a clear disincentive to develop risk intelligence. All the intelligence in the world may be useless if other people think you're stupid.

My friend Geoffrey Miller, a psychologist at the University of New Mexico, was once phoned by a journalist in search of a sound bite. Miller told the journalist he needed some time to think and asked him to call back in a few days' time. When the journalist called back, Miller told him that he had thought long and hard about the question and had finally decided he didn't have anything useful to say about it. That's a great example of risk intelligence, but I bet the journalist never bothered contacting Miller again. The media tend to favor verbose idiots over thoughtful silent types.

FOLLOWING THE HERD

Another of the powerful but generally subliminal ways in which social pressures affect risk intelligence is the widespread tendency to follow the crowd. If several people with similar views get together, they often form a self-reinforcing group, in which each person's faith boosts that of the others and contrary evidence is completely blocked out. Conditions are then ripe for the "madness of crowds," which the Scottish journalist Charles Mackay described in an influential book published in 1841.

A century and a half after publication, Mackay's book is still a rollicking good read, and his accounts of economic bubbles seem more relevant than ever in light of the financial crisis of 2007–2008. Take the Dutch tulip mania of the early seventeenth century, for example. According to Mackay, during this bubble, speculators from all walks of life bought and sold tulip bulbs for ridiculously high prices, and in 1637 some tulip bulbs briefly became the most expensive objects in the world, before the market suddenly collapsed. Mackay may have exaggerated the scale and effects of tulip mania somewhat, but he does paint a compelling picture of the ways in which groups can amplify the irrationality of individuals.

According to Mackay, the growing popularity of tulips in early-seventeenth-century Holland caught the attention of the entire nation, and by 1636 tulips were traded on the exchanges of numerous Dutch towns and cities. Mackay tells of people selling their possessions in order to speculate in the tulip market:

> The epidemic of tulipomania raged with intense fury, the
> enthusiasm of speculation filled every heart, and confidence

was at its height. A golden bait hung temptingly out before the people, and one after the other they rushed to the tulip marts, like flies around a honey pot. Everyone imagined that the passion for tulips would last forever, and that the wealthy from every part of the world would send to Holland and pay whatever prices were asked for them. The riches of Europe would be concentrated on the shores of the Zuyder Zee. Nobles, citizens, farmers, mechanics, seamen, footmen, maid servants, chimney-sweeps, and old-clothes women dabbled in tulips. Houses and lands were offered for sale at ruinously low prices, or assigned in payment of bargains made at the tulip market. So contagious was the epidemic that foreigners became smitten with the same frenzy and money poured into Holland from all directions.

Of course, such a scheme could not last unless someone was ultimately willing to hand over the cash and take possession of the bulbs. In February 1637, tulip traders could no longer find new buyers willing to pay the increasingly inflated prices. As the realization set in, the demand for tulips collapsed and the speculative bubble burst. Some were left holding contracts to purchase tulips at prices now ten times greater than those on the open market, while others found themselves in possession of bulbs now worth a fraction of the price they had paid.

The parallels with the financial crisis of 2007–2008 are not hard to spot. Many commentators have observed that in the years preceding the crisis, optimism about ever-increasing property prices spread like an epidemic from one person to another and from one bank to the next. Mackay's observations about the madness of crowds appear as relevant today as they were 150 years ago.

Yet in recent years an opposing current of thought that emphasizes "the wisdom of crowds" has also gained currency. According to this view, large groups of people are sometimes smarter than a few experts. The classic historical example, often retold, involves a competition to judge the weight of an ox. While visiting a country fair in 1906, the British scientist Francis Galton watched as hundreds of people examined the ox on display and then tried to guess how much it weighed. When Galton later analyzed the guesses, he found that the mean estimate was almost exactly right. The ox was found to weigh 1,198 pounds. The average guess was 1,197 pounds.

The tale of the ox is a good story, but it does not prove anything. If we want to know whether it is indicative of some broader phenomenon and not just a lucky fluke, we have to carry out experiments. Unfortunately, very few experiments have been done, and they are not very convincing. Moreover, the so-called wise crowds in these experiments are not really crowds but collections of individuals. The average estimate tends to be accurate only when all the people in the group figure out their personal estimates on their own. In the weight-judging competition, each participant looked at the ox and wrote down his or her estimate in private. As soon as the members of a group communicate, however, any signs of collective wisdom tend to evaporate, as rumors spread and fashions develop.

Communication tends to inhibit the independent thought that is necessary if the average estimate is to be any good because of the natural tendency to conform to group norms. This explains why the only people not to get swept up in the madness of crowds are the few difficult and obstreperous people who don't care enough about what others think to let their opinions be shaped by the opinions of those around them. As the financial journalist Michael Lewis described in his 2010 book *The Big Short*, while house prices were soaring in the years prior to the financial crisis of 2007–2008, a few wise traders bucked the trend and made a fortune by betting against the market. Michael Burry combed through the prospectuses of mortgage-backed bonds and concluded that lending standards had been corroded. Charlie Ledley and Jamie Mai figured out that credit default swaps on mortgage-backed bonds were massively underpriced.

According to Lewis, the contrarians who made fortunes from predicting the crisis were all oddballs, outsiders, or both. Burry was a one-eyed fund manager with Asperger's syndrome who avoided contact with other people. Cornwall Capital, the fund run by Ledley and Mai, was too small to be taken seriously by most Wall Street firms, which nicknamed it Cornhole Capital. Paradoxically, the only way to restore sanity to a mad crowd may be by sprinkling it with a few "crazy" people. High risk intelligence may go hand in hand with a certain eccentricity, or at least a refusal to bow to peer pressure.

A good example of someone who makes the right decision even when the crowd is calling for the wrong one is New England Patriots coach Bill Belichick. In football it is widely assumed that you should punt on fourth down if you're far away from the other team's end zone. The stats, however, show that it is better "to go for it" in this situation (that is, to try to pick up the first down), and Belichick behaves accordingly, going for it on fourth down more often than any of his colleagues do.

Belichick is often criticized for his refusal to go along with the crowd. In a famous game in November 2009, the New England Patriots faced the Indianapolis Colts, who were undefeated at the time. In the fourth quarter, with New England leading 34–28, they faced fourth and two on their own 28-yard line. Much to the fans' surprise, Belichick ordered his offense to stay on the field. Unfortunately for the Patriots, they failed to make first down. Turnover! The Colts pressed forward and, with seconds to play, scored a touchdown on a one-yard pass to win the game 35–34.

Despite being the most highly regarded coach in the NFL and making the statistically correct choice, Belichick was hammered for his "cowboy tactic" and "needless gamble," but the torrent of criticism didn't faze him. The very next week, when the New England Patriots faced a similar situation in a game with the New York Jets, he made the same decision to go for it. In the press box, commentators were aghast, expressing amazement that Belichick would again buck the conventional wisdom, "especially after what happened the previous week!" This time, however, the Patriots made first down. Was Belichick's decision praised with the same fervor that accompanied the condemnations of the week before? Of course not; as the British economist John Maynard Keynes once observed, "Worldly wisdom teaches that it is better for the reputation to fail conventionally than to succeed unconventionally."

COMMUNICATING ABOUT RISK

Another way in which social processes impact on risk intelligence arises from the ways in which information about risks is presented to us and the conventions we use to characterize it. Many well-intentioned efforts in this area are counterproductive. For example, novel visual formats for communicating about risk may appear more user-friendly at first blush but actually turn out to muddy the waters. A case in point is the infamous color code system for terrorist threats created by Homeland Security Presidential Directive 3 on March 11, 2002, in response to the September 11, 2001, attacks. This system was meant to provide a "comprehensive and effective means to disseminate information regarding the risk of terrorist acts to federal, state, and local authorities and to the American people," but it was abolished in 2011 after Secretary of Homeland Security Janet Napolitano announced that the color-coded system often presented "little practical information."

The system rated the risk of terrorist attacks in terms of five different levels, from "low" to "severe," each of which was assigned a different color (see Figure 13). However, no criteria for the threat levels were ever published, with the result that there was no independent way to tell whether the current threat level was accurate. Moreover, the two lowest threat levels—Green (low risk) and Blue (guarded risk)—were never used, and the system remained at Yellow (elevated risk) for six years, from August 2005 until April 2011, when it was finally abolished. As one group of critics observed, "This static, ambiguous and nonspecific system creates uncertainty, or indifference, among the population it is meant to help protect."

FIGURE 13: THE HOMELAND SECURITY ADVISORY SYSTEM.

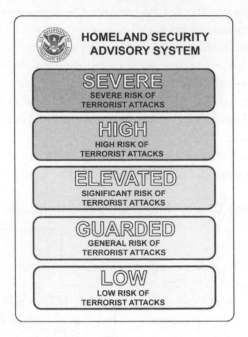

The warning system used in the United Kingdom is just as con-fusing. On Friday, January 22, 2010, for example, the UK terror threat was raised from "substantial" to "severe." Again, it's hard to know what on earth this actually means. The official explanation—that an attack was now "highly likely" rather than merely "a strong possibility"—did not make things any clearer. Given that the threat level had stood at "substantial" since the previous July and there had been no terror-ist attacks during that period, we can infer that "a strong possibility" indicated that an attack had a probability of less than 1 percent per day. But how much greater was the probability now that an attack was "highly likely"? Would it be 2 percent per day or 5 percent? Who knew?

Merely replacing verbal labels with numbers is not enough by itself to make things any better. Take, for example, the case of the

Doomsday Clock. This imaginary device is supposed to help scientists communicate their estimates of the risk of global catastrophe to the general public. Originally, the analogy represented the threat of global nuclear war, but since 2007 it has also reflected the dangers of climate change and new developments in technology. The higher the probability of catastrophe is deemed to be, the closer the scientists move the clock hands to midnight. As Figure 14 shows, the clock hands were reset nineteen times between 1947 and 2010 in response to world events.

FIGURE 14: THE DOOMSDAY CLOCK FROM 1947 TO 2010.

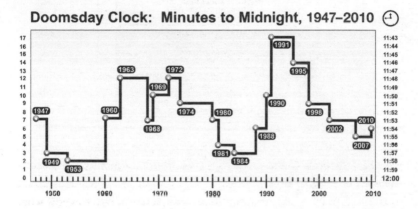

I wonder, however, about the value of the Doomsday Clock as a tool for communicating risk. The problem should be familiar by now; although the clock uses numbers (minutes to midnight), it is unclear what the numbers mean in terms of actual probabilities. How likely is a global catastrophe when the clock shows two minutes to midnight? 10 percent, 20 percent, or more? Or is it in fact less than 5 percent? When it comes to putting numbers on risk, it's not the case that any kind of number will do; it's probabilities that count.

WEASEL WORDS AND VAGUE EXPRESSIONS

A couple of years ago I received the following email from a friend:

Hi Dylan

Unfortunately my father (aged 91) was taken ill with a stroke the night before you first phoned me and, after initially showing some improvement, died on December 26.

Given your interests, you may be able to explain what the specialist stroke nurse meant when she told me that his "prognosis" was "guarded." An exhaustive Google search failed to turn these meaningless words into a meaningful number.

I understand my friend's frustration with the nurse's opaque statement. Why couldn't she have been clearer? But this sort of thing happens all the time. A 1998 study found that physicians preferred to use *words* when communicating information to patients about the chances of a treatment being effective but that the patients preferred receiving the information numerically. The same pattern has also been found among advisers and bettors for gambling on basketball; the advisers tend to use verbal probabilities, while the bettors prefer numerical ones. The reason for the asymmetry between speakers and listeners is not clear, but it may have something to do with the different incentives faced by each. Listeners just want accurate information, but speakers have more complex motives. While they want to provide information, they don't want to be caught out if they are wrong. By choosing a more ambiguous way to present the information, speakers can give themselves wiggle room and thus make it harder for their errors to be detected.

The obvious solution to this problem is to dispense with verbal labels entirely and require risk estimates to be expressed in numerical terms. This is not a new idea; more than a century ago, William Ernest Cooke, the government astronomer for Western Australia, argued that weather forecasters should attach numerical probabilities to their predictions. The idea is often rejected, however, on the grounds that it would be too complicated for most people to understand. That is rubbish. National Weather Service forecasters have been expressing their forecasts of rain in numerical terms since 1965, and, as we saw in chapter 2, they have become pretty good at it. If weather forecasters can do it, why not the rest of us?

It is not enough to supplement verbal labels with numerical translations; the labels should be dispensed with altogether, because people tend to ignore the numerical translations and interpret the labels in their own idiosyncratic ways. For example, the Intergovernmental Panel on Climate Change (IPCC) clearly states that, in its reports on global warming, the term "unlikely" is used to mean a probability of less than 33 percent, while "very likely" means a likelihood of at least 90 percent. Nevertheless, people who read IPCC reports interpret the phrases to mean a wide variety of possible values. Research published in 2009 in *Psychological Science*, a peer-reviewed scientific journal, showed that it was even possible for the label "unlikely" to be interpreted as meaning as much as a 66 percent probability.

When different individuals interpret the same labels to mean very different things, there arises an "illusion of communication." People may describe the probability of a given event with the same verbal label and conclude on that basis that they agree; however, since each person may implicitly attach different probability ranges to the verbal label, their agreement may be illusory. To complicate matters further, the same individual may attach a different probability range to the same label in different contexts. In one experiment, an intelligence analyst was asked to substitute numerical probability estimates for the verbal qualifiers in one of his own earlier articles. The first statement was: "The cease-fire is holding but could be broken within a week." The analyst said he meant there was about a 30 percent chance the cease-fire would be broken within a week. Another analyst who had helped this analyst prepare the article said she thought there was about an 80 percent chance that the cease-fire would be broken. Yet, when working together on the report, both analysts had believed they were in agreement about what could happen.

Sherman Kent, the first director of the CIA's Office of National Estimates, was one of the first to recognize problems of communication caused by imprecise statements of uncertainty. Kent was alarmed by the wide discrepancies between the ways that different policymakers interpreted the term "serious possibility" in a national estimate. Unfortunately, such miscommunication between analysts and policymakers, and between analysts, is still a common occurrence.

Vague labels cause confusion in financial markets too. Credit-rating agencies (CRAs) such as Moody's and Standard & Poor's (S&P) play a key role in such markets by assigning ratings to government bonds and other debt instruments. The credit ratings indicate the agencies' estimates of the chance that the debtor will default. But rather than using numbers to express this probability, confusing labels are employed. For example, the highest rating issued by Standard & Poor's is AAA, which indicates that the debtor has an "extremely strong capacity to meet its financial commitments." Slight increases in the chance of default are indicated by downgrading the rating in successive "notches," first to AA+, then to AA, then to AA-, then to A+, and so on. But the rating agencies never specify in numerical terms exactly how much higher the risk of default becomes at each downgrade.

In order to make some sense of the ratings, Wall Street investors have long assigned their own numbers to them. A bond rated AAA, for example, is typically thought to have less than a 1-in-10,000 chance of defaulting in its first year of existence, while for a bond rated AA the chance is usually thought to be less than 1 in 1,000. But in 2008, the rating agencies claimed that they had never intended their ratings to be taken as such precise measurements. Ratings, they argued, were merely their best guesses at a rank ordering of risk.

That was disingenuous, to say the least. In the early years of the new millennium, the three main agencies did start evaluating certain kinds of financial instruments in more precise ways. Each developed special software to estimate the risk characteristics of collateralized debt obligations (CDOs). The CDO Evaluator software introduced by S&P in 2001, for example, used computer simulations to estimate default rates for different portfolios. Table 2 shows the default rates assigned by this software to the various classes of asset-backed securities issued in 2005–2007. The default probabilities were obtained by "scaling" corporate default probabilities (which were easier to estimate statistically because of the large number of corporate defaults) by factors that reflected overall differences between asset-backed securities and corporate debt.

Table 2 also shows the actual default rate for each category of asset-backed security. As you can see, there is a huge gap between the actual default rates and the estimates. The agencies gave the highest-rated securities (AAA) a mere 0.008 percent chance of defaulting in the next three years (that is, a chance of less than 1 in 10,000). The real chance, it turned out, was 0.1 percent (1 in 1,000). The agencies underestimated the probability of default by more than a factor of 10. With securities rated A+ the error was even worse, with the agencies underestimating the probability of default by more than a factor of 300!

TABLE 2: CDO EVALUATORS' THREE-YEAR DEFAULT PROBABILITY ASSUMPTIONS VERSUS REALIZED DEFAULT RATE OF US ASSET-BACKED SECURITIES ISSUED FROM 2005 TO 2007.

	CDO Evaluator Three-Year Default Probability Assumptions, as of June 2006 (percent)	Realized Incidence of Default, as of July 2009 (percent)
AAA	0.008	0.10
AA+	0.014	1.68
AA	0.042	8.16
AA-	0.053	12.03
A+	0.061	20.96
A	0.088	29.21
A-	0.118	36.65
BBB+	0.340	48.73
BBB	0.488	56.10
BBB-	0.881	66.67

It is now common knowledge that many of the ratings issued by the major CRAs in the decade prior to the financial crisis were wildly optimistic. But it is only when we transform their ambiguous labels into precise numbers that we can see exactly how overconfident the CRAs had become. If we plotted the estimates in Table 2 against the actual default rates as a calibration curve, just as we do for the risk intelligence test, we would see an almost vertical line, indicating very poor risk intelligence indeed. Indeed, you would hardly be able to see the curve, since it would hug the vertical axis of the graph so closely. No wonder that when CalPERS, a pension fund, accused the three biggest rating agencies—Moody's, S&P, and Fitch Ratings—of issuing "wildly inaccurate" ratings, it won court backing to proceed with a fraud suit against them.

The fact that the ratings assigned to many investment products before the financial crisis were so badly off the mark was probably due to a mix of genuine overconfidence and more dubious motives. For one thing, the models used by the rating agencies to rate subprime mortgage bond–backed CDOs were riddled with flaws that the smart bond packagers on Wall Street could exploit. And since the agencies were paid by the institutions whose instruments they rated, there was an obvious conflict of interest: when a bank engineered a new financial instrument, it simply chose the agency it thought would give it the highest rating. In the wake of the financial crisis, an amendment to the financial reform bill put before the US Senate proposed that the choice of which agency to rate new offerings should be up to the Securities and Exchange Commission (SEC), which would rotate assignments among agencies, with those whose ratings proved less accurate being given less business.

If this or a similar proposal were to become law, some means of measuring the accuracy of ratings would have to become part of the regulatory framework. Yet this will be possible only if estimates are given in numerical terms, since measurement is a fundamentally quantitative process. The agencies would have to define their ratings by means of figures such as those shown in Table 2 above—by stipulating, for example, that a credit rating of AAA implies an estimated default rate of 0.001 percent every three years. That would represent a significant change from the present practice of simply providing verbal definitions. For example, Standard & Poor's states that a credit rating of AAA implies "an extremely strong capacity to meet financial commitments," while a rating of BB means that the debtor is "less vulnerable in the near-term but faces major ongoing uncertainties to adverse business, financial and economic conditions." Those definitions are vague and cannot therefore be used to measure the accuracy of the ratings. Only when the credit-rating agencies begin to define their ratings in more precise numerical terms will we be able to plot calibration curves and measure the risk intelligence of their assessments.

At the time of writing (September 2011), there are no such proposals on the table. The Basel Committee on Banking Supervision, which formulates broad supervisory standards for financial institutions around the world, is currently working on a new update to the Basel Accords. Basel II required numerical assessments of both the probability of default and the expected loss given default, and it specifically forbade relying on rating agencies' assessments to estimate them, but the estimates were typically produced by computer models. What if future rounds of the Basel Accords were to include some provision for testing the risk intelligence of bankers?

This could be done in a number of ways. At the institutional level, if credit-rating agencies were required to provide numerical definitions of their ratings, as I have just suggested, the risk intelligence of the agencies could be compared objectively. At the individual level, bankers and traders could be required to estimate the probability that specific loans would go bad or that particular trades would make a profit, and calibration curves could be calculated from those data, allowing the risk intelligence of individual financiers to be compared. Pilots and other professionals whose decisions can have serious effects on the lives of the general public are required to undergo regular testing, so why not bankers?

Another effect of defining the ratings in terms of numbers would be to improve communication. Investors use the ratings to guide their decisions and would benefit from clearer definitions. Junk bonds are riskier than investment-grade bonds, and therefore pay higher rates of interest, but investors can tell whether the greater return is sufficient to compensate them for the higher risk only if they know exactly how much higher that risk is—or at least how much higher the rating agencies *think* it is. At the moment, that is not clear at all.

HOW MUCH DOUBT IS REASONABLE?

Another area in which vague verbal expressions of probability cause concern is in decisions by juries. As we have already seen, the law acknowledges that proof is not a matter of 100 percent certainty and also that different standards of proof are appropriate in different circumstances. In many jurisdictions, criminal cases require that guilt must be established "beyond a reasonable doubt," but in civil cases it is sufficient to show that the evidence points to a conclusion "on the balance of probabilities." The latter metaphor is particularly apt; not only does it call to mind the famous image of justice, blindfolded and holding a set of scales, it also evokes an intuitive notion of the "weight" of evidence. Other standards also exist; in some jurisdictions, for example, "clear and convincing evidence" is a lesser requirement than "beyond a reasonable doubt" but stricter than "the balance of probabilities," which merely requires that the matter asserted seem more likely than not to be true.

The problem is that, like the verbal labels used by the credit-rating agencies, these legal standards can be interpreted in a wide variety of ways. A 1971 study, for example, showed that there was a large variance in the way American jurors interpret the phrase "beyond a reasonable doubt" even when given detailed instructions (the instructions also differed from state to state). The words are subject to the same vagueness and ambiguity that infect terms such as "likely" and "improbable," so judges and jurors can interpret them to mean many different things, giving rise to an illusion of communication that threatens the integrity of due process and equal protection before the law.

Could we solve this problem by quantifying legal standards of proof just as we can quantify words such as "unlikely"? How much evidence does the prosecution have to provide before doubts about the guilt of the accused become *unreasonable*?

A number of studies have attempted to answer this question. For example, in the 1971 study, Rita Simon and Linda Mahan asked judges and jurors to complete the following phrase:

"I would have to believe that it was a ____ out of ten chance that the defendant committed the act [in order to convict beyond a reasonable doubt]."

More than a third of respondents gave the answer as ten out of ten, but that was due at least in part to the fact that they could respond only in increments of 5 percent, so those respondents might merely have been signaling that they took "beyond a reasonable doubt" to indicate a degree of belief nearer 100 percent than 95 percent. The mean response among the judges was 89 percent, while among the jurors it was 83 percent. Simon and Mahan concluded that there were significant discrepancies between the ways in which judges and jurors understood the phrase. In a separate study, Simon found that judges believed that jurors applied the burdens of proof exactly as the judges instructed them, which points to the existence of an illusion of communication; since judges and jurors use the same verbal descriptions, they think they understand each other, but since they attach different probability ranges to the descriptions, their agreement is illusory.

In a third study, Simon took a different approach. First she presented a trial to the participants, and then she asked half to decide whether the defendant was guilty or innocent. The other half were asked to say how likely, in percentage terms, they thought it was that the defendant had committed the crime. She then matched the highest likelihoods of guilt with the guilty verdicts and the lowest likelihoods of guilt with the not guilty verdicts. By assuming that the cutoff for reasonable doubt would fall somewhere between the highest likelihood of guilt matched to a not guilty verdict and the lowest likelihood of guilt matched to a guilty verdict, Simon concluded that the standard was between 70 and 74 percent, a figure regarded as far too low by the judges she interviewed.

Simon also found wide discrepancies between the ways that jurors and judges interpreted the "balance of probabilities" (or "preponderance of evidence") standard applied in civil actions. Strictly speaking, the standard means that the probability of guilt must be greater than 50 percent, but the judges actually put it slightly higher, at 61 percent. Jurors, however, interpreted the standard as meaning that the probability of guilt must be greater than 75 percent. This implies that the jurors saw a much smaller difference between the criminal (beyond a reasonable doubt) and civil (by a preponderance of the evidence) standards than the judges, who made a much sharper distinction between the two standards.

It would appear that the range of different values attached to this standard of proof by judges and jurors is great enough to threaten the integrity of due process. One solution to the problem would be to require jurors to report their degree of belief in the defendant's guilt rather than simply choosing between "guilty" and "not guilty." To convert the probability estimates into a final verdict, judges could average them and convict the defendant only if the result exceeded a prespecified threshold, which would vary depending on the standard of proof required. This would also eliminate the possibility of hung juries and so reduce the number of retrials. Of course, jurors might require some training before they were able to report their degrees of belief in numerical terms, but that itself might be no bad thing.

Yet when Simon discussed similar proposals with the participants in her research, she found marked opposition to them among both judges and jurors. One judge stated that "percentages or probabilities cannot encompass all the factors, tangible and intangible, in determining guilt—evidence cannot be evaluated in such terms." But, as I have been arguing, it is only by quantifying belief and evidence that we can make progress toward more rational decision making.

As this and the previous chapter have revealed, there are many factors that hinder the development of high risk intelligence. The cognitive and emotional mechanisms bequeathed to us by natural selection often lead us astray when assessing probabilities; we're also vulnerable to a range of social pressures and group influences; and probabilities are often communicated by means of vague verbal labels and other spurious formats. Yet, on the flip side, it's also clear that our brains have the fundamental equipment for making good probability assessments in the right conditions, though some people seem to have a good deal more talent in this regard than others. Over the past few hundred years, we've also developed a powerful set of analytical tools that can enhance that skill and assist us in making good judgments, such as statistics and probability theory. They are the subjects of the next chapter, where we'll see that the development of probability theory by mathematicians in the seventeenth and eighteenth centuries extended our cognitive toolkit and gave us new resources to complement and correct our evolved heuristics. The fact that risk intelligence can be developed and improved by means of these new resources shows that it is not a fixed, innate mental capacity, such as face recognition or locomotion. Rather, risk intelligence is heavily dependent on the tools provided by culture. Sure, there must be some basic neural mechanisms that enable us to wield the tools, but risk intelligence is a joint venture between biology and culture, not a feature of the bare biological brain.

CHAPTER 6

Thinking by Numbers

The sign of a truly educated man is to
be deeply moved by statistics.

—GEORGE BERNARD SHAW

In 1682, a thirty-year-old Swiss mathematician by the name of Jacob Bernoulli returned to his native Basel after touring the cities of Europe. On his trip he had learned about the latest discoveries in mathematics and science, and soon afterward he began writing what would become his most famous work, a treatise called "The Art of Conjecturing" (though it was not published until 1713, by which time Bernoulli had been dead for eight years). In this pioneering work, Bernoulli showed how any probability could be represented as a number between zero and one. That is how mathematicians treat probability today, though it is logically equivalent to speak of probabilities in terms of percentages, as I do throughout this book.

Before Bernoulli, the idea that probability could be represented as a number was unheard of. The idea of differing degrees of likelihood had been around for thousands of years, but they were always expressed by vague verbal labels such as "likely" and "improbable." Accustomed as we are nowadays to phrases such as "There's a 20 percent chance of success," it may seem obvious to express probability in numerical terms. We fail to appreciate how radical this would have appeared to Bernoulli's contemporaries.

Take the case of the famous Lloyd's of London. The futuristic Lloyd's building in London, with its twelve glass elevators and huge barrel-vaulted glass roof, could not contrast more starkly with the homely coffeehouse that first housed the eponymous insurance market around 1688. In that crowded bar, Edward Lloyd plied the sailors, merchants, and shipowners who frequented his establishment not only with stimulating beverages but also with the latest news about shipwrecks, plagues, and attacks by pirates. The information was vital to insurers, who would price their policies to reflect the highly volatile conditions of both sea traffic and health that reigned throughout the seventeenth and eighteenth centuries. The policies must have been reasonably well priced, though, since the insurers turned a healthy profit and the shipowners came back for more. Yet none of the tools of the modern insurance industry had yet been developed.

Neither the data that insurers use today, such as mortality tables, nor the mathematical tools that they use to process those data, such as the probability calculus, were available to the men who met to strike deals in Lloyd's coffeehouse. Completely reliant on their intuitive risk intelligence, the insurers would price their policies on a case-by-case basis, weighing the specific circumstances of each voyage in much the same way as the horse handicappers we encountered in chapter 1 weighed up the particular characteristics of each horse in a race.

Today, we would calculate the prices with a formula based on probability theory, using the product of two distinct numbers: the value of the cargo and the probability of its loss at sea. Perhaps the early insurers were doing this in an unconscious, intuitive way, but if so they would have been quite incapable of articulating their thoughts in terms of an equation, for they lacked the crucial cognitive tool that Bernoulli was to provide: a way of representing probabilities as numbers.

As soon as probability is expressed in numerical terms, it becomes possible to reason about it by employing the formidable tools of mathematics. In the decades following Bernoulli's invention, mathematicians from all over Europe constructed a formal system and a set of inference rules for working with numerical probabilities that form the basis of probability theory to this day. As we turn to considering the ways in which insights from this body of work can beef up our risk intelligence, it may seem that our best hope lies in building better computer models and statistical data sets to provide us with ever more powerful analyses based on math. This is true to a degree, and we'll explore some of the amazing progress that's been made in this regard in this chapter. But it's vital in considering how a better grasp of the math of risk intelligence can help us that we not overplay this hand.

The development of probability theory and statistics over the past few centuries, and their ever-ramifying effects on science and society, has been described as a true scientific revolution, just as radical as the more familiar examples named after Nicolaus Copernicus and Charles Darwin. The probabilistic revolution differed from both of those, however, in being much more gradual. Indeed, it may still be regarded as a work in progress. Most of the early work in probability theory focused on the analysis of simple forms of gambling, such as tossing coins and throwing dice, and it allowed mathematicians to calculate the precise odds of winning. It was not long, however, before the pioneers of probability theory realized that the tools they had developed could also be applied to many other problems that had nothing to do with gambling. Today, mathematicians continue to explore the applications of probability theory to fields as diverse as cryptography and quantum mechanics. And the revolution is gathering pace.

The ever-increasing power of modern computers has enabled government agencies and private companies to apply statistical methods, such as multiple regression, to ever more areas of life, often in unexpected ways. In his 2007 book *Super Crunchers*, the law professor Ian Ayres discussed some fascinating examples of these developments, in areas ranging from medicine and education to entertainment and wine collecting. In many of those examples, Ayres showed how statistical models can be used as a supplement to or even a substitute for human intuition.

Take the Bordeaux equation, for example. In the 1980s, the economist Orley Ashenfelter found that he could predict the price of

Bordeaux wine vintages with a model containing just three variables: the average temperature over the growing season, the amount of rain during harvesttime, and the amount of winter rain. Ayres observed that this did not go down well with the professional wine tasters who made a fine living by trading on their expert opinions. All of a sudden, Ashenfelter's equation threatened to make them obsolete.

HIGH-TECH HANDICAPPING

Something similar is now occurring at the racetrack, as computerized models of horse racing increasingly supersede the intuition of handicappers. In chapter 1, we saw how remarkable those intuitions can be. Even the best human handicapper, however, is no match for a well-designed computer model.

Back in the 1980s—in the same year, coincidentally, that Ceci and Liker published their study of expert handicappers—another paper on handicapping appeared. Unlike Ceci and Liker, however, the authors of that paper didn't interview actual handicappers. Instead, Ruth Bolton and Randall Chapman proposed a mathematical model of horse racing that could do the handicapping automatically. In other words, if you had the right data about the horses in a given race, you could feed the data into their equation, and it would spit out each horse's chance of winning.

The idea in itself wasn't completely new. In 1979 a math professor named William Quirin had discussed mathematical models of handicapping in a book called *Winning at the Races: Computer Discoveries in Thoroughbred Handicapping,* and the next year saw the publication of *Beating the Races with a Computer* by the ace programmer Steven Brecher (who later became a poker player, winning more than a million dollars at the WPT Bay 101 Shooting Star tournament in 2009). But though the two books had showed how the process of handicapping could be automated by developing equations with the help of a computer, the paper by Bolton and Chapman spelled out exactly how it could be done in detail.

When Frank Singer (not his real name) read Bolton and Chapman's paper, he immediately grasped its potential. Singer had started out as a casino gambler, playing the card-counting system in blackjack, but, as happened with most other successful blackjack players, it was only a few years before he found himself excluded by all the big casinos, and by 1986 he was looking around for a new source of income. The computerized approaches to handicapping were just what he was looking for.

After raising around $800,000 of investment capital from his friends, Singer moved to Hong Kong to develop his equations. Hong Kong had three big advantages over other markets such as the United States. First, the amount of money wagered on each race in Hong Kong was the highest in the world, allowing Singer to bet hundreds of thousands of dollars on a single race without moving the payout odds too much. Second, the not-for-profit Hong Kong Jockey Club was scrupulously honest, so a horse's history would be a good guide to future performance (race fixing makes a horse's history less relevant to predicting its chances). Last but not least, there were only around a thousand horses running in Hong Kong each season, which was significantly more manageable in terms of data input than the seventy thousand running in the United States; that meant a lot when there were no online data feeds and all the numbers had to be typed into a computer by hand.

Singer spent the first two years in Hong Kong building a database and developing a computer model of horse racing with more than a hundred terms in the equation, each standing for a particular feature of a horse or jockey, such as weight, number of wins in the past two years, amount of money won per race in the past year, and so on. Then he put it to use, looking for "overlays"—bets where the bookies had, according to Singer's model, underestimated a horse's chance of winning and so offered higher odds than they should have. At first his winnings were modest, but each race provided more data that could be used to tweak the model, and by the mid-1990s Singer was making a profit of more than 30 percent. With betting outlays that regularly ran into the hundreds of thousands of dollars per race, the winnings could amount to many millions per year, with the best years being in the tens of millions.

Singer has since moved back to the United States and says he is "currently somewhat diversified into other businesses," but he still derives the bulk of his income from gambling.

Although computerized handicapping systems allowed a few people to make huge fortunes in the 1990s, it was not until the following decade that their influence came to dominate the betting markets. The key event in this development was the launch, in June 2000, of an online betting exchange called Betfair. Unlike bookmakers, which offer bets to punters at fixed odds, betting exchanges allow clients to take bets as well as place them. Betfair merely puts the people offering bets in touch with others who are willing to take them, charging a small commission on the way. Unlike bookies, therefore, Betfair doesn't risk any of its own money.

The growth of Betfair has been phenomenal. Within ten years it had become the largest online betting company in the United Kingdom and the largest betting exchange in the world, with more than two million clients and a turnover in excess of £50 million per week. And it has changed the way that bookies work.

The traditional bookmakers aren't very happy about the changes. As I wandered around the betting ring at Wexford Racecourse in southeast Ireland on one serendipitously sunny day in May 2010, the old hands were struggling to make a profit. "The online exchanges have seriously damaged our business," lamented bookmaker Francis Hyland over a cup of coffee after the last race was over. "I don't know if the on-course bookies can survive much longer."

Predicting the prices of wines and the outcomes of horse races is just the tip of the iceberg in applying mathematical models to areas of analysis that have previously relied on human judgment. Of course, companies have long mined their data to improve sales and productivity. But the huge popularity of social networks such as Facebook offers new opportunities, such as modeling social relationships. In some companies, emails are analyzed automatically to help bosses manage their workers. Employees who are often asked for advice may be identified as good candidates for promotion, for example.

Network analysis is also being used by financial firms to uncover fraud. Risky borrowers can be identified by examining their social networks and Internal Revenue Service records, for example. A person who applies for a loan to launch a type of business that has no links to his social network, education, previous business dealings, or travel history may be a bad risk or even a fraudster. In 2009, the Recovery Accountability and Transparency Board (RATB) began using network-analysis software to look for fraud within the $780 billion financial stimulus program, and within twelve months it had triggered about 250 criminal investigations and 400 audits.

GARBAGE IN, GARBAGE OUT

This application of computer models to so many of the tricky areas of analysis in business is to be applauded. Not only are computers able to handle much more complex mathematical models than human brains can, but computers aren't subject to the biases and social effects we looked at in the previous two chapters. But the fact is that although sophisticated computer models are fine and dandy for companies that have the resources to develop them, they are not likely to be part of the average person's tool kit anytime soon. Besides, they also have a serious downside, as we saw in chapter 1 when we looked at how the proliferation of computer models in Wall Street has led to a de-skilling of the risk process. Some economists worry that an overreliance on computer models drowns out serious thinking about the big questions, such as why the financial system nearly collapsed in 2007–2008 and how a repeat can be avoided. According to the economist Robert Shiller, the accumulation of huge data sets led economists to believe that "finance had become scientific." Conventional ideas about investing and financial markets—and about their vulnerabilities— seemed out of date to the new empiricists, says Shiller, who worries that academic departments are "creating idiot savants, who get a sense of authority from work that contains lots of data." To have seen the financial crisis coming, he argues, it would have been better to "go back to old-fashioned readings of history, studying institutions and laws. We should have talked to grandpa."

Finance is not the only area in which the failure to spot the flaws in mathematical models has led to disastrous consequences. Epidemiological models that predict the spread of disease can also lead to problems if their limitations are not properly understood. Take the 2001 outbreak of foot-and-mouth disease (FMD) in the United Kingdom. FMD is an infectious and sometimes fatal viral disease that affects cattle, sheep, goats, pigs, and other cloven-hoofed animals. It is a severe plague for animal farming, since it is highly infectious and can be spread by infected animals through aerosols, through contact with contaminated farming equipment, and by predators.

In February 2001, a case of FMD was detected in pigs at an abattoir in Essex. Over the next four days, several more cases in Essex were announced, and the European Union imposed a worldwide ban on all British exports of livestock, meat, and animal products. Traditional methods of controlling FMD require the rapid detection and slaughter of infected animals and any susceptible animals with which they may have been in contact. During the 2001 epidemic, this approach was supplemented by a culling policy driven by unvalidated predictive models.

The model that drove the cull was written not by available experts who were familiar with the particular strain of the virus in circulation, but by epidemiologists and biomathematicians who were not. Dr. Paul Kitching, from the main governmental animal health laboratory in Great Britain, was particularly critical of their approach. "The modellers produced some very seductive graphs," he noted drily, but "the problem has been that virtually none of the models have been able to predict what has actually happened, and I feel this is because there hasn't been the data input available, and there hasn't been the expert advice sought to feed into these models." Despite those flaws, the model seems to have played a vital role in driving the cull. The slaughter of approximately 10 million animals provoked widespread public disgust and political resolve to adopt alternative options, notably including vaccination, to control any future epidemics. The UK experience provides a salutary warning of how models can be abused in the interests of scientific opportunism.

As Kitching makes clear, a model is only as good as the data that are fed into it. As the saying goes, "Garbage in, garbage out." And the statistics we need to calculate odds and make decisions are never perfect and may not even be available. The data fed into the model of FMD, for example, had been hurriedly gathered and converted from many different sources to try to create a database of all UK farms. Some of the data were seriously out of date with regard to crucial factors, such as map coordinates, addresses, post codes, local authorities, and counties. Roy Anderson, a leading British epidemiologist, pointed out that several of the farms were, according to official figures, "situated in the North Sea." There were no computer systems available in many local offices at the start, and inexperienced personnel were drafted to copy all the data in from the VetNet system. Inadequate procedures were followed for checking the data for accuracy. The whole thing was a mess.

My point in telling this story is that even an abundance of data does not obviate the need for judgment and estimation. Risk intelligence is required even when sophisticated models and supercrunching computers are in plentiful supply. And true risk intelligence is not achieved simply by making mathematical calculations.

THE PERILS OF PROBABILITY

Many books that purport to help people think more clearly about risk focus on analytical puzzles to train them in the math of probability. Here's one for you to cut your teeth on:

> Every day, Fred gets the 8:00 A.M. bus to work. Ten percent of the time, the bus is early and leaves before 8:00. And 10

percent of the time, the bus is very late and departs after 8:10. The rest of the time, it departs between 8:00 and 8:10. One morning Fred arrives at the bus stop at 8:00 A.M. exactly and waits for ten minutes without the bus arriving. What is the probability that the bus will still arrive?

But although such puzzles can be fun to explore and their solutions are often pleasingly counterintuitive, mastering probability theory is neither necessary nor sufficient for risk intelligence. We know it is not *necessary* because there are people who have very high risk intelligence yet have never been acquainted with the probability calculus. Many of the horse handicappers whom we met in chapter 1, for example, relied on a purely intuitive approach when estimating probabilities. And mastering probability theory is not *sufficient* for risk intelligence either, as is demonstrated by the existence of nerds who can crunch numbers effortlessly yet show no flair for estimating probabilities or for judging the reliability of their predictions.

Probability theory is most relevant in casinos, because there all you need to know is the rules of the game you are playing. You don't need to collect any data or observe how the game is actually played. You can just read the rule book and work out your optimal strategy with pen and paper (though a laptop would often help considerably).

To work out what the odds of a given bet should be at a racetrack, however, it won't help much if you simply read the rule book. You need to gather lots of data about the horses in the race, the jockeys, the racetrack, the likely weather on the day of the race, and who knows what else. You can get those data in all sorts of ways—by reading the "form" of the horses as published in newspapers, looking carefully at the horses with your own eyes, talking to tipsters, listening to the weather forecast, and so on. Then you need to crunch all those data and come up with an estimate of how likely it is that each horse will win.

As we've seen, one way to crunch the data is to use a computer. However, that doesn't require risk intelligence, since the computer does all the work. Risk intelligence involves crunching the data with your brain. You absorb the data by reading, watching, and listening, and then you mull it over in your own head and come up with an estimate of how likely it is that a particular horse will win.

In fact, despite what I said a short while ago about the usefulness of probability theory in casinos, it does not in fact work *perfectly* even there, since real casinos are quite different from the idealized versions of them found in the pages of textbooks. This point is well made by the maverick trader Nassim Nicholas Taleb, who wrote in his insightful book *The Black Swan*:

> In real life you do not know the odds; you need to discover them, and the sources of uncertainty are not defined. Economists, who do not consider what was discovered by noneconomists worthwhile, draw an artificial distinction between Knightian risks (which you can compute) and Knightian uncertainty (which you cannot compute), after one Frank Knight, who rediscovered the notion of unknown uncertainty and did a lot of thinking but perhaps never took risks, or perhaps lived in the vicinity of a casino. Had he taken financial or economic risk he would have realized that these "computable" risks are largely absent from real life! They are laboratory contraptions!

When Taleb states that computable risks are "laboratory contraptions," he means that casinos are artificial entities that have to be deliberately manufactured under sterile conditions, like an unstable element that exists for only a few brief moments in a physics lab. It took thousands of years for the irregular-shaped knucklebones used in ancient Rome and the vibhīdaka nuts used in ancient India to evolve into the precision dice used in modern casinos, with their pips drilled and then filled flush with a paint of the same density as the acetate, such that the six numbers are equally probable. It takes even greater engineering prowess to produce a fair roulette wheel. The manufacturers of roulette wheels perform elaborate tests to ensure that the numbers generated will be truly random, and even then the wheels still have flaws, allowing some cunning players to make a fortune by means of a "biased wheel attack." In 1873, for example, an engineer from Lancashire named Joseph Jagger identified a biased wheel in Monte Carlo and won the equivalent of $70,000 in one day.

Taleb tells a lovely story to illustrate the mismatch between the idealized casinos in probability textbooks and the real ones that people actually go to. A casino in Las Vegas thought it had all the bases covered in risk management. It was sufficiently diversified across the various tables not to have to worry about taking a hit from lucky gamblers. It had a state-of-the-art surveillance system to catch cheats. But the four largest risks faced by the casino in the past few years lay completely outside its risk management framework. For example, it lost around $100 million when its star performer was maimed by the tiger he used in his show.

Probability theory is not completely irrelevant to thinking about risk, of course, but higher-order mathematical calculations are not required for most of the issues we must make decisions about in our daily lives, and mathematical logic is only one part of the overall risk intelligence equation. True risk intelligence involves a curious blend of rational numerical calculation and intuitive feelings in which neither is sufficient on its own.

EPISTEMIC FEELINGS

Nobody knew this better than the famous French philosopher René Descartes. A brilliant mathematician, he was also perhaps the first person in the history of western philosophy to base a knowledge claim on a *feeling* of rightness. As the philosopher Ronald de Sousa has noted, Descartes's famous argument, *"Cogito ergo sum"* ("I think, therefore I am"), rests on a hidden premise that involves a claim about feelings; it was precisely because the thought of his existence *felt* particularly clear and distinct that Descartes was able to *feel* so certain that he did, in fact, exist.

De Sousa goes on to argue that the feeling of certainty is just one of a family of emotions relating to knowledge, and he proposes the term "epistemic feelings" to designate them. Other such emotions include feelings of doubt and recognition. Recognizing someone you know, for example, is a complex process involving both cognitive and emotional components. People with Capgras syndrome can recognize faces on an intellectual level, but lack the feeling of familiarity that normally accompanies this. The woman in front of you looks exactly like your wife, but you don't have the feelings you should have when you usually look at your wife's face. As a result, those with Capgras syndrome may conclude that their spouse, parent, or close friend has been replaced by an identical-looking impostor, or is perhaps an alien in disguise.

Epistemic feelings blur the traditional distinction between reason and emotion. Reason, it seems, cannot function properly without certain emotions. Risk intelligence is no exception; epistemic feelings all play a crucial role here too. Doing a good job of estimating probabilities involves both conscious and unconscious components, and epistemic feelings facilitate communication between them. When we start to ponder the factors that make something more or less likely, it happens in the full glare of conscious awareness. We can name each factor and explain why it is relevant to the question. The process of weighing all the evidence, however, and crunching all the data, happens unconsciously. The expert handicappers we met in chapter 1 and the first Lloyd's insurers were doing multiple regression and solving linear equations, but they didn't know it; they did all of it instinctively. The output of their unconscious calculations was an epistemic feeling whose strength could vary from complete uncertainty to complete conviction. In order to provide a probability estimate, they had to translate that strength of feeling into a number.

High risk intelligence therefore depends on two factors:

1. Well-calibrated epistemic feelings;
2. An ability to translate epistemic feelings into numbers.

Epistemic feelings are well calibrated when they accurately reflect your level of knowledge about a particular topic. If you feel uncertain about a statement when you really know little about it one way or the other, your feeling is well calibrated. If you feel uncertain about a statement that you know a lot about, but the evidence for and against the statement is finely balanced, then your feeling is also well calibrated. Likewise, if you feel very confident that something will happen when you have a lot of information that strongly suggests the event will occur, your feeling is also well calibrated. If, on the other hand, you feel sure about something despite knowing very little about it, or feel uncertain despite having a lot of relevant knowledge that points to a definite verdict, your epistemic feelings are miscalibrated.

Even if your epistemic feelings are well calibrated, however, you won't be able to reliably translate them into accurate decisions about risks unless you can do a good job of expressing those feelings in terms of specific numerical probabilities. That is why, of course, my risk intelligence test focuses on this aptitude. In the next chapter we'll look at some good methods of helping you fine-tune your epistemic feelings, as well as a set of basic concepts from probability theory that can help you do a better job of assessing probabilities on a daily basis. But before getting to those, it's important for you to do a basic assessment of your degree of comfort with such mathematical thinking.

Risk intelligence does require a certain amount of numeracy, and in working to improve our risk intelligence it is important to assess how numerate we are, both in terms of our ability to work with numbers, and how comfortable we feel with mathematical methods and concepts. The simple truth is that some people find putting numbers on things harder than others. At one end of the spectrum there are people such as the Hungarian mathematician Paul Erdős, the "man who loved only numbers" as the title of Paul Hoffman's biography nicely put it. Erdős published more papers than any other mathematician in history. He spent most of his life as a vagabond, traveling between scientific conferences and the homes of other mathematicians. He would show up, unannounced, at a colleague's doorstep and announce "my brain is open," staying long enough to work furiously on a paper or two, before moving on a few days later, leaving his colleague exhausted. He never married, and had no children.

At the other end of the spectrum are people who find numbers utterly foreign. David Boyle's entertaining book *The Tyranny of Numbers* captures the oppressive character that numbers seem to have for this latter group:

> Every time a new set of statistics comes out, I can't help feeling that some of the richness and mystery of life gets extinguished. Just as individual stories of passion and betrayal get hidden by the marriage statistics, or the whole meaning of the Holocaust gets lost in the number 6,000,000. There is a sort of deadening effect, a distancing from human emotion and reality.

Complicating matters is the fact that communication between people at opposite ends of the numeracy spectrum can be fraught with misunderstanding. Those who feel comfortable with numbers tend to perceive those who aren't as muddle-headed and evasive, while those who dislike numbers may view their number-loving friends as cold and unsympathetic. Witness, for example, the following conversation between a number lover and a number hater:

A: Why don't you let your daughter play in the park?
B: There are loads of pedophiles round here!
A: What? In your street?
B: No, in general.
A: You mean in this town?
B: No, you know, in general.
A: You mean in Ireland?
B: Well, yes, okay, then, in Ireland.
A: How many is loads?
B: I don't know, just loads.

A: Just roughly. Ten thousand? A hundred thousand?
  A million?

B: I don't know!

A: Okay, give me an upper and a lower bound. I just want
  to know what you mean by "loads."

B: Don't be a number Nazi!

People aren't distributed evenly across the spectrum, of course. Many more find numbers alien than friendly. When a local health department in the United States tried to calm public fears about hazardous waste disposal by publishing controlled studies showing little evidence of harm, its efforts had no effect because the numbers "had no meaning" for most readers. In fact, the numbers seemed to increase panic. One woman, divorced and with three sick children, looked at the numbers and started crying hysterically: "No wonder my children are sick. Am I going to die? What's going to happen to my children?"

Unsurprisingly perhaps, subjective feelings about numbers correlate quite well with objective tests of mathematical ability. Researchers have taken advantage of this fact to develop a subjective numeracy test, which is much quicker and less onerous than objective tests. Whereas objective tests require people to solve mathematical problems, the subjective test merely asks you to say how good you are at solving them and how you feel about numerical information. The subjective numeracy test developed by Angela Fagerlin and her colleagues, for example, comprises only eight questions and still produces a reliable estimate of your objective numeracy.

The first four questions in this test ask you to say how good you are (on a scale of 1 to 6, where 1 = not at all good and 6 = extremely good) at doing the following things:

1. How good are you at working with fractions?
2. How good are you at working with percentages?
3. How good are wyou at calculating a 15 percent tip?
4. How good are you at figuring out how much a shirt
   will cost if it is 25 percent off?

The remaining four questions ask you to use a similar six-point scale to describe your preferences and feelings about numerical information:

5. When reading the newspaper, how helpful do you find tables and graphs that are parts of a story? (1 = not at all helpful, 6 = extremely helpful)
6. When people tell you the chance of something happening, do you prefer that they use words ("it rarely happens") or numbers ("there's a 1 percent chance")? (1 = always prefer words, 6 = always prefer numbers)
7. When you hear a weather forecast, do you prefer predictions using percentages (e.g., "there will be a 20 percent chance of rain today") or predictions using only words (e.g., "there is a small chance of rain today")? (1 = always prefer words, 6 = always prefer percentages)
8. How often do you find numerical information to be useful? (1 = never, 6 = very often)

To find where you sit on the six-point Subjective Numeracy Scale (SNS), you simply calculate the average of your answers to all eight questions. If you score less than 3.5, you aren't very numerate. In England, one adult in five is innumerate.

Many people would hate to be described as illiterate but could take an accusation of innumeracy with a grain of salt. Some even take a perverse pride in not being good at math while denigrating those with poor verbal skills. Yet to my mind the two disabilities are equally bad. People with poor numeracy are twice as likely to be unemployed as people who are numerate; and they have worse medical outcomes when prescribed medication with complicated dosing regimes, which they find hard to follow. Men with poor numeracy are more likely to get into trouble with authority, and women with poor numeracy are more likely to experience a spell of homelessness.

So although studying probability theory in depth is certainly not required for boosting your risk intelligence, facing up to what may be your unease with thinking in mathematical ways is vital. Doing so will allow you to work on becoming more comfortable with at least a key set of fundamental concepts and simple methods that will help you avoid the most common pitfalls in assessing probabilities. It's to those that we turn in the next two chapters. None of these methods requires complicated mathematical calculation. What I will introduce is, rather, a set of basic ways of thinking and powerful mental devices that will have an immediate effect on helping you make better risk assessments on a daily basis.

But first I'll make good on my earlier promise to reveal the solution to the bus problem posed earlier. Here it is again, to refresh your memory:

> Every day, Fred gets the 8:00 A.M. bus to work. Ten percent of the time, the bus is early and leaves before 8:00. And 10 percent of the time, the bus is very late and departs after 8:10. The rest of the time, it departs between 8:00 and 8:10. One morning Fred arrives at the bus stop at 8:00 A.M. exactly and waits for ten minutes without the bus arriving. What is the probability that the bus will still arrive?

When this question was posed to a group of psychology students at the University of Oslo, they got into trouble. Some claimed that Fred would still have a 90 percent chance of catching the bus, since he had arrived on time. Others insisted that he had only a 10 percent chance, since the bus is rarely more than ten minutes late. In fact, neither of the answers is correct. The correct answer is that Fred has a 50 percent chance of catching the bus.

After Fred has waited for ten minutes, he can eliminate the 80 percent chance of a bus arriving in the period between 8:00 and 8:10, because he knows it did not arrive in that interval. Only two possibilities remain: either the bus arrived ahead of schedule, or it will arrive more than ten minutes late. Both outcomes are rare, but as they are equally rare, we must assign each outcome an equal chance. Since the two outcomes are mutually exclusive, and there are no other possibilities, we should assign each a probability of 50 percent.

Don't worry if you didn't get the answer right. As we've said, an ability to solve analytical puzzles like this is neither necessary nor sufficient for risk intelligence in daily life. Far more important are the basic principles and methods that we'll explore in the next few chapters.

CHAPTER 7

Weighing the Probable

I can see looming ahead one of those terrible exercises in
probability where six men have white hats and six men have
black hats and you have to work it out by mathematics how
likely it is that the hats will get mixed up and in what
proportion. If you start thinking about things like that,
you would go round the bend. Let me assure you of that!

—DR. HAYDOCK, IN *THE MIRROR CRACK'D
FROM SIDE TO SIDE* BY AGATHA CHRISTIE

One of the biggest difficulties that people have with thinking
about probabilities—whether ones reported to them, as with
medical procedures, or ones they've estimated themselves—is knowing how to make use of them. If someone tells you that it will rain
later today, you can simply take your umbrella with you when you
go out, but if they say there's a 70 percent chance of rainfall, it is not
immediately clear whether you should you take your umbrella or not.

There is no point in cultivating better risk intelligence if you don't
know how to use the better probability estimates that will result. Yet
there is little instruction at school or college in how to incorporate
probabilistic information when deciding on a course of action. We'll
explore a number of ways to do so in this chapter and the next, starting with two of the simplest: setting thresholds and bet sizing.

The simplest way to take probabilities into account when making a decision is to set a threshold. For example, I might decide that I
will take my umbrella with me only if there's more than a 65 percent

chance of rain. Different people can choose to set their thresholds at different levels, according to how much they dislike getting wet—and how much they dislike carrying umbrellas.

To take another example, a commanding officer may decide to bomb a building only if intelligence reports suggest that there is more than an 80 percent chance that it is being used by insurgent forces rather than civilians. Again, different commanders might set the threshold at different levels, depending on how keen they are to take out the insurgents and how much they want to avoid civilian casualties.

Setting thresholds is a simple and useful way to make decisions based on probability estimates. It was used, for example, by the Flood Forecasting and Warning Centre (FFWC) in Bangladesh in 2007 and 2008 when providing flood warnings to villagers. Bangladesh sits in the Ganges Delta, which is formed by the confluence of the Ganges, Brahmaputra, and Meghna rivers just before they empty into the Bay of Bengal. Most parts of Bangladesh are less than twelve meters above sea level, and it is therefore highly susceptible to flooding. In 1998, for example, Bangladesh saw the most severe flooding in modern world history, when the Ganges and the Brahmaputra crested simultaneously well above flood level. More than two-thirds of the country was submerged for three months and an estimated one thousand people drowned, with millions left homeless.

The catastrophic floods of 1998 prompted the US Agency for International Development (USAID) to fund an exploratory project to provide advanced warning of flooding in Bangladesh on daily to seasonal timescales. One of the first decisions that the project team took was to issue probabilistic forecasts, so that decisions about how to act on this information could be taken locally. The FFWC of the Bangladesh Water Development Board (BWDB), for example, decided that it would send out flood warnings only when the computer model suggested that the probability of flooding was greater than 80 percent. These warnings were first communicated by cell phone text messages to regional centers, which then relayed them to the villages by a series of flag alerts.

Village leaders were trained to understand and interpret the forecasts in terms of local references and landmarks so that the expected degree of flooding could be communicated clearly to the villagers. Local officials also played a key role in helping the villagers understand the nature of probabilistic forecasts. For example, an imam introduced the concept of probability during prayer time at his mosque. As a result, not only were the flood warnings heeded, but the concept of risk was better understood and widely discussed. Unsurprisingly, perhaps, it seems that people living on the edge understand risk very well, and are happy to accept and use probabilistic forecasts. One Bangladeshi farmer commented that the concept of probability simply made explicit the way that those in rural communities had always had to take chances, though they did so not randomly but on the basis of their perceptions and local knowledge.

While I was writing this book, a director at the UK Met Office (the national weather forecasting service) emailed me to say that, in his experience, the public seemed to hate probabilistic forecasts. But as the Bangladesh project shows, it is not difficult to help people become more comfortable with probabilities, and weather forecasters may be in a unique position to educate the public in this regard. Indeed, there is some evidence that the longer people are exposed to probabilistic weather forecasts, the better they understand probabilities.

SIZE MATTERS

Besides setting thresholds, another simple way to take probabilities into account when making decisions is bet sizing. Bet sizing is the art of knowing how much money to wager on any given bet. Even experienced gamblers can make mistakes when it comes to bet sizing, as the notorious seducer and compulsive gambler Giacomo Casanova discovered to his cost.

In a few mad days at the Ridotto casino in Venice in 1753, Casanova lost 5,000 sequins (gold pieces) playing faro, a card game that first emerged in France in the late seventeenth century. As was his way, Casanova soon recouped his losses, only to lose everything again a few months later. This time, his lover (a nun whose initials were M.M.) gave him all her diamonds to sell. Casanova went straight back to the casino and lost everything all over again. With only five hundred sequins left to her name, M.M. had to abandon her plans to escape from the convent.

Casanova's mistake lay in following a betting strategy known as a Martingale, after Henry Martingale, the proprietor of a British gambling house (though in fact the system was known before Henry was born). The Martingale is a progressive betting strategy used for even-money bets; the gambler doubles his wager after every loss until a win is recorded, at which point he returns to betting the original amount. The strategy guarantees that whenever the player wins, he recoups all his previous losses and earns a profit equivalent to his initial bet.

The fatal flaw of the Martingale, and the reason it ruined Casanova on more than one occasion (and led to the collapse of Barings Bank, when rogue trader Nick Leeson followed something like it), is that it can quickly lead a player to make huge bets. Since a player must double up every time he loses, even a short run of losses can lead the player to wager everything left in his wallet. The Martingale strategy guarantees a profit only if you have an infinite bankroll and the casino doesn't impose any betting limits. There's the rub, of course. Expert gamblers, unlike compulsive nonexperts like Casanova, never forget that their bankroll is finite. They therefore follow various strategies for sizing their bets appropriately, such as the Kelly criterion, which recommends that the amount wagered must never be larger than a certain fraction of the gambler's current bankroll. Another complimentary strategy is to make the size of your bet proportional to your degree of confidence. The more certain you are of something, the more you should bet on it. That is how card counting works in blackjack. The player keeps a running total in his head, which he updates according to every card he sees placed faceup on the table. For example, he might start with zero, add one for every low card (2 to 6), and subtract one for every ten, jack, queen, king, or ace. Midvalue cards (7 to 9) are ignored. The number tells the player how much to bet.

When the count is zero or negative, the player places the minimum bet allowed by the casino. But when it is positive, he places a larger bet, whose size increases as the count rises. By employing systems like this, professional blackjack players can earn millions of dollars in a single year.

Similar strategies can be applied to investing in the stock market by, for example, making sure that the amount of shares you buy in a company is proportional to how strongly you believe that the company will do well. An interesting study from that domain, which confirmed the differences in results for novice versus expert investors, was conducted by a talented high school student named Jacob Pastor. He analyzed data from a website that offered live exotic financial option bets. For example, certain wagers called binary options allowed participants to bet that some stock or index would move higher or lower by at least a certain amount within a short amount of time. The most popular kind of bet was "fast-money bets," binary options over intervals from two to forty-five minutes (the average was eight minutes). That meant the bettor selected an interval and a financial variable and bet whether it would go up or down over the interval.

Pastor drew a random sample of 100 fast-money bettors from the data and found that they had made a total of 16,377 bets. Had they chosen their sides randomly, they would have been expected to win 8,218 (50.2 percent) of these bets, but in fact they had won 8,739 (53.4 percent) of them, which is a huge difference in this context. That means that the bettors as a group must have known some market-beating information. What is more interesting is that further analysis revealed that the valuable information was not distributed evenly among the bettors. When Pastor removed from the sample the eight most successful bettors, the performance of the remaining 92 was hard to distinguish from pure chance. That is not particularly surprising; many markets consist of a majority of noise traders, who know very little, and a few experts. But, confirming the point that even expert betters can make mistakes, Pastor also found that two of the eight experts managed to *lose* money, despite winning 56 percent of their fast-money bets. Their mistake, it turns out, was all to do with betting the wrong amount. If those two bettors had simply bet the same amount each time, for example, they would have made a profit of £1,282 instead of losing £978. If they had bet different amounts in proportion to the accuracy of their information, they would have made even more. The fact that they lost money meant that they were doing the opposite; betting more when they knew less.

How can we make use of the wisdom of bet sizing to boost our risk intelligence in daily life? In addition to helping us make better financial investments, the principle can serve us well in making choices about all sorts of other things, such as how much effort to put into applying for various jobs and how much time to spend preparing for an exam. Take the case of job hunting. The principle of bet sizing suggests that we should spend more time preparing for an interview for a job we have a good chance of getting than for a long shot. When it comes to reviewing for an exam, the situation is slightly more complicated. Clever bet sizing would not mean you should spend more time preparing for an exam you know you will pass than for one that hangs more finely in the balance. That would clearly be wasteful. Bet sizing, in this case, would mean spending more time preparing for the exams where you are more confident that preparation will make a difference.

CALIBRATING EPISTEMIC FEELINGS

In order to do a good job of bet sizing, of course, we first have to do a good job of assessing how confident we are—and this is where risk intelligence comes in. In particular, as we saw in the previous chapter, our epistemic feelings must be well calibrated. To understand how we can achieve this, picture these feelings as the mercury in a thermometer. If they are well calibrated, your epistemic feelings will expand or contract in proportion to how much you know about a particular matter, so the mercury will rise or fall. To help us refine our estimates, and therefore do a better job of calibrating, we have to inscribe a set of notches, associated with probabilities, on the column. Without a fixed scale of this kind, we won't really be doing a rigorous job of calibrating.

To do so best, you should imagine notches for probabilities from 0 to 100 percent and come up with as specific an estimate of the probability as you can. If you think your chances are better than 50 percent, for example, but less than 80 percent, try to pin it down more. Maybe you would end up with an estimate of 72 percent.

Some people think that it can be misleading to express probability in terms of a single number, such as 72 percent, because it conveys a false impression of precision. It's all right if we *know* that there's a 72 percent chance that a company will go bankrupt or a horse will win a race, but what if we have only a vague idea about how likely those things are? Surely it would be more honest in such cases to use verbal labels that at least wear their vagueness on their sleeve? Or, if numbers must be used, might it not be better simply to provide upper and lower bounds for the estimate by stating, for example, that we think that the chance of a horse winning a race is *somewhere between* 60 and 80 percent?

Despite their apparent plausibility, such arguments reveal a fundamental misunderstanding of the nature of probability estimates. The whole point of introducing the apparatus of numerical probabilities is precisely that our knowledge is not perfect. Numerical probabilities merely express that imperfection. And if point estimates (such as 72 percent) give a misleading impression of precision, surely interval estimates (such as "somewhere between 60 and 80 percent") convey an impression of even greater precision, since they provide precise estimates of both the upper and lower bounds of the interval. But how can you be so certain about *that*? Furthermore, if we concede that people can be uncertain about how uncertain they are, why stop there? Why not also concede that they can be uncertain about how uncertain about how uncertain they are, and so on, ad infinitum? Surely we should provide intervals for those upper and lower bounds too, and intervals for those intervals, and so on. The absurdity of this slippery slope should be immediately apparent.

The situation is similar to that of measuring physical magnitudes such as heat or mass, where we are generally quite happy to invoke point values, even though, strictly speaking, our measurements are never exact. When we report someone's weight as, say, 143 pounds, we are employing a form of idealization that nevertheless gives sufficiently accurate results, within an appropriate range of imprecision. The same is true of probability estimates. When we say that there is a 65 percent chance it will rain tomorrow, we are in effect reporting a measurement of our own uncertainty. The device we have used to take the measurement—our brain—has a margin of error just like any other measuring device, from the humble bathroom scale to the muon spectrometer systems at CERN. The latter can track the path of subatomic particles to within the width of a human hair—but that is still a range and not a point value.

A 2010 study seems to confirm that there is little to be gained by using the more complex apparatus of interval probabilities. Researchers gave participants a simulated forecast about a potential terrorist attack in Washington, D.C. One version of the forecast contained only a point estimate: "We estimate that the probability that this attack will occur over the next six months is 5 percent." Another version of the forecast supplemented this information with a probability range: "We estimate that the probability that this attack will occur over the next six months is 5 percent, but the probability could be as low as 1 percent or as high as 10 percent." The participants were then asked to rate the risk associated with the potential attack on an eleven-point scale where 0 = very low risk, and 10 = very high risk.

The researchers found that the extra information provided by the probability range made no difference to the perception of risk; those presented with the interval probability rated the risk the same as those given the simple point estimate. More important, in my opinion, is the misleading nature of the way the interval information was presented. In a statement such as "We estimate that the probability that this attack will occur over the next six months is 5 percent," the subjective nature of probability estimates is pretty clear. But when the statement is supplemented with interval information by cautioning that "the probability could be as low as 1 percent or as high as 10 percent," it begins to sound as if probabilities are objective things that we are measuring imperfectly, such as temperature or mass, rather than subjective feelings. And this is profoundly misleading, for probabilities are merely expressions of subjective uncertainty.

Getting back to our hypothetical mercury thermometer, how precisely we can calibrate probabilities on it will depend in part on how many notches there are on the column. If there are only a few notches, we might be able to estimate probabilities in increments of 10 or 20 percent only. If there are more notches, we will find over time that the more we practice, the better able we will be to make finer distinctions; we might learn to be able to tell the difference, for example, between being 60 percent sure and 63 percent sure of something.

Psychologists refer to this aspect of risk intelligence as "resolution." How finely we can tune our risk intelligence—how many notches we can inscribe and perceive on our epistemic thermometer—is an open question. Indeed, it may be the case that our ability to perceive small differences in probability is subject to basic psychophysical constraints. Psychophysics concerns the limits of our senses and was one of the first areas in psychology to be explored by means of scientific experiments. In the 1840s, for example, the German physiologist Ernst Weber gradually increased the weight that a blindfolded man was holding and asked him to say when he first felt the increase. Weber found that the smallest noticeable difference in weight was proportional to the starting value of the weight. That is to say, if the initial weight was doubled, the threshold at which the subject could perceive a difference also doubled.

Daniel Kahneman and Amos Tversky suggest that something similar operates in the domain of risk intelligence, only here our ability to discriminate between different probabilities varies according to whether the probabilities are extreme or not. This is a powerful finding that we should always keep in mind when weighing risks. It is much easier to perceive differences between extreme probabilities than differences between intermediate ones, and this can lead to flawed decision making. The difference between 0 percent and 1 percent, for example, is much more salient than that between 10 percent and 11 percent, and the difference between 99 percent and 100 percent looms much larger than that between 89 percent and 90 percent. As a result, we tend to overreact to small changes in extreme probabilities and underreact to changes in intermediate probabilities. For example, we will pay far more for a medical operation that increases our chance of surviving from 0 percent to 1 percent than one that increases it from 10 percent to 11 percent. We will also pay more for a lottery ticket that increases our chance of winning from 99 percent to 100 percent than one that increases it from 89 percent to 90 percent.

This oversensitivity to small changes in likelihood at both ends of the probability spectrum explains a well-documented phenomenon in gambling on horse racing; amateurs tend to value long shots more than they should, given how rarely they win, while valuing favorites too little, given how often they win. The result is that they make bigger losses over the long run when they bet on long shots than they do when betting on favorites. That is why bookies rejoice when a long shot wins; it's when they make their biggest profits.

This phenomenon is known as the favorite–long shot bias, and was first noted by the psychologist Richard Griffith in 1949. Since then numerous studies have found evidence of the bias at racetracks and other sports betting markets all around the world. Indeed, it is probably the most discussed empirical regularity in sports gambling markets, and the literature documenting it now runs to well over a hundred scientific papers.

This all leads to a powerful rule of thumb to follow when making decisions regarding probabilities: beware of exaggerating the importance of differences in probability at either extreme of the spectrum, and not sufficiently factoring in differences in the intermediate range. Put as much weight on something that increases your chances from 45 percent to 50 percent as on something that increases your chances from 5 percent to 10 percent, even if it doesn't feel right. For example, suppose you are studying for two exams, one of which is much harder than the other, but which are both equally important to you. You estimate you have a 45 percent chance of passing the easy exam, but only a 5 percent chance of passing the difficult one. You have enough money to pay for a tutor to help you prepare for one of the exams, and you estimate that the tutor could boost your chances of passing by around 5 percent. Which exam should you spend your money on? If you instinctively feel that your money would be better spent preparing for the hard exam, your intuition still needs educating. A person with high risk intelligence would feel indifferent; it wouldn't matter to her which exam she spent her money on. For her, a 5 percent improvement is a 5 percent improvment, and that's that.

THE 100 PERCENT RULE

Another common flaw in thinking about probabilities is breaking the 100 percent rule. According to this rule, all the probabilities assigned to a set of mutually exclusive possibilities can never add up to more than 100 percent. If there are four horses in a race, for example, and we exclude the possibility of a tie, it makes no sense to assign a 30 percent chance of winning to each of them. We have to make sure that we calibrate our estimates of the likelihood of various possibilities by weighing them carefully against one another, and using the rule that the total percentages must come to 100 percent will help us be more rigorous about this and also help us make appropriate adjustments in our estimates of probabilities as new information becomes available.

Suppose you are asked to determine which of a group of guests invited to a country estate murdered one of the other guests. Assuming you can exclude the possibility that all or some of them acted together, as in Agatha Christie's famous *Murder on the Orient Express*, when you first assign a probability to each guest being the murderer, the total should add up to 100 percent. As each suspect is eliminated from the inquiry, the chance of guilt of each of the remaining suspects increases, since the probabilities must still add up to 100 percent. This may seem stating the obvious, but when psychologists presented a group of people with just such a murder mystery, they failed to obey the 100 percent rule.

The participants in this experiment were first divided into two groups. Both groups were told that probabilities could range from

0 to 1 (it makes no real difference whether you use this scale or percentage values between 0 and 100) and given some practice in estimating probabilities. In addition, the members of the second group were informed of the 100 percent rule. Those in the first group were given no information about this rule, as the researchers wanted to find out whether people who were not specifically trained in using the rule would follow it naturally.

The researchers then read murder mystery stories to the participants, beginning with a short plot scenario of a few hundred words that set the scene and introduced the victim and five suspects. To simplify things, the participants were told that the guilty party was definitely one of the five suspects and that there was no conspiracy; the murderer always acted alone. At that point, the participants had to estimate the probability of each suspect's guilt by drawing a slash somewhere along a black line running from 0 (labeled "no chance") to 1 (labeled "sure thing"). Those initial ratings formed the "prior probabilities" assigned to each suspect.

Next the researchers read out a clue that pointed to the guilt or innocence of one particular suspect and asked the participants to rate each suspect's probability of guilt again. They repeated the procedure for a total of thirteen clues, two of which gave a suspect an airtight alibi and thus eliminated him or her from further consideration. The eliminators were presented late in the series, as the eleventh and thirteenth clues. Finally, the researchers revealed who the guilty party was.

When the researchers analyzed the results, they found significant differences between the two groups of participants. In the untutored group, which had not been told about the 100 percent rule, the probabilities of the suspects' guilt regularly added up to more than 1. In the tutored group, by contrast, the ratings added up to 1.

Keeping the 100 percent rule in mind can help you do a consistent job of weighing possibilities against one another. But it won't tell you anything specific about how you should reevaluate the probabilities as you receive additional information. It is this process that makes reading murder mysteries so much fun, as you follow along and try to second-guess the detective while he rethinks each suspect's chance of guilt as new pieces of information accumulate. This is a task in which probability theory has provided a particularly helpful tool called Bayes's theorem.

BAYES'S THEOREM

Surprisingly, perhaps, the question of how much stronger or weaker beliefs should become when we take new information into account has a precise mathematical answer. The man who discovered the formula was a Presbyterian minister who lived in eighteenth-century England. In his spare time, the Reverend Thomas Bayes liked to dabble in mathematics, and the theorem he discovered still bears his name. That formula can be expressed as:

$$P(H \mid E) = \frac{P(E \mid H)\,P(H)}{P(E)}$$

where H stands for the hypothesis, E stands for the evidence, and P stands for "probability of." We can put the theorem into words this way:

The probability P of a hypothesis H given some new evidence E is equal to the probability of the evidence given the hypothesis, multiplied by the probability of the hypothesis, divided by the probability of the evidence.

To clarify this, the expression on the left, $P(H \mid E)$, is the degree of belief you should have in the hypothesis H after you take new evidence E into account. This is also known as the "posterior probability" because it represents the degree of belief in a hypothesis after considering new evidence, as opposed to the "prior probability," which is the degree of belief we had in the hypothesis before we considered the new evidence. Bayes's theorem tells us that, in order to find out how much stronger or weaker our belief in H should become after considering the new piece of evidence E, we first have to know three things:

- $P(H)$: Our prior probability (or simply, our prior): How much do we believe in the hypothesis *before* we consider the new evidence?
- $P(E|H)$: How likely is the new evidence according to the hypothesis?
- $P(E)$: How likely is the new evidence, regardless of the hypothesis?

To see how we can use this basic formula, recall the murder mystery experiment. The participants in this study were told that there were five suspects, but they were not at first given any clues as to who might be guilty. In the absence of such evidence, they should have assumed that each suspect was equally likely to be the murderer and therefore assigned each one a 20 percent probability of guilt. In Bayesian terms, this is the *prior probability* of each hypothesis.

Let's suppose that the first clue the participants were given eliminates Reverend Green from the inquiry but provides no information about any other suspect. The probability of Reverend Green's guilt therefore drops to zero and that of the other four suspects increases to 25 percent each by virtue of the 100 percent rule.

Now let's imagine that we are given a second clue that points to Colonel Mustard being the murderer but has no bearing on any other suspect. Suppose we now think there is a 40 percent chance that Colonel Mustard committed the crime; the probability of guilt of each of the three remaining suspects must therefore drop to 20 percent each.

Finally, let's suppose that a third clue gives Mrs. Peacock a cast-iron alibi, and the probability of her guilt therefore falls to zero. How should we adjust the probabilities for the remaining three suspects so they now sum to 100 percent? One possibility would be to increase them all by the same amount, by adding 6.6 percent to each, but that is not what Bayes's theorem indicates.

The correct way to revise one's beliefs in such circumstances is to adjust the probabilities attached to the remaining suspects in a way that is proportional to their current probability of guilt. Since Colonel Mustard is currently the prime suspect, with a probability of guilt (40 percent) twice as great as that of the other remaining suspects (20 percent each), we should increase his chance of guilt by twice as much as we increase theirs. After eliminating Mrs. Peacock from the inquiry, therefore, Colonel Mustard's probability of guilt stands at 50 percent (an increase of 10 percent), while that of Miss Scarlet and Professor Plum stands at 25 percent each (an increase of 5 percent each). The evolution of our suspicions about the five original suspects can be represented as a graph, as in Figure 15:

FIGURE 15: THE EVOLUTION OF SUSPICION IN A WHODUNIT.

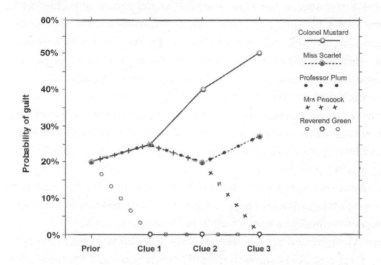

This strikes many people as counterintuitive. Why, after Mrs. Peacock is eliminated from the inquiry, should we adjust the probabilities attached to the remaining suspects in a way that is proportional to their current probability of guilt, rather than simply increasing them all by the same amount? The answer lies in the top line of Bayes's theorem, which states that, in order to find the new probability P

of a hypothesis *H* given some new evidence *E*, we must first *multiply* the probability of the evidence given the hypothesis by the prior probability of the hypothesis. Before we discovered the clue that gave Mrs. Peacock a cast-iron alibi, the probability that Colonel Mustard committed the murder was already double the probability that Miss Scarlet did the deed, so after Mrs. Peacock is ruled out, the revised probability of Colonel Mustard's guilt increases by twice as much as that of Miss Scarlet.

NATURAL BORN BAYESIANS?

Bayes's theorem shows us how we should revise our beliefs in the light of new evidence, but we need not apply the formula consciously or even know it in order to follow its prescriptions. Cognitive scientists have been arguing for decades about whether people are "natural Bayesians"—that is, whether or not people automatically update their beliefs as Bayes's theorem says they should, even when they have never studied probability theory. The first round of studies, carried out in the 1970s and 1980s, tended to answer this question in the negative. Those studies identified a number of specific ways in which people tend to flout Bayesian prescriptions. One of these is the so-called base-rate fallacy.

Suppose you are tested for a disease and the test comes back positive. What is the chance that you actually have the disease? I've posed this question to hundreds of medical students over the past few years, when I have taught Bayesian methods, and most of them have gotten it wrong. Many think that the chance must be pretty high, without even realizing that the question is ill posed. Only a few answer, correctly, that you need more information before you can work out the answer. In particular, you need to know how good the test is and how many people like you have the disease in question. But unless you know something about Bayes's theorem, or at least the logic that underlies it, you probably won't realize that you need more information, let alone which extra information you need.

Let's say I've just been for an HIV test and gotten a positive result. In order to make use of that information, I first have to know how many people like me have HIV. Of course, the phrase "like me" is ambiguous. How much like me do they have to be? Do they have to have brown hair? Philosophers call this "the problem of the reference class," and there is no simple solution. In short, we have to make some rough-and-ready choices. For the sake of argument, I'll stipulate here that my reference class is that of "English men." In other words, I've decided not to take into account my sexual orientation, my history of drug use, and other potentially relevant factors. I can always do that later if I choose.

Let's say about 0.2 percent of English men are HIV-positive; that is the base rate. It is also the probability that I should assign to the hypothesis that I am HIV-positive before I get the test result, if I consider just the facts that I am male and English. As we've already seen, Bayesians would call this the *prior probability* of the hypothesis.

The base rate is not the only piece of information I need to know before I can make use of the evidence provided by the positive test result. I also need to know how good the test is. This means knowing both the hit rate and the false alarm rate. No test is 100 percent accurate. Let's assume that if someone has the virus, there is a 99 percent chance that this particular test will be positive; this is the *hit rate*. We'll also assume that if someone does not have the virus, there is still a 5 percent chance that the test will be positive; this is the *false alarm rate*.

If we plug all this information into Bayes's theorem, we can calculate the posterior probability—the probability that I am HIV-positive after taking into account the new evidence provided by the positive test result. The answer turns out to be just under 4 percent. In other words, the chance that I actually have HIV is still very low, even after I test positive.

Many of my students are surprised by this, even after I go through the details of how to calculate the answer with Bayes's theorem. Their surprise indicates the prevalence of the base-rate fallacy. Time and again, studies have shown that people fail to take sufficient account of prior probabilities or even completely ignore base rates altogether. The positive test result massively increased the probability that I have HIV, from 0.2 percent to almost 4 percent—an increase of almost 2,000 percent! But since we started off with an extremely low prior probability, the posterior probability was still rather low in absolute terms. If the base rate had been higher, then the situation would be very different. If, for example, I were an adult in Swaziland, where the prevalence rate of HIV/AIDS was estimated at over 26 percent in 2008, a positive test result would increase the probability that I have HIV to over 87 percent. It should be clear by now why it is so important to know the base rate when interpreting the results of diagnostic tests—and why ignoring the base rate is a major violation of Bayesian law.

The argument about whether people are natural Bayesians has begun to tilt somewhat in the other direction. Studies in the past decade or so have uncovered evidence that the base-rate fallacy, for example, may not be quite so pervasive as earlier research seemed to suggest. Some have even found examples of the opposite fallacy, in which people put too much weight on the base rate and fail to take adequate account of new information when updating their beliefs. Other studies have identified contexts in which people avoid both extremes and take account of both new evidence and base rates in just the right way.

In 2006, for example, two cognitive scientists, Thomas Griffiths and Joshua Tenenbaum, found that the fallacy disappeared when people were asked to make predictions about familiar things such as how long people tend to live and how much money movies tend to earn at the box office. Griffiths and Tenenbaum suggested that previous conclusions about the prevalence of the base-rate fallacy had been premature, since they had been based largely on laboratory studies that required people to make judgments about things outside their everyday experience. When asked to make predictions about things they were more familiar with, people are much better at taking the base rate into account.

Here are two of the questions that Griffiths and Tenenbaum asked the participants in their research:

- If you made a surprise visit to a friend and found that they had been watching a movie for thirty minutes, what would you predict for the length of the movie?
- Imagine you hear about a movie that has taken in $10 million at the box office, but you don't know how long it has been running. What would you predict for the total amount of box office intake for that movie?

The questions might seem tricky, since they ask you to predict something—a duration or a quantity—based only on a single piece of information. Yet everyday life routinely poses similar challenges—situations in which the true answer cannot be calculated precisely on the basis of the limited data available, yet where common sense suggests at least a reasonable guess.

For each of the questions they posed, Griffiths and Tenenbaum varied the value of the single piece of information they provided. When they asked the question about the duration of the movie, for example, they did not always specify that the friend had been watching it for 30 minutes; sometimes it was 60, 80, 95 or 110 minutes. Likewise with the question about the box-office takings; sometimes they specified that the movie had already taken in $1 million, $6 million, $40 million, or $100 million.

Griffiths and Tenenbaum made sure to ask questions about things with different underlying *distributions*. Movie run times, for example, follow what mathematicians call a Gaussian distribution, in which the values cluster around the mean, while box-office takings follow a power-law distribution, in which there are many minnows and a few blockbusters (see Figure 16). In other words, movie run times and box-office takings have different base rates (different "priors," in Bayesian terms). If people take base rates into account, therefore, the answers they give to questions such as those posed by Griffiths and Tenenbaum will also follow different patterns. And that is exactly what happened. In other words, people used their knowledge about the different statistical properties of movie run times and box-office takings when making predictions about them. When outside the lab, at least, people turn out be rather more Bayesian than psychologists had previously thought.

FIGURE 16: DISTRIBUTION OF MOVIE RUN TIMES (GAUSSIAN DISTRIBUTION) AND BOX-OFFICE TAKINGS (POWER-LAW DISTRIBUTION).

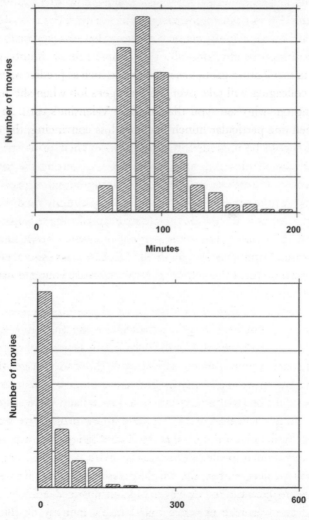

What does all this have to teach us about risk intelligence? The first thing to emphasize is that it is not necessary to master the complex math of Bayesian theory to develop high risk intelligence. Nevertheless, it can be useful to keep in mind some of the counterintuitive consequences that follow from Bayes's theorem, and apply these insights in a rough and ready way. Recall, for example, how after eliminating Mrs. Peacock from the whodunit, we had to adjust the probabilities attached to the remaining suspects in a way that was proportional to their current probability of guilt. This simple rule of thumb can be applied to many other problems in daily life, such as predicting which of your colleagues will take over the manager's job when she retires, or finding out who sent you that mystery Valentine's card. In each case, when one particular hunch becomes less convincing, the other hunches should be upgraded in proportion to their prior strength. If you no longer think Bob has a hope in hell of getting the top job, then you should reallocate the little remaining faith you previously had in him to the other candidates, in order to comply with the 100 percent rule. But you shouldn't necessarily re-allocate this quantum of faith equally among the other candidates; if you already thought Cheryl was the front-runner, you should increase your estimate of her chances by more than the amount that you increase your estimates of her competitors.

Likewise, never forget the base rate! We've already seen how optimism bias can lead us to underestimate the time it will take to complete a task, whether it be writing an essay or building a new transport system. But the tendency to think we can get things done faster than we really can—which psychologists call "planning bias"—can also be attributed to the base-rate fallacy. When estimating how long it will take us to complete a new project, we tend to focus on the details of the project itself, and ignore our experience of previous similar projects. For many years, I never completed a research project within the initially estimated time frame, but continued to commit to unreasonably optimistic deadlines. Even though I knew from experience that I rarely met my deadlines, I didn't learn from this experience. I continued to ignore the evidence of many similar projects in the past, and to estimate completion dates that I rarely met.

Daniel Kahneman and Amos Tversky developed a method for overcoming the planning fallacy that they called reference class forecasting. This involves forcing yourself to make explicit assumptions about the base rate when estimating the time it will take to complete a project, based on your experience of similar projects in the past. For example, suppose your boss wants to know when you can deliver the new marketing plan he has just asked you to write. If you've written several marketing plans in the past, you should start by recalling how long it took you to finish them. But what if you've never written a marketing plan before? In that case, you should still try to draw on previous experience, if at all possible, but to do so you'll have to select a different reference class. You might recall the essays you wrote at college, for example, and make any necessary adjustments for the novelty of the material, or the different number of words expected. What you should definitely *not* do is focus entirely on the nature of the new task, and completely ignore all your past experience. Any similar ventures that you have already undertaken are grist to your mill. By framing the forecasting problem and making use of previous experience, you are leveraging what you already know to make a better estimate than you would if you focused only on the task at hand.

In this chapter we've seen how the insights of probability theory can help us avoid a set of basic errors when estimating probabilities. We've also seen how we can take probabilities into account when making informed decisions by using simple strategies such as setting thresholds and bet sizing. But those methods will get us only so far and may not be relevant to many of the most important decisions we face in life, where we must often consider multiple criteria and objectives. In such circumstances we must employ a more sophisticated approach. In the next chapter we'll look at the most powerful method of decision making yet devised, the theory of expected utility. And we'll see how yet more lessons for good decision making may be derived from the study of gambling, which is so closely related in its evolution to the theory of probability. Though gambling proper is for most people an ill-advised exercise in losing money, the scientists who have studied gambling, and expert gamblers themselves, have much to teach us about weighing odds.

CHAPTER 8

How to Gamble and Win

A number of moralists condemn lotteries and refuse to see anything noble in the passion of the ordinary gambler. They judge
gambling as some atheists judge religion, by its excesses.

—CHARLES LAMB

When Galileo wanted to put Aristotle's theory of motion to the test, he cut a groove in a wooden board, propped the board up at an angle, and let a brass ball roll down the groove. Aristotle's theory predicted that the speed of the ball would be constant, but Galileo found that the speed increased as the ball rolled down the slope. The reason, as Isaac Newton later showed, is that the ball is accelerated by gravity.

Galileo's experiment was a stroke of genius because it stripped away the things he wasn't interested in, such as friction, thereby allowing the phenomenon of interest to be studied in isolation. In a similar way, what Galileo's inclined plane was to the study of gravity, gambling is to the study of decision making. Gambling provides a simplified "toy world" in which all the extraneous factors are stripped away, allowing the fundamental forces to stand out more clearly. In gambling, the process of decision making is boiled down to its barest essentials and expressed in a quantitative form that allows precise mathematical analysis. The conditions can be held constant more easily, so experiments are eminently repeatable.

In fact, the very origins of decision theory lie in the analysis of optimal gambling behavior by seventeenth-century mathematicians such as Blaise Pascal—and Galileo himself, who wrote a small treatise on dice. The most important book about decision making ever published, *The Theory of Games and Economic Behavior* (1944) by John von Neumann and Oskar Morgenstern, draws many lessons from the analysis of poker. The ideas presented in their book are, in my view, on a par with Albert Einstein's theory of general relativity in terms of their scientific importance and sheer genius. Unlike Einstein, however, von Neumann and Morgenstern are not household names, and few nonspecialists would have even the roughest understanding of their theory.

To carry the analogy one step further: what Einstein did for space, time, and gravity, von Neumann and Morgenstern did for rationality. They provided, in other words, a rigorous mathematical theory of rational choice. It may come as a shock to some people to discover that the theory is based largely on an analysis of optimal gambling behavior. Many people view gambling as, at best, frivolous and, at worst, downright sinful, but in my view it is neither. It is, in fact, one of the best scientific tools we have for studying rational decision making.

At the heart of the theory developed by von Neumann and Morgenstern is the concept of expected utility. This involves making a basic calculation: you multiply the probability of winning by the potential gains and multiply the probability of losing by the potential losses. Adding the two figures together gives you the expected utility of a gamble.

For example, let's suppose you are offered a wager with a 60 percent chance of winning $300. To calculate the expected utility of the wager, you first multiply $300 by 60 percent, which is $180. Let's also say you have put $400 on the table in order to make the bet, so that's your potential loss. You must now multiply this figure by the probability of losing, which is 40 percent, and arrive at a figure of minus $160. Finally, to calculate the expected value of the bet, you add the two figures together (or subtract $160 from $180) to arrive at $20.

The basic rule in gambling is to wager money only on bets with a positive expected value, so in this example, an expert gambler would go ahead and make the bet. Most casino games and national lotteries have negative expected values, so it's best—if money is your primary concern, rather than the fun of playing—not to bet on them.

But, as you may have said to yourself in reading this, is the expected gain of $20 really worth the risk? After all, if you lose, you'll be $400 worse off. It's worth it to an expert gambler, because he knows he'll be making many, many more similar wagers, and this calculation is actually premised on playing an infinite number of times. The math behind the theory of expected utility assumes that we could go on gambling forever, and expert gamblers play often enough that this is a good approximation of the results they can expect.

Focusing on the expected utility of a bet, rather than on the maximum possible profit or loss, allows expert gamblers to look beyond the moment and view each gamble in the context of a much longer time horizon. This in turn allows them to avoid one of the biggest mistakes so many novice gamblers make: trying to make up for losses by making more risky bets. As one expert gambler, the Irish horse-race bettor J. P. McManus, told me, a novice who has lost all his bets at the racetrack in the morning may be so desperate to back a winner before going home that he stakes everything on a horse he has never heard of in the last race of the day. J.P., on the other hand, could always take it or leave it. His motto was "There's always another race."

But as I've said, most of us aren't making bets nearly as continuously as expert gamblers, even if we're quite regular gamblers, and of course the relevance of this calculation for most of our day-to-day decision making is also limited by the fact that so many of our decisions about risks have nothing to do with money to be won or lost. This is where the theory of expected utility comes into its own.

As with all great scientific theories, at the heart of von Neumann and Morgenstern's theory is a very simple yet very powerful idea. The idea is that many of our choices in life, especially those that involve risks, can be thought of as the choice of whether or not to gamble.

They are choices that have a chance of leaving us better off than we are now, and a chance of leaving us worse off, and we can see that there are four elements in any risky choice (see Figure 17):

1. **The status quo:** This is our current situation, which will persist for sure if we choose not to take the gamble.
2. **The potential gain:** This is our reward if the gamble pays off. By definition, it must be better than the status quo.
3. **The potential loss:** This is what we lose if the gamble doesn't pay off. By definition, it must be worse than the status quo.
4. **The chance of winning:** This is the probability of the gamble paying off (by implication it also tells us what the chance of the gamble *not* paying off is).

FIGURE 17: THE ANATOMY OF A GAMBLE ACCORDING TO VON NEUMANN AND MORGENSTERN. You choose whether or not to gamble, but the outcome of the gamble itself is determined by chance. The symbol *p* stands for the probability of winning, here expressed as a number between 0 and 1; because of the 100 percent rule, the probability of losing is therefore 1 - *p*.

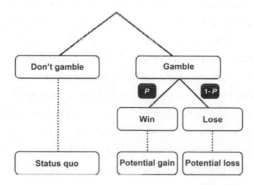

To come up with an estimate of the expected utility of any such choice, then, we must calculate the potential gains and losses and subtract the latter from the former. If the result is a positive number, the theory recommends that you should take the gamble. If the number is negative, you'd be better off staying with the status quo.

It's all very well to analyze roulette and the lottery in terms of their expected utility, but the whole point of decision theory is that the same quantitative analysis can—and should—be applied to many other areas of our lives that might seem at first to have little or nothing to do with gambling.

In order to apply expected utility theory to decisions involving nonmonetary losses and gains, we have to put numbers on intangible things such as happiness, health, and suffering. Some people object to this on the grounds that such things are impossible to quantify. But at some level, our brains are always making judgments about the relative value of seemingly intangible things. The only question is whether we attempt to make the process explicit or not.

Oscar Wilde quipped that a cynic is a man who knows the price of everything but the value of nothing. But whether you're a cynic or not, you can't be a good gambler unless you at least *try* to put a price on everything. We can measure such prices in terms of a single imaginary currency called "utility" in which all possible gains and losses can be quantified, regardless of whether they involve money or less tangible things such as health and happiness. When Einstein said, "Not everything that counts can be counted," he was wrong.

For example, let's say you find a classmate quite attractive but you aren't so impressed by his or her conversational ability, so you rate a date with him or her as worth about 10 utility points to you. On the other hand, you find embarrassment and rejection very unpleasant indeed, so you rate the experience at minus 20 utility points. Let's say you estimate the chance of the person saying "yes" at about 30 percent. So:

- The expected utility of winning is 10 multiplied by 30 percent, which is 3 utility points.
- The expected utility of losing is minus 20 multiplied by 70 percent, which is –14 utility points.
- The expected utility of the gamble is therefore 3 utility

points minus 14 utility points, which comes to –11 utility points. That number is below 0, so you should not ask the person out on a date.

If this strikes you as just too rational, that's precisely the point. My aim in this book is to help you make your decisions on a more rational basis. If you want to be irrational, you might as well stop reading now and go and do something beautifully senseless, such as betting your life savings on a single spin of a roulette wheel or crossing the street with your eyes shut.

But what about gut feelings? Actually, the theory of expected utility does not involve eliminating feelings. On the contrary, feelings are essential to the process of estimating the utility of potential gains and losses. Utility is an entirely subjective thing that each person calculates by consulting his or her own feelings, values, and preferences.

HANNAH'S CHOICE

Of course the specific numbers we put on most potential gains and losses in our lives are crude approximations. But the exercise of thinking through what all the losses and gains might be and struggling to weigh them up and estimate their probabilities can be extremely clarifying. To see how powerful this method of decision making can be, consider the case of Hannah Jones, a British teenager whose story hit the headlines in the United Kingdom in November 2008 when she turned down a heart transplant that might have saved her life. Instead, she left the hospital and went home, where she expected to die in the company of her parents, her younger brother, and her two sisters.

When a child protection officer was called in to determine whether it was really Hannah's decision or her parents had been putting undue pressure on her, Hannah was clear and articulate. "I put my point straight across," she told reporters after the interview with the protection officer. "I said, I don't want this and it's not my choice to have [the operation]. I just decided there were too many risks and even if I took it there might be a bad outcome afterwards.

"I'm not a normal thirteen-year-old," she continued. "I'm a deep thinker. I've had to be, with my illness. It's hard at thirteen, to know I'm going to die, but I also know what's best for me."

The decision to refuse further medical treatment is entirely rational if the expected utility of continuing with the treatment is less than the expected utility of stopping. If we analyze Hannah's choice according to von Neumann and Morgenstern's model, we must first identify her potential gains and losses. The potential gains are all the good things that will happen to Hannah if she takes the gamble of the heart transplant and the gamble pays off. They would include getting a new heart that works well and going on to lead a much more healthy and enjoyable life. The potential losses are all the bad things that will happen to Hannah if she takes the gamble of the heart transplant and the gamble doesn't pay off. They would include undergoing a major surgical procedure, with multiple subsequent invasive treatments, and finding that after all the pain and suffering, the heart doesn't work properly, with the result that she dies shortly afterward, perhaps in the hospital and away from her family.

Having identified the potential gains and losses, Hannah would have to put numbers on them to convert them into the currency of utility. This is an entirely subjective matter. The numbers depend on the person's own values and preferences, and nobody else can decide these numbers for him or her. Von Neumann and Morgenstern assume that each person is the best judge of his or her own happiness.

Next, Hannah must estimate her chance of "winning"—which means, in this context, the chance of the operation being successful. Finally, having assigned numbers to her potential gains, her potential losses, and her chance of winning, the final step is to calculate the expected utility of the gamble. To do this, she would multiply her potential gain by her chance of winning, multiply her potential loss by her chance of losing, and add the results together. If the expected utility is negative—if, that is, the final figure is less than zero—the rational choice is not to undergo the operation.

Now, I'm not suggesting that Hannah really made her decision in such a formal way. But I would argue that this method captures something important about her decision; namely, that it is that it may be perfectly rational and consistent with her best interests for her to choose to die peacefully at home rather than submitting herself to a major surgical procedure, with no guarantee that it will work, and maybe even dying in the hospital, away from her loved ones. Hannah probably weighed the various costs and benefits of each option implicitly, but when the stakes are high, we may prefer to structure the problem formally and evaluate multiple criteria explicitly.

Thankfully, Hannah's story has a happy ending. Six months after she refused the transplant, doctors found that she had grown stronger and said the operation would be less risky than previously thought. Hannah changed her mind and asked to be placed on the waiting list for a new heart. "I know I decided I definitely didn't want this," she said, "but everyone's entitled to change their mind." Within days, Hannah was taken to London's Great Ormond Street Hospital and given a new heart in a six-and-a-half-hour-long operation. The operation was hailed as a total success, and it is believed that the organ could add twenty-five years to her life.

THE EXPECTED UTILITY OF INVADING IRAQ

The theory of expected utility is not restricted to making intensely personal decisions, as in Hannah's case, but can also be applied to making huge political decisions that affect the lives of millions. The US decision to invade Iraq in 2003 is a case in point.

Put yourself in the position of President George W. Bush in early 2002. Together with the Northern Alliance, US forces have recently defeated the Taliban regime and mustered support for a new government in Afghanistan. An interim administration has been formed and Hamid Karzai sworn in as the country's leader. After a fierce battle with US forces in the mountains of Tora Bora, a number of Al Qaeda operatives, probably including Osama bin Laden, have escaped into Pakistan. With the attacks of 9/11 still fresh in everyone's minds, the United States has widespread sympathy and support. The federal budget is nearly in balance, making ambitious projects feasible, and the US military is at full strength and well prepared.

As the journalist James Fallows pointed out, this would have been an ideal time for President Bush to step back and think more broadly about the United States' strategic options:

> As the fighting wound down in Tora Bora, the administration could in principle have matched a list of serious problems with a list of possible solutions. In his State of the Union Speech, in late January, President Bush had named Iran, Iraq, and North Korea as an "axis of evil." The administration might have weighed the relative urgency of those three threats.

This was an opportunity created by crisis. The United States had enough reserves of both hard and soft power to take out one of the three members of the axis of evil if it so desired. The question was—which one?

According to Fallows, there is no evidence that President Bush even considered this question or that he ever discussed the opportunity costs and trade-offs when deciding to invade Iraq. The only evidence of any serious attempt by anyone in the administration to identify the ways in which an invasion might backfire is a memo by Donald Rumsfeld to Bush dated October 15, 2002, which later became known as the "parade of horribles." Several of the points in Rumsfeld's memo mention the danger of neglecting other threats:

> 7. While the United States is engaged in Iraq, another rogue state could take advantage of US preoccupation—North Korea, Iran, PRC in the Taiwan Straits, other?
>
> 8. While preoccupied with Iraq, the US might feel compelled to ignore serious proliferation or other machinations by North Korea, Russia, PRC, Pakistan, India, etc., and thereby seem to

tacitly approve and acquiesce in unacceptable behavior, to the detriment of US influence in the world.

9. Preoccupation with Iraq for a long period could lead to US inattentiveness and diminished influence in South Asia, which could lead to a conflict between nuclear armed states.

As Rumsfeld also noted in his memo, however, a fully informed decision would also have to consider a similar list of "all the potential problems that need to be considered if there is *no* regime change in Iraq" (emphasis added). After drawing up a list of the pros and cons of invading Iraq, a rational decision maker could then have weighed the expected utility of this option.

Let's consider the potential benefits of invading Iraq from the point of view of the Bush administration in early 2002. One such benefit would clearly have been toppling the regime of Saddam Hussein. That was important for a variety of reasons, of which removing the threat of WMD was just one. There was a long list of other charges against Saddam Hussein's regime, including its attacks on US pilots in the no-fly zones, its violation of the UN Security Council resolutions, and its crimes against its people. In addition to toppling Saddam Hussein, other benefits of invading Iraq, from the US point of view, would include the possibility of establishing long-term military bases there, securing access to Iraqi oil reserves, and encouraging the spread of democracy in the Middle East.

Having drawn up a list of the potential benefits of invading Iraq, the next step would be to assign probabilities and utilities to each one. This would, of course, involve a lot of guesswork, but there's nothing wrong with that, and it's certainly better than refusing to make any estimates at all. It's especially hard to put a value on such intangible things as spreading democracy in the Middle East or weakening global support for the United States, but even a crude system is better than nothing, so let's just invent a currency called "US utility" to represent some measure of advancing US interests. We might assign 10 US utility points to removing Saddam from power, for example, 8 points to establishing long-term military bases in Iraq, and so on.

We then estimate the probability that invading Iraq would lead to each of these benefits and multiply the probability by the number of utility points to arrive at the expected utility of each potential benefit. Finally, we add up the results to find the overall expected utility of all the potential benefits of invading Iraq (Table 3).

TABLE 3: THE POTENTIAL BENEFITS OF INVADING IRAQ, FROM THE US PERSPECTIVE.

Benefit	US utility	Probability	Expected US utility
Regime change	10	98%	9.8
Military bases in Iraq	8	85%	6.8
Access to Iraqi oil	6	70%	4.2
Spreading democracy	10	25%	2.5
TOTAL			23.3

Next we do the same for the potential costs of invading Iraq. Again, it is important to view this from the perspective of the Bush administration in early 2002, without the benefit of hindsight. So although we should include the risk of civil war, which was considered in advance but which did not in fact occur until three years after the invasion, it would not be fair to include the risk of an organized insurgency, which did later develop but which nobody foresaw prior to the invasion. It has to be expected that we're not always going to identify all of the potential gains and losses at play in any given choice. But the framework provided by expected utility theory can alert us to the need to factor in new information about possible gains and losses as that information arises, which may tilt the balance of costs and benefits in the other direction and lead the decision maker to change his mind. Without that, decision makers will never cut their losses; they will be forced to stick with failed policies to prove they were good ideas in the first place.

Returning to the costs that were clearly foreseeable at the time, the potential casualties on both sides should obviously be included, as well as the financial costs of the war, with large margins of error to reflect our uncertainty about them. Last but not least, another potential cost of the invasion that was clearly foreseeable was the possible erosion of global support for the United States. Rumsfeld also noted this in his memo of October 15, 2002:

20. US alienation from countries in the EU and the UN could grow to levels sufficient to make our historic post World War II relationships irretrievable, with the charge of US unilateralism becoming so embedded in the world's mind that it leads to a diminution of U.S. influence in the world.

After listing the potential costs of invading Iraq, we assign probabilities and utilities to each one, just as we did when considering the potential benefits. We then estimate the probability that invading Iraq would lead to each of these costs and multiply the probability by the number of utility points to arrive at the expected utility of each potential cost. Finally, we add up the results to find the overall expected utility of all the potential costs of invading Iraq (Table 4).

TABLE 4: THE POTENTIAL COSTS OF INVADING IRAQ, FROM THE US PERSPECTIVE.

Cost	US utility	Probability	Expected US utility
Civil war	-4	25%	-1
Casualties	-5	80%	-4
Financial cost	-35	80%	-28
Loss of global support	-3	25%	-0.75
TOTAL			-33.75

The last step is to add the expected utility of all the potential benefits to the expected utility of all the potential costs. We are then left with a number that represents the expected utility of invading Iraq. If we assign the utilities and the probabilities as I have done in Tables 3 and 4, the overall expected utility of invading Iraq, from the US perspective in early 2002, was minus 10.45 utility points (23.3 – 33.75). Since this number is negative, a rational decision maker would not have gone ahead with the invasion.

Does this imply that President Bush's decision to invade Iraq was therefore irrational? Not necessarily. It may well be that Bush simply envisioned lower financial costs and fewer casualties than I have done here, or used a different "exchange rate" when converting the costs and benefits into US utility points, or took other benefits into account that I have not considered, or estimated the probabilities differently. Utility is a subjective quantity, and what seems irrational to one person may therefore be quite rational to someone else with different values and preferences. The theory of expected utility does not pretend to reveal what the "objectively optimal" course of action is. But by forcing decision makers to spell out their assumptions, it keeps them honest, and makes their reasoning more transparent. If someone had presented the foregoing analysis of the pros and cons of invading Iraq to President Bush in early 2002, it would have been incumbent upon him to explain which of the various assumptions he disagreed with, and why, on pain of exposing himself to the charge of irrationality.

But even supposing President Bush was able to demonstrate that, from his point of view, the overall expected utility of invading Iraq was a positive number, this would not necessarily mean that the invasion was rational, for he would also need to go through a similar set of calculations with regard to military action against the other two members of the axis of evil. Only if the expected utility of invading Iraq, as perceived by the Bush administration in early 2002, was *both* positive *and* greater than that of attacking Iran or North Korea, should Operation Iraqi Freedom have been authorized.

What threats did Iran and North Korea pose to US interests in

HOW TO GAMBLE AND WIN

2002? In October of that year, a delegation of Americans in Pyong-
yang found that North Korea's nuclear weapons program was actually up and running. In December, North Korea reactivated a nuclear
processing plant it had closed eight years earlier, and soon afterward
it expelled inspectors from the International Atomic Energy Agency
and announced that it would withdraw from the Nuclear Non-
Proliferation Treaty. Meanwhile, in August an Iranian opposition
group had revealed the existence of two previously secret nuclear
facilities. Of the three members of the axis of evil, Iraq had made the
least progress toward developing nuclear weapons. Even if the worst
suspicions about Saddam's WMD—the existence of mobile bioweapons labs—had turned out to be true, the stakes would still have been
lower than those in North Korea or Iran.

Even without the benefit of hindsight, even if we consider only
the information available to President Bush in early 2002, it seems
plausible that the expected utility of invading Iraq was lower than that
of attacking North Korea or Iran. Of course, it was not obligatory to
launch military action against any of the members of the axis of evil.
But if military force was to be used, it should not have been wasted on
toppling Saddam.

THE RATIONAL TERRORIST

The apparatus of expected utility could equally well be used by the
enemies of America and to help do a better job of anticipating their
next moves. Put yourself, for example, in the shoes of a terrorist leader
planning an attack in the continental United States. Let's suppose
your senior advisers have mapped out a range of options, including
releasing anthrax in a major sports arena, detonating a dirty bomb
in a major city, and shooting down a domestic airliner with a stinger
missile. Which target should you select?

A rational terrorist might proceed by calculating the expected
utility of each attack. He might start by listing what he would perceive
to be the potential benefits of each attack, such as causing American

casualties, damaging the US economy, increasing the level of fear among the US population, and attracting more recruits to the terrorist organization. The potential costs to consider might include the possibility of increasing worldwide support for the United States, the loss of popular support for the terrorist organization, the loss of the operatives themselves, and of course the financial costs. As before, the next step would be to assign probabilities and utilities to each potential benefit and cost. The terrorist leader might assign 10 utility points per American casualty, for example, and one point for each million dollars of damage to the US economy. He could then estimate the probability that each option would lead to each of these benefits and multiply the probability by the number of utility points to arrive at the expected utility of attacking each target. Next he could do the same for the potential costs and subtract the total from the expected utility of the benefits. He would then be left with a set of numbers representing the expected utility of each option.

The same methodology could also be used by the Department of Homeland Security to anticipate likely terrorist targets, argue Heather Rosoff, a policy analyst, and Richard John, a cognitive psychologist. Current methods of terrorism risk assessment tend to focus on target vulnerability, terrorist resources, and the consequences of a successful attack, but neglect the influence of terrorists' values and beliefs. By modeling the terrorist leader mind-set in terms of expected utility theory rather than simply assuming that terrorists are irrational, security services might be able to better assess the possible threats and so allocate their resources more effectively.

Rosoff and John point out that this is not a zero-sum game. The benefit of an attack for a terrorist organization is not the mirror opposite of our costs. Terrorist objectives are generally not directly related to our antiterrorist objectives. For example, though the 2001 attack on the World Trade Center was costly to the United States in terms of lives lost and economic impacts, there were many other potential targets that would have resulted in more casualties and greater financial consequences. The twin towers had a powerful symbolic value, however, as icons of Western capitalism. Clearly, terrorist organizations have other objectives, not directly related to lives and economics, that drive their decisions about targets and modes of attack.

The pros and cons of the September 11 attacks were the subject of heated debate within the senior ranks of Al Qaeda, with many concerned that they could prove counterproductive. Most worrying was the possibility that US retaliation might eliminate the safe haven and training camps that Al Qaeda had secured in Afghanistan. If Bin Laden thought this was a risk worth taking, it must have been because he placed less value on having such a territorial base, or more value on the potential benefits of such a spectacular operation, than did the other senior figures in Al Qaeda. In fact, extreme retaliation was itself a benefit from Bin Laden's point of view. "We want to bring the Americans to fight us on Muslim land," he told the Palestinian journalist Abdel Bari Atwan in 1996. By provoking the United States to send troops to Afghanistan, Bin Laden hoped to beat the infidel forces on that inhospitable terrain just as he and his fellow Mujahideen had defeated the Soviet Army after their invasion of Afghanistan in 1979.

But the chance of a military victory was not the only, nor indeed the most important, reason why Bin Laden wanted to tempt US forces to invade Afghanistan. The presence of large numbers of American soldiers on Muslim soil would, he hoped, enrage the *umma*, the worldwide Muslim community, and encourage more young men to join the jihad. Most important, by engaging the United States in a long war of attrition, Bin Laden hoped to inflate the American military budget and eventually bankrupt the US economy. If Bin Laden really thought there was a good chance of an Afghan war bankrupting the United States, he was clearly being overconfident. Fortunately for Al Qaeda, however, the United States did not stop with Afghanistan, but went on to invade Iraq, a far costlier enterprise, which did indeed contribute significantly to the fiscal deficit. At the time when the attacks of September 11 were being planned, nobody in Al Qaeda imagined that they would eventually lead to a war in Iraq. Just as the Bush administration failed to foresee the insurgency that would become perhaps the worst consequence of invading Iraq, from the US point of view, so Bin Laden failed to predict the invasion of Iraq itself, which from his point of view, would become the best consequence of 9/11.

As already noted, there will always be the potential gains and losses that we fail to foresee when making a decision. The framework provided by expected utility theory cannot remedy this by itself. But it can alert us to the need to factor in new information about possible gains and losses as that information arises. We can only judge the quality of the decision by the light of the information available at the time; if we discover new facts that change the cost-benefit equation, the only wise thing to do is to make a different decision. As the great British economist, John Maynard Keynes, is reputed to have said, "When the facts change, I change my mind. What do you do, sir?"

RATIONING HEALTH CARE

Just like the high-powered mathematical programs whose pitfalls we looked at earlier, calculations of expected utility are only as good as the estimates we make about gains, losses, and the probabilities of each. No matter how good any equation is, it can never transmute lead into gold; if you put garbage in, you will get garbage out. Unfortunately, this means that expected utility calculations are sometimes used in problematic ways.

Take the case of one of the UK National Health Service's methods of determining whether or not to give patients potentially lifesaving treatments. Researchers for the service have conducted interviews with the public that aim to measure the quality of life associated with various health states. An interview might go something like this.

The researcher hands a sheet of paper to the volunteer. "First I'd like you to read this description of what it's like to be on kidney dialysis," she says. "Imagine that you will have to spend the rest of your life in this condition unless you elect to have an operation. If you have the operation, there is a chance that you will be completely cured of your kidney problems and you'll be healthy for the rest of your life. But there's also a chance that the operation might kill you."

The researcher takes a colored disc out of her bag. "Now," she says, "I have a device here called a probability wheel. The wheel is divided into two sectors, a blue sector and a yellow sector. If you choose to have the operation, I'll spin this pointer on the wheel. If it stops on blue, the operation is successful, but if it stops on yellow, you die during surgery."

The researcher adjusts the wheel so it is half blue and half yellow.

"Okay," she says, "now, would you choose to have the operation or not?"

The volunteer pauses for a moment. "Well, dialysis sounds pretty bad, so, yes, I think I'd take my chances and go for the operation."

The researcher now adjusts the wheel so it is 40 percent blue and 60 percent yellow. "Now the pointer has a greater chance of stopping on yellow," she says, "in which case the operation kills you. Would you still go for the operation?"

The volunteer nods.

"Okay, now I'll adjust the wheel again so it is 30 percent blue, 70 percent yellow. Would you still choose to have the operation?"

"No, I don't think so. That's too risky now. I'd rather keep on living with the dialysis."

The researcher makes a note in her logbook: "Utility of dialysis = 0.35."

By conducting interviews like this, researchers aim to measure the quality of life associated with various health states. Each health state is assigned a number called a "quality weight" on a scale between 0 (death) and 1 (perfect health). In the example above, the quality weight associated with being on kidney dialysis is 0.35.

The numbers can be a matter of life and death. In the United Kingdom, the National Institute for Health and Clinical Excellence (NICE) uses them to decide whether or not to recommend state funding for potentially lifesaving treatments. The quality weights of health states with and without a given treatment are used to calculate how many so-called QALYs the treatment would give you. QALY stands for "quality-adjusted life-year." A drug that could raise your quality of life from 0.7 to 0.9 for five years would give you one QALY (0.2 multiplied by five). If that drug costs £5,000 per year, it would cost £25,000 per QALY. NICE does not usually recommend funding for treatments that cost more than £30,000 per QALY.

Given the importance of the quality weights, it is worth asking how reliable the procedures are by which they are measured. Quality weights can be measured by a variety of methods, but I'll focus on the particular method just described, which is known as the "standard gamble."

The underlying principles of the standard gamble are impeccable. It is based directly on the model of risky choice developed by von Neumann and Morgenstern (see Figure 17). The model has an interesting consequence; if we measure utility on a scale of 0 to 1 where the maximum potential loss has a value of 0 and the maximum potential gain a value of 1, it follows that when you are indifferent between the gamble and the status quo, the chance of winning (measured on a scale from 0 to 1) will exactly equal the utility of the status quo. The proof of this is rather complex, so you'll have to take it on trust for now. The main point is that this equation allows us to measure the utility that someone assigns to his or her current situation. All we have to do is to vary the chance of winning until we discover a person's "indifference point"—that is, the point at which he or she cannot decide whether to take the gamble or stay with the status quo.

That is what the researcher was doing in the case of the kidney dialysis. Since the interviewee switched her choice between two adjacent questions—one in which the chance of success was 40 percent and another in which the chance of success was 30 percent—the indifference point is taken to be halfway between, which is why the researcher wrote down 0.35 as the utility of dialysis. That is the utility this person assigns to the condition of being on kidney dialysis, measured on a scale from 0 (death) to 1 (perfect health).

When I told some computer scientists about QALYs, they were amazed that the theory of expected utility was regularly used in a practical setting such as medicine to make life-and-death decisions.

As well they might have been. We should have serious concerns about this method of assigning quality values to health states.

For one thing, the method assumes that most of us have a good intuitive feeling for probabilities. Yet this, we have seen, is far from universal. Without some independent confirmation of people's risk intelligence, there is no reason we should assume that their decisions in imaginary life-and-death situations reveal anything about how they would actually decide in a real life-and-death situation.

Another problem with using the standard gamble to measure the subjective value that people assign to various health states is that the method does not control for variations in risk appetite. My decision about whether to undergo dangerous surgery to cure a painful condition is determined not just by how much I think my current pain reduces my quality of life and the probability of dying in surgery but also by my appetite for risk. Strictly speaking, von Neumann and Morgenstern showed only that when I'm indifferent between the gamble and the status quo, the utility of the status quo will be equal to the chance of winning *if I am risk-neutral*. But this is often not the case, so without also testing risk appetite, the utilities elicited by means of the standard gamble cannot be taken at face value.

Even worse, it makes no sense to average across the preferences of many people. Utilities are, by definition, subjective. Each person is taken to be the best judge of his or her own preferences, and there is no such thing as a "right" answer. So when the National Institute for Health and Clinical Excellence uses QALY weights to decide whether or not to recommend state funding for potentially lifesaving treatments, it is doing so on the basis of a mythical "average person" whose preferences are mere abstractions.

Perhaps most worrying of all, this way of ascertaining QALY weights assumes that people can predict how they would feel if they were to get various diseases. This flies in the face of abundant evidence showing that most people are pretty bad at predicting their own feelings. Affective forecasting, as psychologists call it, involves predicting how you would feel were certain events to occur in the near future. For example, how happy would you feel if you won $10 million in the lottery, and for how long would you feel that way? How upset would you be, and for how long, if you became paralyzed for life?

It's not hard to guess how those events would make us feel, but when it comes to predicting how long the feelings would last, most people get it badly wrong. Almost everyone overestimates how long both good and bad feelings last. Dozens of studies have shown that common events such as getting married and losing one's job make people happier or sadder for only a few months. Even uncommon events, such as losing a child in a car accident, being diagnosed with cancer, or being sent to a concentration camp, have less impact on long-term happiness than most people think. In short, most people are reasonably happy most of the time, and most events do little to change that for long. Yet most people persist in thinking that powerful events must have long-lasting emotional consequences. They suffer from what psychologists call "durability bias" when trying to predict their emotional reactions.

Durability bias has several possible explanations, but one particularly important factor is the common tendency to underestimate our ability to adapt. When imagining how we might feel if we became paralyzed for life, for example, we fail to consider our capacity to get over bad experiences. When we think that winning the lottery would solve all our problems, we fail to realize how quickly people get used to being rich.

One particularly dramatic example of the ability to adapt comes from a study published in the *British Medical Journal* in 2011. A team of researchers in France and Belgium studied the self-reported quality of life in sixty-five people with locked-in syndrome (LIS). LIS sounds horrific. It involves near-total paralysis, including of the muscles of speech, so you are mute, and the inability to move all four limbs, while remaining perfectly conscious. The only muscles to remain under conscious control are those around the eyes, so that making vertical eye movements or blinking is the only means of communication. That is how the journalist Jean-Dominique Bauby wrote his famous memoir, *The Diving Bell and the Butterfly*. He wrote the entire book by blinking his left eyelid; a transcriber repeatedly recited a French-language frequency-ordered alphabet (E, S, A, R, I, N, T, U, L, etc.), until Bauby blinked to choose the next letter. The book took about 200,000 blinks to write, and an average word took approximately two minutes to "dictate" in this way.

Bauby died of pneumonia three days after the book was published, but, given appropriate medical care, patients with LIS can survive for decades. Of the sixty-five patients who responded to all the questions posed by the French and Belgian researchers, forty-seven professed happiness and eighteen unhappiness. The longer they had been paralyzed, the more likely they were to be happy. Only 7 percent expressed a wish for euthanasia. The researchers concluded that when patients who have recently become paralyzed say they want to die, they should be assured that there is a high chance that they will regain a happy and meaningful life. End-of-life decisions should not be avoided, but if the decisions are to be well informed, they should not be contaminated by durability bias. Patients with LIS should wait at least a few months, until their mood has reached a steady state, before making any dramatic choices. The research shows that they are likely to be pleasantly surprised.

Despite its flaws, the methodology of the standard gamble is at least transparent, so decisions taken on the basis of QALY weights assigned in this way can be publicly analyzed and criticized. If we disagree about their role in making decisions about which medical treatments to fund, it is precisely the explicit nature of the criteria that allows us to formulate our disagreements clearly. Public debate is advanced by such transparency, so that even in this instance, putting numbers on things is helpful in a certain way.

The theory of expected utility is a powerful thinking device that can help us make better decisions if used wisely. This, however, depends crucially on making good enough initial estimates about the value of potential gains and losses and the probabilities of each. It takes practice to get a feel for how to put numbers on such apparently intangible things, and we should always be prepared to go back and revise our estimates whenever we realize we have made a mistake. If you persist, however, you will find that expected utility theory gradually becomes second nature, and you will begin to see the world in a whole new light. The clarity of thinking that comes with a feel for expected utility theory can be quite astonishing.

As powerful as the insights we've explored from probability theory and decision science are, however, an even more fundamental aspect of risk intelligence is assessing how much we really know on a given topic. In the final chapter, we'll take a look at how to do the best job we can of working out how much information we have in any given situation and gauging the limits of our knowledge.

CHAPTER 9

Knowing What You Know

He who does not know may still have true notions
of that which he does not know.

—PLATO

In 1894, the physicist Albert Abraham Michelson was so confident that all the fundamental laws of physics had been discovered that he relegated the future of science merely to "adding a few decimal places to the results already obtained." The physicist Lord Kelvin was only slightly more circumspect. A few years after Michelson's brazen prediction, Kelvin also claimed that physics was nearly complete, but he did note "two clouds on the horizon"—two anomalies that couldn't be explained by the physics of his day. The observation was remarkably prescient; the two anomalies he identified (the Michelson-Morley experiment and black-body radiation) led subsequently to the two biggest revolutions in physics since Newton: relativity theory and quantum mechanics. By focusing exclusively on the questions he understood and failing to consider the possibility that there might be other questions of which he was unaware and whole areas of knowledge yet to be discovered, Michelson was dramatically overconfident about how much he knew.

The danger of failing to consider that we may not merely lack vital information, but may also be unaware that such gaps in our knowledge even exist, was noted by then US defense secretary Donald Rumsfeld at a press briefing in February 2002. When asked about possible links between the Iraqi government and the supply of weapons of mass destruction to terrorist groups, Rumsfeld observed:

> There are known knowns; there are things we know that we know. There are known unknowns; that is to say, there are things that we now know we don't know. But there are also unknown unknowns; there are things we do not know we don't know.

The statement was criticized by some people as an abuse of language and was even awarded a "Foot in Mouth" award by the Plain English Campaign, which hands out the prize each year for the most nonsensical remark made by a public figure. Others, however, saw the statement as expressing a profound, almost philosophical truth, and Rumsfeld continues to stand by it to this day and alludes to it in the title of his autobiography.

UNKNOWN UNKNOWNS

Known unknowns are bits of information that we don't yet possess but that we know we need to find out. They are the answers we are currently seeking to questions we are already asking, such as the few extra decimal places that Michelson thought were all that remained for science to discover in 1894. *Unknown unknowns*, however, are the answers to questions that have *not yet been asked*. Not only do we not possess these bits of information; we don't even realize that we need them. If and when such information is ever discovered, its discovery tends to blindside us, because we weren't even aware that it was there to be found. For Michelson, relativity theory and quantum mechanics were two very large unknown unknowns. Within a few decades of his rash remark, physics had been utterly transformed by the very sort of revolutionary advances that he had confidently ruled out.

How can we avoid Michelson's mistake? There is, in fact, no fail-safe solution. Philosophers have discussed this problem under various guises for centuries, but we need not concern ourselves too much with the logical complexities. As long as we temper our confidence by keeping Rumsfeld's caveat in mind, we can carry on estimating probabilities in the rough-and-ready way we already do. Regular risk intelligence testing will help to keep us on track, but there will always be surprises.

For example, let's say you are trying to guess how likely it is that a particular foreign power is working on a covert nuclear weapons program. You might begin by identifying the relevant things you know—what Rumsfeld would call the known knowns. For example, you may have various pieces of intelligence, of varying reliability, that suggest that a weapons program is indeed under way. If you are wise, you will also identify the things you don't know. You may not have much idea, for example, of how reliable some of the intelligence is that you have received from your spies—after all, they might be double agents. Those are the known unknowns—the gaps in your knowledge that you are aware of.

It might appear that your degree of confidence—and therefore your probability estimate—will be proportional to the ratio of the number and weight of known knowns to the number and weight of the known unknowns. But that isn't the whole picture. The spirit of Rumsfeld whispers in your ear that there may be other factors you have not even considered: the unknown unknowns. So your probability estimate should really be proportional, not to the ratio of the known knowns to the known unknowns, but to the ratio of the known knowns to everything else, including the unknown unknowns.

By definition, however, the last are unknown. In other words, we can never really know how much relevant information we have failed to take into account. It would thus seem that we can never provide reliable probability estimates outside the idealized casino worlds of math textbooks. We might discover the answer to all the questions we have identified but fail to identify all the relevant questions. If we don't consider this possibility, we will tend to be overconfident. And that's the key. Life requires that we estimate probabilities all the time, and usually we don't have the luxury of doing so with complete information. We still have to hazard some guess, but we can do so much more judiciously if we check our confidence by recalling the warning about unknown unknowns.

A good illustration of the problem of unknown unknowns is provided by the Scottish writer Iain M. Banks in his science fiction novel *Excession*. The story concerns the mysterious appearance of a blackbody sphere (the Excession of the title), which seems to be older than the universe itself and which resists all attempts to probe it. The appearance of the sphere constitutes what Banks calls an "Outside Context Problem," the kind of problem that "most civilisations would encounter just once, and which they tended to encounter rather in the same way a sentence encountered a full stop" (or, in American English, the same way a sentence encountered a period). Such problems are generally not considered until they occur, and it may be impossible or at least very difficult even to imagine them in advance:

> The usual example given to illustrate an Outside Context Problem was imagining you were a tribe on a largish, fertile island; you'd tamed the land, invented the wheel or writing or whatever, the neighbours were cooperative or enslaved but at any rate peaceful and you were busy raising temples to yourself with all the excess productive capacity you had, you were in a position of near-absolute power and control which your hallowed ancestors could hardly have dreamed of and the whole situation was just running along nicely like a canoe on wet grass . . . when suddenly this bristling lump of iron appears sailless and trailing steam in the bay and these guys carrying long funny-looking sticks come ashore and announce you've just been discovered, you're all subjects of the Emperor now, he's keen on presents called tax and these bright-eyed holy men would like a word with your priests.

Banks's concept of Outside Context Problems is similar to Nassim Taleb's notion of "black swans." Before 1697, when the Dutch explorer Willem de Vlamingh spotted one in Western Australia, Europeans had never seen black swans, so the birds are a good metaphor for surprising events of all kinds. But there is more to Taleb's notion of black swans than surprise. Not only are such events outliers, they also have a massive impact. Taleb thinks that most important scientific discoveries, historical events, and artistic accomplishments, from the rise of the internet to the terrorist attacks of September 11, 2001, are black swans.

A vivid example of an unknown unknown at an individual level occurs in Anton-Babinski syndrome. People who suffer from this syndrome are blind, not because of any problem with their eyes (which are fine) but because brain damage in the occipital lobe has destroyed the neural circuits responsible for vision. Yet they seem quite unaware of their blindness and declare—often quite adamantly—that they can see. When they collide with pieces of furniture or try to walk through a closed door, they explain away such mishaps with elaborate excuses, which they seem to believe wholeheartedly.

Anton-Babinski syndrome is not the only example of what neurologists call "anasognosia"—being unaware of a disability—but it is a particularly dramatic one. In 1999, two psychologists, Justin Kruger and David Dunning, proposed that incompetence, like anasognosia, causes not only poor performance but also the inability to recognize that one's performance is poor. Those who lack competence in a given domain, they argue, suffer a dual burden: not only do they make bad choices, they also fail to realize how bad their choices are. Instead, like those with Anton-Babinski syndrome, they are left with the impression that they are doing just fine. The unskilled therefore suffer from illusory superiority, rating their ability as above average, much higher than it actually is. This double whammy is now known as the Dunning-Kruger effect.

For example, socially incompetent boys may be largely unaware of their lack of social graces. Not only do they lack the social skills needed to fit in with their peers, but they are not even aware that they lack those skills. As a result, they are blissfully ignorant of their social gaffes.

According to Dunning and Kruger, the only way out of this trap is to become more competent. Since the skills that engender competence in a particular domain are the same skills needed to evaluate competence in that domain, it follows that the way to help the incompetent gain insight into their shortcomings is, paradoxically, by making them more competent.

As people become knowledgeable in a given domain, they may also become more aware of the limits of their knowledge. As the sphere of knowledge expands, so does the surface area marking the frontier of the unknown, which bristles with ever more questions, and thus more unknown unknowns are converted into known unknowns. They are still unaware of the answers, but now they are at least aware of the questions, and this awareness can spur further inquiry. As Socrates told Meno, awareness of our ignorance is the beginning of wisdom. But as Meno's dejection shows, greater awareness of our limits may weaken our self-confidence more than it should. This can lead to a paradoxical situation in which less competent people rate their own ability as higher than that of more competent people. In fact, this is exactly what Kruger and Dunning found: the growing realization of one's weaknesses that comes with greater competence led the most highly skilled people to err in the other direction and underrate their own abilities, with the result that they suffered from illusory inferiority. As Darwin noted, "Ignorance more frequently begets confidence than does knowledge." Or, as the poet William Butler Yeats put it:

The best lack all conviction, while the worst
Are full of passionate intensity

KNOWN UNKNOWNS

Awareness of the limits of our knowledge turns *unknown* unknowns into *known* unknowns. There are still many things we don't know, but at least we are now aware that we don't know them. This is a common trait among the expert gamblers I have studied; they are under no illusions about their blind spots.

When I started researching this book I found it wasn't easy to track down expert gamblers. Most professional gamblers shun publicity and don't talk to journalists. Those who chose to talk to me did so largely for two reasons. First, I offered them anonymity if they wanted it. Second, I wasn't a journalist, I was an academic doing scientific research.

The first expert gambler I interviewed was J. P. McManus, a multimillionaire who has almost mythical status in Ireland today. The "luck of the Irish" may have run out with the death of the Celtic tiger, but this cliché still contains a grain of truth; it points to the Irish fascination with chance, fortune—and gambling.

On my way to interview McManus at his stud farm near Limerick, I asked a local policeman the way to Martinstown. The officer took one look at me, dressed in my best suit, and guessed where I was going. "On your way to see J.P.?" he asked with a smile.

Ten minutes later I was seated opposite J.P. in his office, which looked out onto a sunny paddock in which an elegant racehorse was quietly grazing. It was Istabraq, three times winner of the Champion Hurdle race at Cheltenham and J.P.'s favorite horse, now retired.

As a teenager, J.P. worked as a farmhand and laborer on the very fields that now make up the four hundred acres of his stud farm. In those days, he would head off to the bookies as soon as he finished work at noon on Saturdays and spend his meager weekly earnings betting on horses. He wasn't very successful at first, but, unlike most gamblers, he learned from his mistakes. After building up a fortune from betting on horses, he applied his risk intelligence to a different kind of gambling: trading currencies on the foreign exchange markets. His personal fortune is now estimated at more than a billion dollars.

He rarely gambles these days, but his public battles with the infamous Scottish bookmaker "Fearless" Freddie Williams have become legendary. On March 16, 2006, J.P. won more than a million pounds from Williams at the Cheltenham Festival, the pair's favorite battle-ground.

The thing that most struck me about J.P. was his willingness to admit his blind spots. When playing backgammon, he told me, he would make a few deliberate mistakes to see how well his opponent would exploit them. If the other guy played well, J.P. would stop playing. That way, he wouldn't throw good money after bad. In other words, J.P. knew something that most gamblers don't: he knew when *not* to bet.

This turned out to be a frequent characteristic of the expert gamblers who agreed to let me interview them. They all knew their strengths and weaknesses very well and were brutally honest with themselves. Many of them kept accurate and detailed records of their earnings and their losses, and they reviewed their strategies regularly to learn from their mistakes.

UNKNOWN KNOWNS

Most of the commentary on Rumsfeld's most famous remark has focused on the unknown unknowns—the things we don't know we don't know. But, as the Slovenian philosopher Slavoj Žižek has pointed out, there is a fourth category implicit in Rumsfeld's statement that is perhaps just as important: the *unknown knowns* (see Table 5). Fascinated as he is by psychoanalysis, Žižek describes this category as "the disavowed beliefs, suppositions and obscene practices we pretend not to know about, even though they form the background of our public values," but there is no need to invoke the arcane Freudian concept of repression to recognize that we may at times underestimate the true extent of our knowledge. The unknown knowns are bits of information you possess but fail to use when solving a problem. The reason you fail to use the information is not because you can't retrieve it from memory but because you don't see how it could help you solve the problem. You fail, in other words, to see its relevance.

TABLE 5: RUMSFELD'S MATRIX.

		Do I *possess* relevant information?	
		Yes	No
Am I *aware* that this information is relevant?	Yes	Known knowns	Known unknowns
	No	Unknown knowns	Unknown unknowns

We cannot use the information we possess to solve a given problem if we don't realize that it is relevant. But seeing the relevance can be hard, because the logical chains that connect various bits of information to the solution of a given problem may involve many links. For example, you might think that the possibility of discovering life on Mars in the next few years would have no bearing whatsoever on the question of whether humans will ever colonize the galaxy. As the Swedish philosopher Nick Bostrom has pointed out, however, there is an important logical chain that connects these two possibilities. Can you work out what it is? Put the book down for a moment and hazard a guess.

One vital link in the logical chain identified by Bostrom is what he calls "the Great Filter." Since the galaxy appears devoid of intelligent aliens, despite the abundance of planets on which aliens could have emerged and the amount of time they have had to evolve, we should conclude that some kind of filter is in place that prevents life from developing to the stage at which it is capable of exploring distant solar systems. The Great Filter can be thought of as a probability barrier that consists of one or more evolutionary obstacles that a species must overcome at great odds if it is to progress. Alien life may have germinated in many of the billions of hospitable planets, but the Great Filter has prevented any of those life-forms from developing to the point of colonizing the portion of the galaxy that we can observe:

> The Great Filter must therefore be sufficiently powerful—which is to say, passing the critical points must be sufficiently improbable—that even with many billions of rolls of the dice,

one ends up with nothing: no aliens, no spacecraft, no signals. At least, none that we can detect in our neck of the woods.

Bostrom then goes on to pose a vital question: just where might this Great Filter be located? There are two possibilities: it might be behind us, somewhere in our distant past. Or it might be ahead of us, somewhere in the decades, centuries, or millennia to come. The former is clearly preferable to the latter; let's hope the filter resides in our past and that we have already overcome highly improbable odds to get where we are today. It would be very disturbing to think that the Great Filter still awaits us in the future, for that would imply there's some kind of technologically instigated event that exists out there and that no species can avoid it:

> If the Great Filter is ahead of us, we have still to confront it. If it is true that almost all intelligent species go extinct before they master the technology for space colonization, then we must expect that our own species will, too, since we have no reason to think that we will be any luckier than any other species. If the Great Filter is ahead of us, we must relinquish all hope of ever colonizing the galaxy, and we must fear that our adventure will end soon, or at any rate that it will end prematurely.

Now, what has all this to do with finding life on Mars? For one thing, the discovery that life had evolved independently on another planet in our own solar system would suggest that the emergence of life is not a very improbable event. If it happened independently twice here in our own backyard, it must have happened millions of times across the galaxy. That would mean that the Great Filter is less likely to occur in the early life of planets and is therefore more likely still ahead of us. Such a discovery would therefore be a crushing blow to any hope that humans might someday colonize the galaxy.

People got very excited in 2004 when NASA's Opportunity rover discovered evidence that Mars had once been wet. Where there is water, there may be life. But Bostrom hopes that our space probes will discover nothing. If they discovered traces of some simple extinct life-form—a bacterium, for example, or some algae—it would be bad news. If the probes found fossils of something even more advanced, such as a trilobite or even the skeleton of a small mammal, it would be even worse. Any such discovery would be scientifically interesting, but it would also be dire news for the future of the human race.

Most people would probably fail to see the relevance of discovering life on Mars for the long-term future of humanity. They may be in possession of all the facts that play a role in Bostrom's line of reasoning but fail to join the dots. These facts thereby become *unknown knowns*—bits of knowledge that could help us solve the problem if we knew how to make better use of them but that we ignore like the proverbial swine, unaware of the value of the pearls in front of them.

People with risk intelligence are good at identifying the nuggets of information lurking in the recesses of their minds whose relevance to the problem at hand may not at first be apparent. We often possess more clues than we are aware of, but they are buried in unconnected information silos, so we fail to make use of them. Risk intelligence involves liberating relevant facts from the information prisons to which we often consign them.

Our ability to draw on the full range of our knowledge, and make use of information whose relevance may not be immediately apparent, will always remain limited. Our cognitive horizons will always have limits, and we will therefore always be prone to what the economists Nicola Gennaioli and Andrei Shleifer call "local thinking": we can't think of everything when imagining the future, so some ideas will always come to mind more easily than others. But we can learn to extend our mental horizons bit by bit, and become—if not truly global in our thinking—at least somewhat more regional.

THE ART OF ESTIMATION

One way in which the ability to draw connections between apparently isolated chunks of information can be developed is by trying to solve Fermi problems. The Italian physicist Enrico Fermi would surprise his students at the University of Chicago by asking them strange questions such as how many piano tuners there were in the city. It was not the sort of question they expected in a physics class, and they would often shrug their shoulders. But Fermi would persist, helping them arrive at an answer by breaking the problem down into a variety of subproblems. The question can, for example, be decomposed into two smaller ones; how many pianos are there in Chicago, and how many pianos can each tuner care for? Each of those questions can then be broken down further. To estimate the number of pianos, we need to estimate the population of the city, the proportion of people in the city who own a piano, and the number of schools, concert halls, and so on that have a piano. It often turns out to be much easier to estimate the answers to such subproblems, and when we multiply all the answers, we arrive at an answer to the original question. And this answer is often a pretty good approximation of the true value.

This method works by transforming *unknown* knowns into *known* knowns. You may not, at first blush, think that you have any idea how many piano tuners there are in Chicago, but you probably have some idea of how many people live in that city, and you can hazard a reasonably good guess as to what proportion of them own a piano. You probably know, for example, that there must be more than a million people in Chicago, since that's the size of an ordinary big city, and you know it must be fewer than a hundred million since there are only three hundred million people in the whole of the United States. Having estimated the lower and upper bounds of the answer, you can average the two to arrive at an answer. The geometric mean is a better average to use here than the arithmetic mean, since it is the same factor away from the lower and upper bounds, so we arrive at an estimate of ten million. The real answer is three million, but our estimate is within a factor of ten, which is all we're aiming at here.

If you didn't already know that an ordinary big city had around a million inhabitants, you could break that problem down further, until you arrived at a number you felt you could estimate with some degree of confidence. The trick is identifying the knowledge you already have that can be linked with the answer you're trying to guess by means of a series of intermediate steps. In this way, you often realize that you know more than you first thought.

Fermi questions are increasingly used by top companies to test the ability of job candidates to think on their feet. At job interviews, Microsoft and Goldman Sachs interviewers ask questions such as: What's the market size for disposable diapers in China? How long a hot dog could you make from a typical cow? The point is that the interviewee is unlikely to have learned the answers beforehand. To answer such questions, therefore, the candidate will be forced to break them down into smaller subquestions and draw on other relevant knowledge to estimate the answers to those.

Take the question about the hot dog, for example. You might start by breaking it down into the following subquestions:

1. How much larger is a cow than a human?
2. What's the volume of a human?
3. What's the thickness of a hot dog?
4. How long would that hot dog have to be for its volume to be the same as that of the cow?

By linking the size of a cow to that of a human, the first question draws on something familiar (the size of a human) to help us think about something slightly less familiar (the size of a cow). If we estimate cows to be about ten times bigger than humans, all we then need to do is estimate the size of a person and multiply that by ten. If the volume of a typical person is around 100,000 cubic centimeters, a typical cow will have a volume of about one cubic meter.

Now we need to estimate the volume of a hot dog. Calculating the volume of a cylinder is hard without a calculator because it involves factoring in *pi*, which is an irrational number, so let's simplify matters by treating hot dogs as cuboid instead. Basic geometry tells us that we can find the volume of a cuboid by multiplying its length by the square of its thickness. A typical hot dog is around two centimeters thick, so to arrive at an answer to our original question we can simply divide the volume of a typical cow (one cubic meter) by two centimeters squared. That gives us a figure of two kilometers. That's a very long hot dog! Of course, the calculation assumes that every little bit of the cow is ground up to make the hot dog, which would be pretty disgusting.

Tackling Fermi questions is a great way to develop your ability to leverage your existing knowledge and bring it to bear on apparently unrelated problems. As a result, there will be fewer unknown knowns—bits of information that you possess but fail to take advantage of. And you will be less likely to utter that awful, misleading, lazy phrase "I have no idea."

I hate it when people answer questions this way, because it's rarely true that they have no clue. They almost always have *some* idea what the answer is, even if it's only a rough and hazy one; it's just that they can't be bothered to do any thinking. For example, suppose I tell you that my sister lives in England and ask you to estimate the probability that she lives on Coronation Street. I very much doubt you have *no idea* about the answer. If that were true, you would have to rate the probability at 50 percent, which is equivalent to saying you have absolutely no idea whether the statement is true or false. That's what a probability estimate of 50 percent means.

If you think 50 percent is too high, therefore, you must have *some* idea, some nugget of information that you think is relevant. Perhaps you have heard of the UK soap opera called *Coronation Street*, in which case you can guess that it is probably not an uncommon street name. How many common street names are there in the United Kingdom? Probably more than a thousand but less than ten thousand. If you ignore uncommon names—that is, names that are used only once— you might start by estimating there to be a 0.03 percent probability that my sister lives on Coronation Street.

Laziness is not the only reason why people may state, misleadingly, that they have "no idea" what the answer to a particular question is; another possible explanation is that they are being evasive. For example, in the months prior to Operation Iraqi Freedom, senior officials in the Bush administration consistently refused to hazard even the vaguest guesses as to what the financial costs of the war might be. On February 27, 2003, for example, with combat less than three weeks away and the uncertainties therefore growing smaller by the day, then US deputy secretary of defense Paul Wolfowitz told the House Budget Committee, "Fundamentally, we have no idea what is needed unless and until we get there on the ground." As James Fallows noted:

> Before the war the administration exercised remarkable "message discipline" about financial projections. When asked how much the war might cost, officials said that so many things were uncertain, starting with whether there would even be a war, that there was no responsible way to make an estimate.

But in such circumstances it was irresponsible *not* to make an estimate. Despite the many uncertainties, there were lots of known knowns that could have been leveraged to make a reasonable guess. The projected troop numbers were known, as was the cost of keeping each soldier in the field each day. The cost of transporting troops to and from the theater of war was known. The amount of fuel and ammunition that would likely be used per day of operations was known. In short, anyone who really wanted to make an estimate had plenty of information on hand.

Indeed, in December 2002 the Yale economist William Nordhaus published an article in *The New York Review of Books* in which he made a thoroughgoing attempt to estimate the likely cost of invading Iraq. He addressed the uncertainties head-on by making upper and lower estimates for each unknown quantity, such as how long the war would last and what its impact on the world economy would be. Nordhaus concluded that over the course of a decade the total cost of the war to the United States could be as low as $121 billion or as high as $1.6

trillion. At the time of writing (September 2011), those estimates still look remarkably good.

IN PRAISE OF SPECULATION

When I ask my students a question that they can't answer immediately, their most common response is "I don't know." But that is usually just the all-or-nothing fallacy rearing its ugly head; all they really mean is that they don't know the answer with complete certainty. If you define knowledge that way, of course, then you'd have to answer "I don't know" to almost every question anyone ever asks you. After all, you don't even know whether the world around you is real with complete certainty; it's just possible that you are really a brain in a vat, or living in a computer simulation, like the characters in *The Matrix*, a science fiction film.

So I often persist and press my students to make an educated guess. It never ceases to amaze me how reluctant many of them are to do this. But on further reflection, perhaps I should not be so surprised. Their previous education has probably taught them not to indulge in speculation, lest they be humiliated for saying something wrong. In fact, our whole education system seems particularly bad at fostering risk intelligence. The brightest students are allowed, even encouraged, to become overconfident, while the rest are discouraged from speculating at all.

Speculation is a dirty word in financial contexts as well as epistemological ones. I suspect that this is no accident and the same implicit attitudes are at the root of the hostility to speculation in both these spheres. The dislike of speculators—whether hedge fund managers or daring thinkers—is all down to risk aversion. Speculators are risk lovers, and if there's one thing risk avoiders hate more than risk itself, it's people who love risk. The risk avoider sees in the risk lover the living indictment of his timidity and blandness, and he feels shamed by the comparison. He envies the risk lover but can't bear to admit it and so condemns him for vices he wishes he had.

The opprobrium heaped upon hedge funds (none of which had to be rescued by governments or received any public money) in the wake of the credit crunch was merely another manifestation of a long-standing prejudice against financial speculation. The figure of the evil speculator is still a powerful cultural icon and often goes hand in hand with anti-Semitism. Only a few years ago, in 2003, Malaysia's prime minister, Mahathir Mohamad, blamed his country's problems on the machinations of Jewish speculators, and even the Nobel Prize–winning economist Paul Krugman seemed to concur.

Risk takers are lionized in times of plenty and scapegoated when things go bad. Few people seem prepared to admit that you can't have the former without the latter. The only alternative to the cycle of boom and bust is not untrammeled growth but stagnation and gradual decline. Without the risk takers, we'd all still be scratching out a living on the African savanna. Nothing ventured, nothing gained. "If you want to succeed, double your failure rate," said Thomas J. Watson, the founder of IBM.

Financial speculators play a vital role in a market economy. As Victor Niederhoffer, a hedge fund manager, explains:

> When a harvest is too small to satisfy consumption at its normal rate, speculators come in, hoping to profit from the scarcity by buying. Their purchases raise the price, thereby checking consumption so that the smaller supply will last longer. Producers encouraged by the high price further lessen the shortage by growing or importing to reduce the shortage. On the other side, when the price is higher than the speculators think the facts warrant, they sell. This reduces prices, encouraging consumption and exports and helping to reduce the surplus.

In other words, in their search for profits, speculators send signals to producers and consumers that convey useful information about levels of supply and demand. Short selling simply accelerates this process of price discovery. And when short sellers are wrong they are punished for their mistakes even more severely than other speculators because they are more highly leveraged.

To illustrate his point, Niederhoffer refers to the siege of Antwerp by the Spanish in 1585. In response to the blockade, nearby farmers grew more grain, which was smuggled into Antwerp at great peril. Speculators, guessing that bread was going to be scarce, pushed up prices through shrewd purchases, and the bakers responded by baking even more.

But the Antwerp politicians disapproved of the greedy speculators profiting from war. They set a very low ceiling on the price of bread and prescribed severe penalties for violators. The result? The bakers could no longer afford to pay the smugglers, who stopped running the blockades, and the supply of grain dried up. The Antwerpers surrendered, and the city was annexed by Spain.

Just as financial speculation plays a vital role in the economy, so intellectual speculation plays a crucial part in the advance of science. Without daring thinkers willing to challenge our cozy assumptions, knowledge would never progress. There are also, it is true, some people who are overfond of speculation, who should just shut up, and much of this book has been about the dangers of overconfidence, of thinking we know more than we actually do. But there are others with interesting ideas who suffer from the opposite problem and who should speak up more.

MACHIAVELLI AND LADY LUCK

Throughout this book I've argued that risk intelligence is vital in our personal and professional lives, and crucial to making wise public policy. But I want to end with a caveat. Even perfect risk intelligence is no guarantee of success. The very idea of a guarantee is, in fact, somewhat at odds with the probabilistic world to which risk intelligence opens our eyes. In this world, nothing is certain or impossible; there are only degrees of likelihood. Even the wisest decisions can backfire through bad luck.

In his notorious political treatise *The Prince*, Niccolò Machiavelli claimed that chance "is the arbiter of one-half of our actions" and compared fortune to "one of those raging rivers, which when in flood overflows the plains, sweeping away trees and buildings, bearing away the soil from place to place; everything flies before it, all yield to its violence, without being able in any way to withstand it." Machiavelli's depiction of Lady Luck as a malevolent force was a salutary counterpoint to the conventional representations of his day, which treated Fortuna as a mostly benign, if fickle, goddess, who could shower people with gifts as well as dragging them down to ruin. Yet both of those portrayals suggest that we can bend chance to our will. Those who see Lady Luck in more benign terms might suggest that we cozy up to her and seduce her. Machiavelli, with his more pessimistic view, recommended a different strategy:

> For my part I consider that it is better to be adventurous than cautious, because fortune is a woman, and if you wish to keep her under it is necessary to beat and ill-use her; and it is seen that she allows herself to be mastered by the adventurous rather than by those who go to work more coldly. She is, therefore, always woman-like, a lover of young men, because they are less cautious, more violent, and command her with more audacity.

Though the means are different, the end is the same: whether through charm or force, one seeks to master chance.

But this is just superstition. The whole point about chance is that it is beyond our control. Risk intelligence merely boosts our chances of navigating the raging river; it does not eliminate the danger. The illusion of control is a pervasive feature of human thought, however. The advance of science has not banished it but merely dressed it up in different clothes. Whereas priests in ancient Rome would attempt to divine the future by inspecting the livers of sacrificed birds, today statisticians construct probabilistic models.

In his aptly named book on the history of statistics, *The Taming of Chance*, the philosopher Ian Hacking argued that the development of probability theory gave rise to a sense that chance could be understood and so came to seem less capricious. Paradoxically, as the world began to appear less deterministic, the more we began to expect control over our lives. For writers such as Frank Furedi, this trend has now reached such extremes that we demand government intervention in ever more aspects of life, but even as life becomes ever safer, we become more alarmed about the risks that remain. It's as if our worry about bad luck follows the "water bed principle": flatten it down in one place, and it will merely pop up somewhere else.

The irony here is that the very tools that can help enhance risk intelligence—the mathematics of probability theory and the collection of statistical data—have sometimes led to an overconfidence all of their own, a sense that we can finally master Lady Luck through science. But as the financial crisis of 2007–2008 reminded us, the models we build to manage risk are always fallible. There is no such thing as an absolute guarantee, since the guarantor can always go bankrupt, and there is no such thing as rock-solid insurance, since the insurer can become insolvent. If such thoughts make you panic, you have yet to come to terms with the irreducibility of chance. As Nick Pulovski, the character played by Clint Eastwood in *The Rookie*, says, "If you want a guarantee, buy a toaster."

Make your peace with chance. Accept that you can never control her or cajole her. Acknowledge her whimsical nature. Recognize that she doesn't care about you and never will, but don't despair. As Damon Runyon once said, "The race is not always to the swift, nor the battle to the strong—but *that's the way to bet.*"

ACKNOWLEDGMENTS

Writing this book was like rolling a giant snowball; it took ages to accumulate the first few layers, but then it grew rapidly. It took more than a year to turn the original idea into a decent proposal, and during that time I did 90 percent of the thinking that went into the final draft. Throughout this period, my agent, Will Francis of Janklow and Nesbit, worked tirelessly to help me refine my thoughts, forcing me to rewrite and restructure the nascent proposal dozens of times. It is no exaggeration to say that the book would not be what it is without his input.

Once I had finally rolled a large but uneven snowball, my editor at Free Press, Emily Loose, took an ax to it and hacked it to pieces. Then she helped me construct an elegant snowman from the debris. I'd never had the benefit of such thoughtful and detailed editing before, and it was a wonderful experience to see my book take on a new and better shape under Emily's careful hand.

I could not have gathered the data reported in Appendix 4 without the help of my friend and colleague Benjamin Jakobus. Benne (as he is known to his friends) wrote all the code for the risk intelligence test and set up the website. He challenged me whenever I was guilty of sloppy thinking and supported me with huge doses of enthusiasm. Benne cofounded Projection Point Limited with me to offer risk intelligence services on a commercial basis and is now the company's chief technology officer.

Nor could I have done the research without the assistance of the many expert gamblers who let me interview them. For people who shun publicity, talking to me was a risk without potential reward, and I have accordingly used their names only if they gave me their written consent. You know who you are; I am extremely grateful to you. I would also like to thank James Grosjean for being so gracious when I vomited while interviewing him; luckily, I missed him (narrowly), and yes, I'd made the mistake of accepting all those free drinks they plied me with in the casino the night before.

Nick Bostrom, Dave Cliff, Philip Davies, Anthony Glees, Richard John, Dominic Johnson, Michael Massa, Heather Rosoff, and Nic Wilson read various excerpts from the first draft and gave useful feedback. Aaron Brown, Louise Burgoyne, James Carney, Ann Grand, Astrid Hopfensitz, Douglas Hubbard, Nick Maughan, Geoffrey Miller, and David Spiegelhalter all read entire drafts. Their comments helped me improve the text in all sorts of ways. They also helped me avoid some dreadful mistakes; those that remain are wholly my responsibility.

The following people provided me with useful feedback about the online risk intelligence test: Imogen Bertin, Jan Dyre Bjerknes, Susan Blackmore, Adrian Bowyer, Aaron Brown, Joanna Bryson, Louise Burgoyne, Jenny Burgoyne, Paul Clayton, Chloe Evans, Dermot Golden, Steve Grand, Donna Gresh, Claudia Hammond, Douglas Hubbard, Jonathan Jewell, Marek Kohn, Nick Maughan, P. J. Myers, Kathy Neal, Bonnie Ray, Genevieve Shanahan, Dan Sperber, David Spiegelhalter, Robert Karl Stonjek, Jonathan Trout, and many anonymous online commentators.

My ideas about risk intelligence benefited greatly from discussions with my former colleagues in the IBM Risk Management Collaboratory, especially Bonnie Ray, Donna Gresh, and Lea Deleris. Thanks too to my former PhD student Emma O'Reilly for her help with locating source material; I wish her good luck in her new path.

Another of my PhD students, Richard Morrisroe, helped me reanalyze the data reported in Appendix 4, as did another of my students, Scott Siskind.

Thanks to my legal team at Johnsons, especially John Kerr and Paul Tweed; to Michelle Ní Longáin of Byrne Wallace; and to my barristers, Brian Kennedy, Emily Egan, Helen Callanan, and Niall

Buckley, for all their help and support during two unwelcome distractions while writing this book. I'm also grateful to Dr. Isaac Sundeep for encouraging me at a time when I thought I'd never be able to write again. I also wish to thank Angela and Surya for providing such a wonderful place to work on the final draft, high up in the Alpujarras in southern Spain.

Last but not least, I'd like to thank my beautiful wife, Louise Burgoyne; she has been the anchor that has kept me moored to the real world while writing this book and stopped my drifting off into the ether, from which I might never have returned. She has put up with my many foibles with extraordinary patience and grace. Louise also helped analyze the data gathered via the online risk intelligence test. This book is dedicated to her.

RISK INTELLIGENCE TEST

⊞

This appendix provides a pencil-and-paper version of the online risk intelligence test that is available at www.projectionpoint.com. The pencil-and-paper version is for readers who don't have internet access or who wish to learn more about how the online test works.

INSTRUCTIONS

Please estimate the probability of each of the fifty statements below according to the following rules:

- If you are absolutely sure that a statement is true, your estimate should be 100 percent.
- If you are completely convinced that a statement is false, your estimate should be 0 percent.
- If you have no idea at all whether it is true or false, your estimate should be 50 percent.
- If you are fairly sure that it is true but you aren't completely sure, your estimate should be 60 percent, 70 percent, 80 percent, or 90 percent, depending on how sure you are.
- If you are fairly sure that it is false, but you aren't completely sure, your estimate should be 40 percent, 30 percent, 20 percent, or 10 percent, depending on how sure you are.

STATEMENTS

The statements below are those used in the original 2010 version of the online risk intelligence test as described in Appendix 4. The current version of the online test now draws statements at random from a large database.

50 1. A one followed by 100 zeros is a Googol.

0 2. Africa is the largest continent.

70 3. Alzheimer's accounts for under half the cases of dementia in the US.

0 4. An improper fraction is always less than one.

50 5. Armenia shares a common border with Russia.

70 6. There have been over 40 US presidents.

80 7. In 1994, Bill Clinton was accused of sexual harassment by a woman named Paula Jones.

100 8. Canberra is the capital of Australia.

50 9. Zinedine Yazid Zidane played on the French national team for over five years.

100 10. Christianity became the official religion of the Roman empire in the third century A.D.

60 11. Commodore Matthew Perry compelled the opening of Japan to the West with the Convention of Kanagawa in 1870.

50 12. El Salvador does not have a coastline on the Caribbean.

80 13. Gout is known as "the royal disease."

60 14. *Harry Potter and the Goblet of Fire* tells the story of Harry Potter's third year at Hogwarts.

50 15. Lauren Bacall was Humphrey Bogart's third wife.

50 16. In 2008, the population of Beijing was over 20 million people.

50 17. In the Old Testament, Jezebel's husband was Ahab, King of Israel.

50 18. Iron accounts for over 30 percent of the Earth's composition.

19. It is possible to lead a cow upstairs but not downstairs, because a cow's knees can't bend properly to walk back down. *50*

20. Lehman Brothers went bankrupt in September 2008. *50*

21. LL Cool J got his name from the observation "Ladies Love Cool James." *50*

22. Male gymnasts refer to the pommel horse as "the pig." *50*

23. Mao Zedong declared the founding of the People's Republic of China in 1949. *50*

24. The only stringed symphonic instrument that has a pedestal and a crown is a double bass. *30*

25. More than 10 American states let citizens smoke marijuana for medical reasons. *50*

26. "Spanish Flu" killed more people in the 1918–1919 world-wide pandemic than did the First World War. *100*

27. Most of the terrorists who carried out the attacks on 9/11 were from Saudi Arabia. *100*

28. Purified natural gas has an odor. *50*

29. Mozart composed over 1,000 works. *50*

30. Of all Arab nations, Lebanon has the highest percentage of Christians. *20*

31. Over 40 percent of all deaths from natural disasters from 1945 to 1986 were caused by earthquakes. *50*

32. Over 50 percent of Nigeria's population lives on less than one dollar per day. *50*

33. Stalagmites grow down, and stalactites grow up. *0*

34. The Italian musical term *adagio* means that the music should be played quickly. *70*

35. The Euphrates river runs through Baghdad. *100*

36. The face on a $100,000 bill is that of Woodrow Wilson. *50*

37. The Islamic Resistance Movement is better known to Palestinians as Hizbollah. *50*

38. The Japanese were largely responsible for building most of the early railways in the US West. *50*

39. The last Inca emperor was Montezuma. *80*
40. The most frequently diagnosed cancer in men is *20* prostate cancer.
41. The president of Russia is Vladimir Putin. *100*
42. The San Andreas Fault forms the tectonic boundary between the Pacific Plate and the North American Plate. *80*
43. The US civil war broke out the same year the federal government first printed paper money. *20*
44. The US Declaration of Independence begins: "We the People of the United States . . ." *50*
45. The word "robot" was coined by the American science fiction writer Isaac Asimov. *70*
46. The world's highest island mountain is Mauna Kea. *50*
47. The Taj Mahal was built by Emperor Shah Jahan in memory of his favorite wife. *100*
48. There are more people in the world than chickens. *50*
49. There are no diamond fields in South America. *50*
50. Wikipedia was launched in 1999 by Jimmy Wales and Larry Sanger. *50*

HOW TO SCORE THE TEST

It's cumbersome and time-consuming to score this test manually, so I strongly recommend that you take the online version or use the online RQ score calculator at http://www.projectionpoint.com/index.php/calculator/rq_calculator, but if you don't have internet access, or if you simply wish to know more about how the online version calculates your RQ score, here's how to score the test:

1. Start by counting all the times you assigned a likelihood of 0 percent to a statement, then count how many of those statements were actually true (the truth values of each statement from the test are below). Then divide the former into the latter and express the answer as a percentage. For example, if there are five statements that

you estimated had a 0 percent chance of being true and exactly one of these statements was true, divide five into one, which is 0.2 (or 20 percent). Since you can't divide by zero, if none of the statements was true, just put 0 percent.

2. Do the same for each of the other categories (10 to 100 percent).

3. Find the difference between each of the results you have calculated so far and the value of that category. For example, if 20 percent of the statements to which you assigned a probability of 0 percent were actually true, the difference is 20. If 30 percent of the statements to which you assigned a probability of 20 percent were actually true, the difference is 10. These are the "residuals."

4. Subtract each residual from 100.

5. Multiply the results from step 4 by the number of times you used the relevant category. For example, if the residual of the 20 percent category is 10, and you assigned a probability of 20 percent to seven statements, multiply 90 by 7.

6. Add up the results from step 5.

7. Divide the result of step 6 by the total number of probability estimates. If you answered all the questions in the test, it is the same as dividing the result from step 6 by the number of questions. This is the weighted mean.

8. Find the square of the result from step 7, and divide it by 100. This is your RQ score.

You can download an Excel spreadsheet that automates these steps from www.projectionpoint.com. Go the section of the website that is dedicated to this book and click on the Readers' Resources page. Table 6 is an example of this spreadsheet being used to calculate the RQ score of a person with a fairly high level of risk intelligence.

TABLE 6: SPREADSHEET SHOWING HOW RQ SCORES ARE CALCULATED.

Category	Estimates	True	Percent True	Residuals (**R**)	100 – **R**	Column F x Column B
0	10	1	10	10	90	900
10	10	1	10	0	100	1000
20	10	2	20	0	100	1000
30	10	4	40	10	90	900
40	10	4	40	0	100	1000
50	10	5	50	0	100	1000
60	10	7	70	10	90	900
70	10	7	70	0	100	1000
80	10	6	60	20	80	800
90	10	8	80	10	90	900
100	10	8	80	20	80	800
TOTAL	110					10,200
WEIGHTED MEAN						93
RQ SCORE						86

The "Estimates" column shows how many times a particular category (0 percent, 10 percent, etc.) was used. The "True" column shows how many of the statements in that category were in fact true. The "Percent True" column divides the third column ("True") into the second ("Estimates") and expresses the result as a percentage. The "Residuals" column shows the difference between column 1 ("Category") and column 4 ("Percent True"). Column 6 ("100 – *R*") is simply column 5 ("Residuals") subtracted from 100. Column 7 multiplies column 6 ("100 -*R*") by column 2 ("Estimates"). We then add all the numbers in column 7 and divide the result by the total number of estimates. The last step is to find the square of that and divide by 100 to arrive at the RQ score.

I chose to use this approach, rather than the better-known Brier score, for three reasons. Firstly, my approach is easier to understand for a lay audience. Secondly, the Brier score is a composite measure of calibration, resolution, and knowledge, whereas I wish to measure only calibration. Finally, I find some of the statistical properties of the Brier score to be unsatisfactory. For example, the Brier score places a premium on extreme forecasts, so that a 100 percent forecast of rainfall is rewarded more when it does, in fact, rain than is a 90 percent forecast of rainfall. That may make sense in the context of weather forecasting, which is what this scoring method was designed for, since it may be the case that in this context "the most useful forecasts are those which fall into the extreme classes," as Brier argued. But when estimating probabilities in general I see no particular value in valuing more extreme probability estimates more highly than intermediate ones. Indeed, I think this smacks of the need for closure and some of the related problems discussed in chapter 3. Even Brier's remark about the greater usefulness of extreme forecasts may be valid only for populations with low risk intelligence. When people are more comfortable with intermediate probabilities and know how to incorporate probabilistic information into their decisions, extreme probability estimates should be no more useful than intermediate ones.

Here are the truth values of the fifty statements in the risk intelligence test above that we used to score the test in 2010. Some of the values may have changed by the time you read this book. For example, Vladimir Putin may have become the president of Russia again.

A one followed by 100 zeros is a Googol.	T
Africa is the largest continent.	F
Alzheimer's accounts for under half the cases of dementia in the US.	F
An improper fraction is always less than one.	F

Armenia shares a common border with Russia.	F
There have been over 40 US Presidents.	T
In 1994, Bill Clinton was accused of sexual harassment by a woman named Paula Jones.	T
Canberra is the capital of Australia.	T
Zinedine Yazid Zidane played on the French national team for over five years.	T
Christianity became the official religion of the Roman empire in the third century A.D.	F
Commodore Matthew Perry compelled the opening of Japan to the West with the Convention of Kanagawa in 1870.	F
El Salvador does not have a coastline on the Caribbean.	T
Gout is known as "the royal disease."	F
Harry Potter and the Goblet of Fire tells the story of Harry Potter's third year at Hogwarts.	F
Lauren Bacall was Humphrey Bogart's third wife.	F
In 2008, the population of Beijing was over 20 million people.	F
In the Old Testament, Jezebel's husband was Ahab, King of Israel.	T
Iron accounts for over 30 percent of the Earth's composition.	T
It is possible to lead a cow upstairs but not downstairs, because a cow's knees can't bend properly to walk back down.	T
Lehman Brothers went bankrupt in September 2008.	T
LL Cool J got his name from the observation "Ladies Love Cool James."	T
Male gymnasts refer to the pommel horse as "the pig."	T
Mao Zedong declared the founding of the People's Republic of China in 1949.	T
The only stringed symphonic instrument that has a pedestal and a crown is a double bass.	F
More than 10 American states let citizens smoke marijuana for medical reasons.	T
"Spanish flu" killed more people in the 1918–19 worldwide pandemic than did the First World War.	T

Most of the terrorists who carried out the attacks on 9/11 were from Saudi Arabia.	T
Purified natural gas has an odor.	F
Mozard composed over 1,000 works.	F
Of all Arab nations, Lebanon has the highest percentage of Christians.	T
Over 40 percent of all deaths from natural disasters from 1945 to 1986 were caused by earthquakes.	T
Over 50 percent of Nigeria's population lives on less than one dollar per day.	T
Stalagmites grow down, and stalactites grow up.	F
The Italian musical term *adagio* means that the music should be played quickly.	F
The Euphrates river runs through Baghdad.	F
The face on a $100,000 bill is that of Woodrow Wilson.	T
The Islamic Resistance Movement is better known to Palestinians as Hizbollah.	F
The Japanese were largely responsible for building most of the early railways in the US West.	F
The last Inca emperor was Montezuma.	F
The most frequently diagnosed cancer in men is prostate cancer.	T
The president of Russia is Vladimir Putin.	F
The San Andreas Fault forms the tectonic boundary between the Pacific Plate and the North American Plate.	T
The US civil war broke out the same year the federal government first printed paper money.	T
The US Declaration of Independence begins "We the People of the United States . . ."	F
The word "robot" was coined by the American science fiction writer Isaac Asimov.	F
The world's highest island mountain is Mauna Kea.	T
The Taj Mahal was built by Emperor Shah Jahan in memory of his favorite wife.	T

There are more people in the world than chickens.	F
There are no diamond fields in South America.	F
Wikipedia was launched in 1999 by Jimmy Wales and Larry Sanger.	F

PERSONAL PREDICTION TEST

This appendix provides a personalized prediction test so that readers can test their ability to make accurate predictions about events in their own lives. In this way, you can measure your risk intelligence in the context of your day-to-day life and identify the biases that lead you to underestimate or overestimate probabilities.

First, write down a series of predictions in column one of the table below. The predictions can be about anything that you directly observe in your personal or professional life or in your local environment, but they must be reasonably crisp. In other words, it must be fairly easy to tell whether they become true or false. "I'll get a pay raise next week" is crisp because it doesn't leave much room for discussion about whether or not it actually came true. "I'll have a good day tomorrow" is not crisp because it leaves a lot of wiggle room; many days could be described as both good and bad. "I'll see a gray bird this evening" is similarly ambiguous; some birds are clearly gray and others are not, but others are in a fuzzy area in between, where sensible people can disagree about whether to call them gray or not. If your predictions are not reasonably crisp, it's easy to reinterpret them in whichever way matches the facts after the event; the prediction expands to accommodate the event. That is how astrologers and palm readers manage to fool people; when their predictions are couched in sufficiently fuzzy terms, it's always possible to construe them as accurate no matter what happens.

Philosophers call words such as "good" and "gray" *vague concepts*, and they use the term in a very precise way. Concepts are vague, in this specific sense, when they allow borderline cases. Words such as "many" and "few" are vague, but the phrase "fewer than ten" is not, because it creates a sharp division between two classes of numbers. It is hard to devise predictions that are perfectly crisp, because vagueness thoroughly pervades language and because the crisper our predictions get the less they tend to matter; "Tension will grow between China and India this year" is vaguer than "India will expel more than two Chinese diplomats this year" but also more interesting. Crafting predictions that are interesting yet not too vague is a skill that needs to be worked at.

Your predictions should not concern matters of opinion; they should refer to matters of fact, so that everyone would agree on whether or not they come true.

It should also be possible to reason about your predictions. That is, when you estimate the probabilities of each prediction, they should be educated guesses based on things you already know or information you can easily acquire, not random stabs in the dark. Risk intelligence is not some mystical ability to estimate probabilities of things you know nothing about. It involves building mental models, usually unconsciously and always patiently, so that we can extrapolate a reasonable guess about something we don't yet know on the basis of things we do. Constructing predictions that have this feature is also a skill that takes time to acquire.

It's also important to build some kind of expiry date into your predictions. "It will rain" lacks this important feature; it will almost certainly rain sometime. "It will rain tomorrow" is bolder. Make sure all your predictions expire within a few weeks; otherwise you'll have to wait a long time before you can score the test.

After you have written down some predictions in column 1, you should estimate the probability of each prediction coming true by writing down percentage values in column 2. For ease of scoring, restrict your estimates to increments of ten percentage points (i.e., use 0 percent, 10 percent, 20 percent, and so on, and not, say, 24 percent).

Then, over the next few weeks, note whether the predictions come true or not by putting check marks or Xs in column 3. When all the predictions have expired, you can calculate your risk intelligence score in the same way as for the general-knowledge version of the test (see Appendix 1 for details).

After calculating your RQ, review the predictions in more detail, focusing on the events you thought were very likely but didn't happen and on those you thought were highly unlikely but did occur. Can you identify any faulty assumptions that might have led you astray?

Prediction	Estimated probability	Did the prediction come true?

2010 PREDICTION GAME

In January 2010, Benjamin Jakobus and I created an online "Prediction Game" to see whether the scores people obtained by taking the risk intelligence test described in Appendix 1 correlated with their ability to estimate the likelihoods of future events. The format of the prediction test was similar to that of the original risk intelligence test described in Appendix 1; participants were given a few dozen statements and asked to say how likely they thought each of them were by providing a probability estimate. The only difference was that the statements referred to possible future events rather than to items of general knowledge whose answer was already known.

In order to come up with predictions that were plausible but not trivial, I scoured *The World in 2010*, a report published in December 2009 by *The Economist*. This collection of essays speculating about likely developments in politics and business around the world yielded a crop of ideas, to which I added a sprinkling of my own. The full set of fifty-five predictions, together with their eventual truth values, was as follows (the time-frame for all predictions was the year 2010):

A cap and trade system for carbon emissions will be established in the United States.	F
All American combat troops will leave Iraq (excluding those who stay to train Iraqi soldiers and police).	F
All remaining prisoners will be transferred from Guantánamo Bay.	F

Amy Winehouse will release a new album.	F
An earthquake will hit Tokyo.	F
Angelina Jolie and Brad Pitt will split up.	F
Aung San Suu Kyi will be freed from house arrest.	T
Australia will win back the ashes.	F
Ayatollah Ali Khamenei will cease being Supreme Leader of Iran.	F
Carbon footprint labels will be made mandatory for some products in the EU.	F
China's GDP growth rate will fall below 8 percent.	F
David Cameron will become prime minister of the UK.	T
Dilma Rousseff will win Brazil's presidential election.	T
England will win the FIFA World Cup.	F
France will get a new prime minister.	F
Global airline traffic will grow by more than 4 percent.	T
Global average temperature will be higher than for any previous year on record.	*
Global sales of music CDs will be lower than in 2009.	T
Gorillaz will release a new album.	T
Greece will default on its sovereign debt.	F
Inglourious Basterds will win at least one Oscar.	T
Ireland will default on its external sovereign debt.	F
Israel will carry out an overt air strike against Iran.	F
Kevin Rudd will call and win a general election in Australia.	F
Khalid Sheikh Mohammed will be put on trial in New York City.	F
More than a million people will die of swine-flu (H1N1).	F
Norway, Sweden, or Finland will win the Eurovision Song Contest.	F
Osama Bin Laden will be captured or killed.	F

Prince Charles will become King of England.	F
Roger Federer will win the Men's Singles at Wimbledon.	F
Roman Polanski will be extradited to the United States.	F
Russia will cut off gas supplies to Ukraine for at least one day.	F
Scientists will announce they have cloned a famous person.	F
Scientists will observe the Higgs boson particle.	F
Silvio Berlusconi's reign as Prime Minister of Italy will come to an end.	F
Spain will win the FIFA World Cup.	T
Terrorists will blow up an aeroplane while flying in US airspace.	F
The Arctic ice cap will shrink to under 4 million square kilometres.	F
The Democrats will retain their majority in the House of Representatives in US mid-term elections.	F
The Dow Jones Industrial Average will close at 8500 or lower on at least one day.	F
The Federal Reserve will keep US interest rates below 1 percent.	T
The New York Times will announce that aliens have landed on earth.	F
The Nissan Leaf electric car will go on sale in Japan.	T
The Nobel peace prize will be won by an Arab.	F
The number of active users on Facebook will surpass 500 million.	T
The price of oil will go over $100 per barrel for Brent crude.	F
The price of sugar will rise by more than 10 percent.	T
The total assets of Islamic banking will top one billion US dollars.	T
The UK credit rating will be downgraded by at least one credit rating agency.	F
The UK pound will fall below parity with the euro.	F
The US will win the most gold medals at the Vancouver Winter Olympics.	F
Tiger Woods will play in a PGA tour event.	T

UK house prices will end the year more than 1 percent lower than at the start.	F
US combat troops will be sent to Yemen.	F
Someone will be charged with killing Michael Jackson.	T

*The item about global average temperature was excluded when we calculated the final score for participants in the prediction game in January 2011, because the data were not available at the time.

RESEARCH DATA

In December 2009, my colleague Benjamin Jakobus and I created an online version of the risk intelligence test described in Appendix 1 and promoted the website through press releases, media interviews, blogs, and internet discussion forums.

After participants had completed the test, they were asked if they would like to take part in our study. If they declined, they were given their test results, and then their data were deleted from the server. If they agreed, they were asked to specify the following demographic details: gender, nationality, age, highest level of academic education, and profession. They were then given their test results. Ethical approval for this research was granted by the Social Research Ethics Committee of University College Cork.

The test results were calculated according to the procedure described in Appendix 1.

PARTICIPANTS

Between January 1, 2010, and February 14, 2011, a total of 50,070 people visited the website, of whom 38,888 took the online risk intelligence test and gave us permission to use their data in our research. Before analyzing the data set, we deleted the data from all participants who:

1. Estimated the probability of fewer than forty-five statements;

2. Failed to specify their gender or profession;
3. Were members of the test or development team; or
4. Had a K factor of less than 10.

To calculate the K factor, we awarded one K point each time a person used the categories 10 percent, 20 percent, 30 percent, 40 percent, 60 percent, 70 percent, 80 percent, or 90 percent. When he or she used 0 percent, 50 percent, or 100 percent, he or she got 0. The maximum K factor was therefore 50 for a fifty-question test. The K factor gives an indication of how reliable the RQ score is as an indicator of risk intelligence.

A total of 24,594 participants (63 percent of the sample) were removed by these adjustments, leaving a total of 14,294 participants for our analysis. Tables 7 and 8 show the composition of this sample by age, gender, and educational achievement.

TABLE 7: COMPOSITION OF THE RESEARCH SAMPLE BY AGE.

Age	Number of Participants
0–10	674
11–20	1,006
21–30	4,899
31–40	3,720
41–50	2,283
51–60	1,236
61–70	397
71–80	67
81–90	6
90+	6

TABLE 8: COMPOSITION OF THE RESEARCH SAMPLE BY GENDER AND EDUCATION.

Education	Men	Women	Total
Primary or less	108	31	139
Secondary	2,163	521	2,684
First degree	5,486	1,475	6,961
Master's	2,335	755	3,090
PhD	1,134	286	1,420
Total	11,226	3,068	14,294

Our data set is an order of magnitude larger than any previous study of risk intelligence. We were able to collect such a large amount of data by using an online risk intelligence test rather than a pencil-and-paper version. Most previous research on risk intelligence involved much smaller samples because it was conducted prior to the development of the internet. It appears that interest in risk intelligence testing began to decline after 1980 and has not progressed much since then. We feel that this area of research is ripe for revival, especially now that the internet allows risk intelligence testing to be easily automated and data collected online.

RESULTS

The mean RQ score of the entire sample of 14,294 was 63.58 (standard deviation: 13.15). The distribution of RQ scores is shown in Figure 18. Table 9 shows the RQ scores obtained by the participants in our study, broken down by gender and education.

FIGURE 18: DISTRIBUTION OF RQ SCORES IN THE RESEARCH SAMPLE.

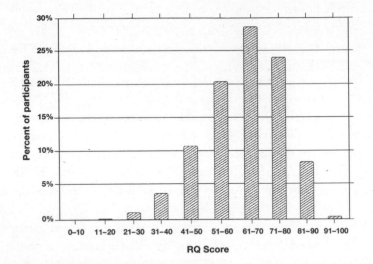

TABLE 9: RQ SCORES BY GENDER AND EDUCATION.

Education	Men		Women	
	Mean RQ	Standard Deviation	Mean RQ	Standard Deviation
Primary or less	58.52	14.95	56.42	14.58
Secondary	61.80	14.00	60.87	14.20
First degree	63.94	12.74	61.60	13.55
Master's	64.93	12.46	62.29	13.60
PhD	67.41	11.58	65.21	13.38
All	64.04	12.95	61.93	13.73

2010 PREDICTION GAME

As discussed in chapter 2 and Appendix 3, early in 2010 we also set up another risk intelligence test on www.projectionpoint.com, but this time with a set of predictions rather than statements about known facts. During the first few months of 2010, more than two hundred people who had already taken the basic risk intelligence test (the general-knowledge version) estimated the probability of each prediction. Over the rest of the year, whenever any of the predictions became true or false, my colleague Benjamin Jakobus would enter the details in the system accordingly. At the end of the year, we had enough data to calculate RQ scores for the prediction game, which we did in the same way as for the general-knowledge version of the test.

A total of 205 people took part in the 2010 prediction game. However, some of them neglected the intermediate categories of 10 to 40 percent and 60 to 90 percent, so we removed everyone with a K factor of less than 10 in either test. We also removed five participants who scored more than 99 in the original (general-knowledge version) of the risk intelligence test, on the grounds that they might have googled the answers. After those adjustments, a total of 132 participants remained.

The mean RQ score of those 132 participants was 61. That is significantly worse than the score that would have been attained simply by assigning a 50 percent probability to every prediction (which would have resulted in a score of 73).

Figure 19 shows the scores those participants achieved in the 2010 Prediction Game plotted against the scores they achieved in the general-knowledge test. The fact that the slope of the regression line is not very steep indicates that the correlation between the two sets of scores is not very high. The fact that the regression line is not completely horizontal means that the correlation is nonzero.

FIGURE 19: RQ SCORES FROM THE 2010 PREDICTION GAME PLOTTED AGAINST RQ SCORES FROM THE GENERAL-KNOWLEDGE TEST.

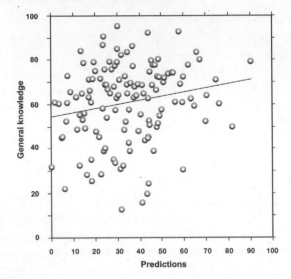

We used Spearman's rank correlation to measure the association between participants' scores in the general-knowledge version of the risk intelligence test and their scores in the prediction game. As shown in Table 10, although the correlation of .185 is low, it is nonetheless statistically significant (Spearman's rho (132) = 0.185; $p < 0.05$).

TABLE 10: CORRELATION BETWEEN SCORES ON THE 2010 PREDICTION GAME AND SCORES ON THE GENERAL-KNOWLEDGE TEST.

CORRELATIONS			Game	Test
Spearman's rho	GAME	Correlation coefficient	1.000	.185*
		Sigma (2-tailed)		.034
		N	132	132
	TEST	Correlation coefficient	.185*	1.000
		Sigma (2-tailed)	.034	
		N	132	132

*Correlation is significant at the 0.05 level (2-tailed).

꓿

CHAPTER 1: WHY RISK INTELLIGENCE MATTERS

2 fifty years of research: This research has been summarized in dozens of popular books. For a recent and accessible overview, see Dan Gardner, *Risk: The Science and Politics of Fear* (London: Virgin Books, 2008) and Baruch Fischhoff and John Kadvany, *Risk: A Very Short Introduction* (Oxford: Oxford University Press, 2011). For a more technical overview, see the papers collected in *Judgment Under Uncertainty: Heuristics and Biases*, ed. Daniel Kahneman, Paul Slovic, and Amos Tversky (Cambridge, England: Cambridge University Press, 1982).

2 Diane is overconfident: Throughout this book, I use the terms "overconfident" and "overconfidence" to refer to a cognitive phenomenon in which people express more certainty than is strictly warranted, and not to feelings of self-esteem. This is explained in more detail in chapter 2.

4 unrealistic expectations: Monica Robbers, "Blinded by Science: The Social Construction of Reality in Forensic Television Shows and Its Effect on Criminal Jury Trials," *Criminal Justice Policy Review* 19, no. 1 (2008): 84–102.

4 Bernard Knight: Knight's comments are reported in "The 'CSI Effect,' " *The Economist*, April 22, 2010, http://www.economist.com/node/15949089.

5 In 2010, a study: Evan Durnal, "Crime Scene Investigation (As Seen on TV)," *Forensic Science International* 199, no. 1 (2010): 1–5.

5 Christophe Champod: Cited in Laura Spinney, "The Fine Print," *Nature* 464 (March 18, 2010): 344–346.

6 the case of Shirley McKie: Iain McKie and Michael Russell, *Shirley McKie: The Price of Innocence* (Edinburgh: Birlinn, 2007). A wealth of information about this case is also available online at www.shirleymckie.com. I have also drawn on an article by David Jones, "Flawed Fingerprint Evidence Led to a Travesty of Justice," *Daily Mail*, April 25, 2007, www.dailymail.co.uk/femail/article-450737/Flawed-finger print-evidence-led-travesty-justice.html.

8 poll conducted by Rasmussen Reports: Matthew Bandyk, "What Airport Security Costs You," *U.S. News & World Report*, January 11, 2010, http://money.usnews.com/money/business-economy/articles/2010/01/11/what-airport-security-costs-you.

9 described the security procedures: Cited in "Airport Attack," *The Economist*, October 30, 2010, 65.

9 "security theater": Bruce Schneier, *Beyond Fear: Thinking Sensibly About Security in an Uncertain World* (Berlin: Springer, 2003).

9 illusion of control: Ellen Langer, "The Illusion of Control," *Journal of Personality and Social Psychology* 32, no. 2 (1975): 311–328.

9 a ritual aspect: I owe this suggestion to Bruce Schneier (personal communication).

10 Robert Poole: Cited in Bandyk, "What Airport Security Costs You."

10 $8 billion a year: This is probably an underestimate. Poole assumed that an hour of time is worth $50 for business travelers and $15 for everyone else, but there is evidence that time is worth more than this. One survey found that business travelers in the United States would be willing to pay $70 to cut their journey time by one hour, while other fliers would pay around $31.

10 2,300 more road fatalities: Garrick Blalock, Vrinda Kadiyali, and Daniel Simon, "Driving Fatalities After 9/11: A Hidden Cost of Terrorism," *Applied Economics* 41, no. 14 (2009): 1717–1729.

11 terrifies kids: Björn Lomborg, "Scared Silly over Climate Change," *Guardian Online*, June 15, 2009, www.guardian.co.uk/commentisfree/cif-green/2009/jun/15/climate-change-children.

13 argues Cass Sunstein: Cass Sunstein, "Throwing Precaution to the Wind," *The Boston Globe*, July 13, 2008, www.boston.com/boston globe/ideas/articles/2008/07/13/throwing_precaution_to_the_wind/.

13 Sunstein has also argued: Cass Sunstein and Richard Zeckhauser, "Overreaction to Fearsome Risks," *Environmental and Resource Economics* 48, no. 3 (2011): 435–449.

14   A famous study: Philip Tetlock, *Expert Political Judgment: How Good Is It? How Can We Know?* (Princeton, N.J.: Princeton University Press, 2005).

15   According to Aaron Brown: Aaron Brown, *Red-Blooded Risk: The Secret History of Wall Street* (Hoboken, N.J.: Wiley, 2011).

16   according to Stephen O'Sullivan: Quoted in "Silo but Deadly," *The Economist*, December 3, 2009, http://www.economist.com/node/15016132.

18   "in the greatest part": John Locke, "Of Judgement," in *An Essay Concerning Human Understanding*, book IV, chapter 14 (1690).

18   "when man is capable": Keats proposed the idea of "negative capability" in a letter to his brothers dated Sunday, December 21, 1817.

19   "Which horse do you think": The text of the interview is recorded in the appendix of Stephen Ceci and Jeffrey Liker, "A Day at the Races: A Study of IQ, Expertise, and Cognitive Complexity," *The Journal of Experimental Psychology: General* 115 (1986): 255–266.

21   multiple types of intelligence: Howard Gardner, *Frames of Mind: The Theory of Multiple Intelligences* (New York: Basic Books, 1983).

22   "emotional intelligence": Daniel Goleman, *Emotional Intelligence: Why It Can Matter More than IQ* (New York: Bantam Books, 1995).

CHAPTER 2: DISCOVERING YOUR RISK QUOTIENT

23   estimate probabilities accurately: The concept of probability is the focus of fierce debate between "subjectivists," who take probabilities to express degrees of belief, and "frequentists," who take probabilities to refer to objective facts about the world. For the subjectivist, the statement that "there is a 50 percent chance of this coin landing on heads" is an expression of his or her own uncertainty. For the frequentist, however, the statement does not have anything to do with anyone's beliefs; rather, it means that, in the long run, the coin will land heads up half of all the times it is tossed. For reasons that are too technical to go into here, I think the frequentist view is fundamentally flawed; this book is, among other things, a call to return to the older, subjectivist view of probability. According to the subjectivist view, there is no such thing as a "true" probability, in the sense of some objective fact existing out there in the world; probabilities are just ways of quantifying our subjective degree of belief. I suppose a subjectivist could say that a probability estimate is "true" when it accurately expresses the strength of one's conviction—

indeed, that is a vital part of risk intelligence—but that is a far cry from the frequentist view of probabilities as facts. So although I often talk loosely of "making accurate probability estimates," strictly speaking, this phrase is incoherent. The accuracy of an estimate can be measured only by comparing it to some objective fact, and such facts do not exist in the case of probabilities. This is why experts who study risk intelligence usually prefer to speak of "well calibrated" probability estimates rather than of accurate ones. A more precise definition of risk intelligence would therefore be: the ability to provide well calibrated probability estimates. We'll look at how to measure calibration later in this chapter, when I discuss how risk intelligence tests work.

24 according to Aristotle: Aristotle, *Nichomachean Ethics*, ed. Roger Crisp (Cambridge, England: Cambridge University Press, 2000).

24 "No problem": Scott Plous, *The Psychology of Judgment and Decision Making* (New York: McGraw-Hill, 1993), 217.

25 David Apgar, for example: David Apgar, *Risk Intelligence: Learning to Manage What We Don't Know* (Cambridge, Mass.: Harvard Business School Press, 2006), 67.

25 "the ability to effectively distinguish": Cited in Erick Krell, "RiskChat: What Is Risk Intelligence?," June 21, 2010, http://businessfinancemag.com/article/riskchat-what-risk-intelligence-0621; see also Frederick Funston and Stephen Wagner, *Surviving and Thriving in Uncertainty: Creating the Risk Intelligent Enterprise* (New York: Wiley, 2010).

26 absolutely sure: To be more precise, you don't have to be *absolutely* certain to use the 100 percent category, you just have to be more than 95 percent sure. Since the test only allows you to estimate probabilities in increments of 10 percent, the 100 percent category covers the range from 95 percent to 100 percent, and the 90 percent category covers the range from 85 percent to 95 percent.

26 website will calculate: Full details about how the test is scored can be found in Appendix 1.

31 overconfident: As already noted, the terms "overconfident" and "overconfidence" are used throughout this book to refer to a cognitive phenomenon and not to feelings of self-esteem. Even with this proviso, there is room for some ambiguity. Don Moore and Paul Healy argue that research in this area has been hampered by conflicting definitions of overconfidence and distinguish three main senses in which it is used:

(1) overestimating one's ability to perform various tasks, (2) overestimating one's ability relative to that of other people, and (3) excessive certainty regarding the accuracy of one's beliefs. Whenever I use the term "overconfidence" in this book, I always mean it in the third sense. That is, when I say people are overconfident (or underconfident) I mean that they express more (or less) certainty than is strictly warranted, and as a result their calibration curves are biased in systematic ways (see Figure 9 in chapter 3). See Don Moore and Paul Healy, "The Trouble with Overconfidence," *Psychological Review* 115, no. 2 (2008): 502–517.

34   the first study: Allan Murphy and Robert Winkler, "Reliability of Subjective Probability Forecasts of Precipitation and Temperature," *Journal of the Royal Statistical Society, Series C (Applied Statistics)* 26, no. 1 (1977): 41–47.

34   the second study: Jay Christensen-Szalanski and James Bushyhead, "Physicians' Use of Probabilistic Information in a Real Clinical Setting," *Journal of Experimental Psychology: Human Perception and Performance* 7, no. 4 (1981): 928–935.

36   several factors favor: Sarah Lichtenstein, Baruch Fischhoff, and Lawrence Phillips, "Calibration of Probabilities: The State of the Art to 1980," in *Judgement Under Uncertainty: Heuristics and Biases*, ed. Daniel Kahneman, Paul Slovic, and Amos Tversky (Cambridge, England: Cambridge University Press, 1982), 306–334; see p. 322.

37   A 1987 study: Gideon Keren, "Facing Uncertainty in the Game of Bridge: A Calibration Study," *Organizational Behavior and Human Decision Processes* 39 (1987): 98–114.

38   he or she will make a bid: There are exceptions to this rule of thumb. Expert players sometimes bid a contract they know they probably won't make in the hope that the points they lose this way will be fewer than the other team would win by making the final bid. This is quite different, of course, from overconfidence; expert players make such bids in full awareness of the low probability of winning the contract. Their risk intelligence is still apparent in their private evaluations of the chance of winning.

38   According to my calculations: I calculated RQ scores for the expert and amateur bridge players using the scoring algorithm described in Appendix 1. I measured the residuals by blowing up a copy of the graph in Keren's paper (reproduced as Figure 5) and using a ruler. The figures I arrived at were as follows:

	Experts		Amateurs	
Category	Estimates	Residuals	Estimates	Residuals
0%	39	3	37	19
10%	28	4	9	11
20%	29	1	13	9
30%	35	9	13	13
40%	43	1	29	4
50%	53	1	105	5
60%	84	14	48	7
70%	56	14	63	11
80%	53	0	87	10
90%	37	2	71	20
100%	11	0	196	22

40 Royal Dutch Shell introduced: J. Edward Russo and Paul Schoemaker, "Managing Overconfidence," *Sloan Management Review* 33, no. 2 (Winter 1992): 7–17.

43 scoring methods are deeply flawed: Douglas Hubbard and Dylan Evans, "Problems with Scoring Methods and Ordinal Scales in Risk Assessment," *IBM Journal of Research and Development* 54, no. 3 (2010): 2:1–2:10.

44 correcting for "optimism bias": Bent Flyvbjerg, *Procedures for Dealing with Optimism Bias in Transport Planning* (London: British Department for Transport, 2004).

CHAPTER 3: INTO THE TWILIGHT ZONE

50 ambiguity intolerance: Sebastien Grenier, Anne-Marie Barrette, and Robert Ladouceur, "Intolerance of Uncertainty and Intolerance of Ambiguity: Similarities and Differences," *Personality and Individual Differences* 39, no. 3 (2005): 593–600. This concept should not be confused with the much more technical notion of ambiguity *aversion* proposed by Daniel Ellsberg in his seminal paper "Risk, Ambiguity, and the Savage Axioms," *The Quarterly Journal of Economics* 75, no. 4 (1961): 643–669.

50 dog-cat test: Else Frenkel-Brunswik, "Tolerance Towards Ambiguity as a Personality Variable," *American Psychologist* 3 (1949): 268.

50 a sixteen-item scale: Stanley Budner, "Intolerance of Ambiguity as a Personality Variable," *Journal of Personality* 30, no. 1 (1962): 29–50.

50 Others have proposed: Grenier, Barrette, and Ladouceur, "Intolerance of Uncertainty and Intolerance of Ambiguity."

51 AsiaOne News blamed: "Tokyo Stocks Down 0.15 Percent on Nuclear Uncertainty," *AsiaOne News*, March 24, 2011, http://news.asiaone .com/News/Latestpercent2BNews/Business/Story/A1Story20110324-269866 .html.

51 BP and Caltex cited: "Petrol Prices in NZ Rise amid Global Uncertainty," *TVNZ Online*, March 22, 2011, http://tvnz.co.nz/national -news/petrol-prices-in-nz-rise-amid-global-uncertainty-4078446.

51 Whether uncertainty: G. I., "Of Red Tape and Recessions," *The Economist Free Exchange Blog*, September 6, 2011, www.economist.com/ blogs/freeexchange/2011/09/regulation.

53 need for closure: Donna Webster and Arie Kruglanski, "Individual Differences in Need for Cognitive Closure," *Journal of Personality and Social Psychology* 67, no. 6 (1994): 1049–1062.

53 can be measured: Steven Neuberg, T. Nicole Judice, and Stephen West, "What the Need for Closure Scale Measures and What It Does Not: Toward Differentiating Among Related Epistemic Motives," *Journal of Personality and Social Psychology* 72, no. 6 (1997): 1396–1412.

57 "worst-case thinking": Bruce Schneier, "Worst-Case Thinking," Schneier on Security (blog), May 13, 2010, www.schneier.com/blog/ archives/2010/05/worst-case_thin.html.

57 "If there's a 1 percent": Ron Suskind, *The One Percent Doctrine: Deep Inside America's Pursuit of Its Enemies Since 9/11* (New York: Simon & Schuster, 2006).

57 "Every decision has costs": Bruce Schneier, "Worst-Case Thinking," Schneier on Security (blog), May 13, 2010, www.schneier .com/blog/archives/2010/05/worst-case_thin.html.

58 "there will either be": John Kemeny, *Report of the President's Commission on the Accident at Three Mile Island* (Washington, DC, 1979), 12, www.threemileisland.org/downloads/188.pdf.

58 originally required discussion: Cass Sunstein and Richard Zeckhauser, "Overreaction to Fearsome Risks," *Environmental and Resource Economics* 48, no. 3 (2011): 435–449.

58 "Any fear that would make": Bruce Schneier, "Worst-Case

Thinking Makes Us Nuts, Not Safe," CNN Website, May 12, 2010, http://edition.cnn.com/2010/OPINION/05/12/schneier.worst.case .thinking/.

59 "Movie-Plot Threat Contest": Bruce Schneier, "Announcing: Movie-Plot Threat Contest," Schneier on Security (blog), April 1, 2006, www.schneier.com/blog/archives/2006/04/announcing_movi.html.

59 "We all do it": Bruce Schneier, "Terrorists Don't Do Movie Plots," Wired.com, September 8, 2005, www.wired.com/politics/security/ commentary/securitymatters/2005/09/68789.

59 in his challenging book: Frank Furedi, *Paranoid Parenting: Why Ignoring the Experts May Be Best for Your Child* (Chicago: Chicago Review Press, 2002).

60 "fever phobia": Barton Schmitt, "Fever Phobia: Misconceptions of Parents About Fever," *American Journal of Diseases of Children* 134 (1980): 176–181.

61 attitudes had not changed: Michael Crocetti, Nooshi Moghbeli, and Janet Serwint, "Fever Phobia Revisited: Have Parental Misconceptions About Fever Changed in 20 Years?," *Pediatrics* 107, no. 6 (2001): 1241–1246.

62 subsequently dropped: Associated Press, "Will Autism Fraud Report Be a Vaccine Booster?," *The Washington Times*, January 6, 2011, www.washingtontimes.com/news/2011/jan/6/will-autism-fraud-report -be-a-vaccine-booster/.

63 events of 9/11 were orchestrated: See Thierry Meyssan, *9/11: The Big Lie* (Chatou: Editions Carnot, 2003), and Michael Meacher, "This War On Terrorism Is Bogus," *The Guardian*, September 6, 2003, www .guardian.co.uk/politics/2003/sep/06/september11.iraq.

63 secret cabal of Jews: This theory was popularized by *The Protocols of the Elders of Zion*, which purports to be the minutes of a late-nineteenth-century meeting of Jewish leaders discussing their plans for world domination. It was exposed as a fake by *The Times* in 1921, and subsequent investigations have suggested that it was originally produced in Russia between 1897 and 1903 as a piece of anti-Semitic propaganda. It never ceases to amaze me how many otherwise intelligent people believe this rubbish; it remains, for example, one of the most widely read books in the Arab world, and its authenticity has even been endorsed by a number of Arab regimes.

65 interview with John Humphrys: A full transcript of the interview is available online at http://news.bbc.co.uk/today/hi/today/ newsid_9309000/9309320.stm.

66 Nebraska Standard: O'Connor decision in Victor v. Nebraska, 114 S. Ct., 1239 (1994), cited in Katie Evans, David Osthus, and Ryan Spurrier, "Distributions of Interest for Quantifying Reasonable Doubt and Their Applications" (research paper, Valparaiso University, 2006), www.valpo.edu/mcs/pdf/ReasonableDoubtFinal.pdf.

67 secular fundamentalist: Dylan Evans, "Secular Fundamentalism," in *Debating Humanism*, ed. Dolan Cummings (Exeter, England: Societas Imprint Academic, 2006), 12–21. See also Dylan Evans, "The 21st Century Atheist," *The Guardian*, May 2, 2005.

67 *The God Delusion*: Richard Dawkins, *The God Delusion* (London: Bantam Press, 2006), 73.

68 somewhat less: One can disagree about the precise values of the cutoff points. A friend who wishes to remain anonymous told me he would regard 5 to 95 percent as indicating a "play-it-safe" believer (don't violate most of the commandments most of the time unless you really want to). But the verbal labels are not the point. I think we would be better off abandoning them altogether and simply saying how likely we think it is that a god exists.

68 "describe herself": Jack Smart, "Atheism and Agnosticism," *Stanford Encyclopedia of Philosophy*, 2004, http://plato.stanford.edu/entries/atheism-agnosticism/.

68 "I just took it": This comment was posted online in response to a brief piece about my research in *The Economist*'s Cassandra blog published on January 21, 2011; see www.economist.com/blogs/theworldin2011/2011/01/predictions_and_risk_intelligence.

CHAPTER 4: TRICKS OF THE MIND

73 Optimism bias: Tali Sharot, *The Optimism Bias: A Tour of the Irrationally Positive Brain* (New York: Pantheon Books, 2011).

73 availability heuristic: Amos Tversky and Daniel Kahneman, "Availability: A Heuristic for Judging Frequency and Probability," *Cognitive Psychology* 5, no. 2 (1973): 207–232.

73 media reporting in Scotland: Alasdair Forsyth, "Distorted? A Quantitative Exploration of Drug Fatality Reports in the Popular Press," *The International Journal of Drug Policy* 12, no. 5 (2001): 435–453.

74 equine accidents: see David Nutt, "Equasy: An Overlooked Addiction with Implications for the Current Debate on Drug Harms," *Journal of Psychopharmacology* 23, no. 1 (2009): 3–5.

74 these experiments show: Derek Koehler, "Explanation,

Imagination, and Confidence in Judgment," *Psychological Bulletin* 110, no. 3 (1991): 499–519.

74   winning the election: John Carroll, "The Effect of Imagining an Event on Expectations for the Event: An Interpretation in Terms of the Availability Heuristic," *Journal of Experimental Social Psychology* 14, no. 1 (1978): 88–96.

75   In one study: Maryanne Garry, Charles Manning, and Elizabeth Loftus, "Imagination Inflation: Imagining a Childhood Event Inflates Confidence That It Occurred," *Psychonomic Bulletin and Review 3*, no. 2 (1996): 208–214.

75   Increased confidence was found: This may be due to the repetition effect; merely asking twice about a purported fact seems to make people more confident that it is true. See Hal Arkes, Catherine Hackett, and Larry Boehm, "The Generality of the Relation Between Familiarity and Judged Validity," *Journal of Behavioral Decision Making 2*, no. 2 (1989): 81–94.

76   hackers could figure out: "Rethinking Cybersecurity," *C4ISR Journal*, May 12, 2011, www.c4isrjournal.com/story.php?F=6185369.

77   examples of optimism bias: David Armor and Shelley Taylor, "When Predictions Fail: The Dilemma of Unrealistic Optimism," in *Heuristics and Biases: The Psychology of Intuitive Judgment*, ed. Thomas Gilovich, Dale Griffin, and Daniel Kahneman (Cambridge, England: Cambridge University Press, 2002), 334–347.

78   when people are depressed: Lauren Alloy and Lyn Abramson, "Judgment Of Contingency In Depressed And Nondepressed Students: Sadder But Wiser?," *Journal of Experimental Psychology: General* 108, no. 4 (1979): 441–485.

78   we'll be luckier: Neil Weinstein, "Unrealistic Optimism About Future Life Events," *Journal of Personality and Social Psychology* 39, no. 5 (1980): 806–820.

78   "not pessimistic enough": David Dunning and Amber Story, "Depression, Realism, and the Overconfidence Effect: Are the Sadder Wiser When Predicting Future Actions and Events?," *Journal of Personality and Social Psychology* 61, no. 4 (1991): 521–532.

78   his excellent book: Robert Sloan, *Don't Blame the Shorts: Why Short Sellers Are Always Blamed for Market Crashes and How History Is Repeating Itself* (New York: McGraw-Hill, 2009).

79   "appraisers should": HM Treasury, *The Green Book: Appraisal and Evaluation in Central Government* (London: Stationery Office, 2003), www.hm-treasury.gov.uk/d/green_book_complete.pdf, 85.

79   optimism bias uplifts: Bent Flyvbjerg in association with Cowi, *Procedures for Dealing with Optimism Bias in Transport Planning: Guidance Document* (London: British Department for Transport, 2004).

80   this particular episode: Episode 2 of season 2.

80   "Downing Street memo": The memo is available online on various sites, including http://downingstreetmemo.com/memos.html.

80   "September Dossier": "Iraq's Weapons of Mass Destruction: The Assessment of the British Government" (London: Stationery Office, 2002), www.fco.gov.uk/resources/en/pdf/pdf3/fco_iraqdossier.

81   profoundly secret: This point is well made in Anthony Glees and Philip Davies, *Spinning the Spies: Intelligence, Open Government and the Hutton Inquiry* (London: Social Affairs Unit, 2004), 11–13.

81   "sexing up": We have the BBC journalist Andrew Gilligan to thank for popularizing this vulgar expression. Gilligan claimed that the UK government had published statements about Iraqi WMD that it knew to be false, and exaggerated ("sexed up") the information that was available. A subsequent inquiry conducted by Lord Hutton cast serious doubt on Gilligan's account. As Anthony Glees and Philip Davies observed, it would seem that Gilligan was guilty of the very charges he had leveled at the politicians: "making things up, gilding the lily and sacrificing accuracy for effect in order to put the desired spin on the story." See Glees and Davies, *Spinning the Spies*, 9. Gilligan is by no means the only journalist with a log in his eye; many others also wrote with passionate conviction about decisions and events regarding which they knew very little. Ironically, some US journalists lambasted those planning the invasion for being overconfident and arrogant.

81   "the real fault lay": Douglas Murray, *Neoconservatism: Why We Need It* (New York: Encounter Books, 2006), 131.

81   Curveball confessed: Martin Chulov and Helen Pidd, "Defector Who Triggered War on Iraq Admits: 'I Lied About WMD,'" *The Guardian*, February 16, 2011.

82   Colin Powell relied heavily: Powell would later blame others for failing to warn him about the unreliability of the intelligence sources. "There were some people in the intelligence community," he told Barbara Walters of ABC News in 2005, "who knew at that time that some of these sources were not good, and shouldn't be relied upon, and they didn't speak up. That devastated me." (Quoted in Steven Weisman, "Powell Calls His UN Speech a Lasting Blot on His Record," *The New York Times*, September 9, 2005.) This is disingenuous; did Powell really expect lower-ranking intelligence officials to go above the head of the director of the

CIA and communicate their doubts directly to the secretary of state? The intelligence officers themselves had already hedged the information from Janabi with multiple caveats and probably assumed that these caveats had been passed on to Powell. It is unlikely that the failure to pass on the caveats was due to deliberate deception on the part of any individual; as Donald Rumsfeld would later put it, "Powell was not duped or misled by anybody, nor did he lie about Saddam's suspected WMD stockpiles. The President did not lie. The Vice President did not lie. Tenet did not lie. Rice did not lie. I did not lie. The Congress did not lie. The far less dramatic truth is that we were wrong." (*Known and Unknown: A Memoir* [New York: Sentinel, 2011], 449). The refusal of some antiwar protesters even to consider this possibility is a far better example of overconfidence than Powell's mistake. When the British activist Tariq Ali whipped up protesters by calling the British prime minister a "Blair-faced liar," he was clearly guilty of the mind-reading illusion that is discussed later in this chapter.

82 Dale Griffin and Amos Tversky: Dale Griffin and Amos Tversky, "The Weighing of Evidence and the Determinants of Confidence," *Cognitive Psychology* 24 (1992): 411–435.

83 the sleeper effect: Carl Hovland and Walter Weiss, "The Influence of Source Credibility on Communication Effectiveness," *Public Opinion Quarterly* 15, no. 4 (Winter 1951–52): 635–650.

84 "The human understanding": In book 1 of *Novum Organum*. See Francis Bacon, *Selected Philosophical Works*, ed. with an introduction by Rose-Mary Sargent (Indianapolis: Hackett, 1999), 97.

84 One of the most famous: Peter Wason, "On the Failure to Eliminate Hypotheses in a Conceptual Task," *Quarterly Journal of Experimental Psychology* 12, no. 3 (1960): 129–140.

85 a revealing study: Asher Koriat, Sarah Lichtenstein, and Baruch Fischhoff, "Reasons for Confidence," *Journal of Experimental Psychology: Human Learning and Memory* 6, no. 2 (1980): 107–118.

90 Eli Pariser argues: Eli Pariser, *The Filter Bubble: What the Internet Is Hiding from You* (London: Penguin, 2011).

92 first people to study hindsight bias: Baruch Fischhoff and Ruth Beyth, "I Knew It Would Happen: Remembered Probabilities of Once-Future Things," *Organizational Behavior and Human Performance* 13, no. 1 (1975): 1–16.

93 a study of 705 people: Gavin Cassar and Justin Craig, "An Investigation of Hindsight Bias in Nascent Venture Activity," *Journal of Business Venturing* 24, no. 2 (2009): 149–164.

93 Baruch Fischhoff wondered: Baruch Fischhoff, "An Early History of Hindsight Research," *Social Cognition* 25, no. 1 (2007): 10–13.

93 *Being Wrong*: Kathryn Schulz, *Being Wrong: Adventures in the Margin of Error* (London: Portobello Books, 2010), 19–20.

96 "A lot of different signs": Cited in Dina Temple-Raston, "Spotting Lies: Listen, Don't Look," National Public Radio, August 14, 2009, www.npr.org/templates/story/story.php?storyId=111809280.

96 "Nervousness, fear, confusion": David Simon, *Homicide: A Year on the Killing Streets* (Boston: Houghton Mifflin, 1991), 219.

96 A 1997 review: Bella DePaulo, Kelly Charlton, Harris Cooper, James Lindsay, and Laura Muhlenbruck, "The Accuracy-Confidence Correlation in the Detection of Deception," *Personality and Social Psychology Review* 1, no. 4 (1997): 346–357.

96 One of the studies: Bella DePaulo and Roger Pfeifer, "On-the-Job Experience and Skill at Detecting Deception," *Journal of Applied Social Psychology* 16, no. 3 (1986): 249–267.

97 this research is flawed: Mark Frank, Melissa Menasco, and Maureen O'Sullivan, "Human Behavior and Deception Detection," in *Wiley Handbook of Science and Technology for Homeland Security*, ed. John Voeller (Hoboken, N.J.: Wiley, 2008).

97 In one study: Saul Kassin and Christina Fong, "'I'm Innocent!': Effects of Training on Judgments of Truth and Deception in the Interrogation Room," *Law and Human Behavior* 23, no. 5 (1999): 499–515.

97 the Reid technique: John E. Reid and Associates offers training programs, seminars, and videotapes on the 9-Step Reid Technique. In the study referred to in the previous note, Kassin and Fong cite the third edition of Reid's manual of interrogation methods, Fred Inbau, John Reid, and Joseph Buckley, *Criminal Interrogation and Confessions*, 3rd ed. (Baltimore, Md.: Williams and Wilkins, 1986).

98 Friends and lovers: Geoff Thomas, Garth Fletcher, and Craig Lange, "On-Line Empathic Accuracy in Marital Interaction," *Journal of Personality and Social Psychology* 72, no. 4 (1997): 839–850.

99 A 1995 study: William Swann, David Silvera, and Carrie Proske, "On 'Knowing Your Partner': Dangerous Illusions in the Age of AIDS?," *Personal Relationships* 2 (1995): 173–186.

99 "Did she know everything": Stephen King, "A Good Marriage," in *Full Dark, No Stars* (London: Hodder & Stoughton, 2010), 259–336.

100 "illusion of transparency": Thomas Gilovich, Kenneth Savitsky, and Victoria Medvec, "The Illusion of Transparency: Biased Assessments of Others' Ability to Read One's Emotional States," *Journal of Personality and Social Psychology* 75, no. 2 (1998): 332–346.

100 "Did Porfiry wink at me": Fyodor Dostoevsky, *Crime and Punishment*, 1866, trans. Constance Garnett, Project Gutenberg ebook, www.gutenberg.org/files/2554/2554-h/2554-h.htm.

101 A study published in 1998: Gilovich, Savitsky, and Medvec, "The Illusion of Transparency."

CHAPTER 5: THE MADNESS OF CROWDS

104 war puzzle: James Fearon, "Rationalist Explanations for War," *International Organization* 49, no. 3 (1995): 379–414.

105 actually beneficial: Dominic Johnson, *Overconfidence and War: The Havoc and Glory of Positive Illusions* (Cambridge, Mass., and London: Harvard University Press, 2004). See also Dominic Johnson and James Fowler, "The Evolution of Overconfidence," *Nature* 477, no. 7364 (2011): 317–20.

107 "My first surprise": Nassim Nicholas Taleb, *The Black Swan: The Impact of the Highly Improbable* (London: Allen Lane, 2007), 126.

107 BLIRT: William Swann and Peter Rentfrow, "Blirtatiousness: Cognitive, Behavioral, and Physiological Consequences of Rapid Responding," *Journal of Personality and Social Psychology* 81, no. 6 (2001): 1160–1175.

108 "Early in the semester": Cited in Robin Gerrow, "Utterly Blirtatious! Your Verbal Reactions can Affect Personal Relationships and Health," September 2003, www.utexas.edu/features/archive/2003/blirt .html.

109 an influential book: Charles MacKay, *Memoirs of Extraordinary Popular Delusions and the Madness of Crowds* (London: Richard Bentley, 1841).

109 Mackay may have exaggerated: See Peter Garber, "Famous First Bubbles," *Journal of Economic Perspectives* 4, no. 2 (Spring, 1990): 35–54, and Mike Dash, *Tulipomania: The Story of the World's Most Coveted Flower & the Extraordinary Passions It Aroused* (London: Victor Gollancz, 1999).

110 "the wisdom of crowds": James Surowiecki, *The Wisdom of Crowds: Why the Many Are Smarter Than the Few* (London: Little, Brown, 2004).

111 his 2010 book: Michael Lewis, *The Big Short: Inside the Doomsday Machine* (New York: Norton, 2010).

112 The stats: Tobias Moskowitz and Jon Wertheim, *Scorecasting: The Hidden Influences Behind How Sports Are Played and Games Are Won* (New York: Crown Archetype, 2011): 46–50.

113 "Worldly wisdom": John Maynard Keynes, *The General Theory of Employment, Interest and Money* (Basingstoke, England: Palgrave Macmillan, 1936), 158.

113 "This static, ambiguous": Raphael Sagarin, Candace Alcorta, Scott Atran, Daniel Blumstein, Gregory Dietl, Michael Hochberg, Dominic Johnson, Simon Levin, Elizabeth Madin, Joshua Madin, Elizabeth Prescott, Richard Sosis, Terence Taylor, John Tooby, and Geerat Vermeij, "Decentralize, Adapt and Cooperate," *Nature* 465 (May 20, 2010): 292–293.

116 A 1998 study: Wibecke Brun and Karl Teigen, "Verbal Probabilities: Ambiguous, Context-Dependent, or Both?," *Organizational Behavior and Human Decision Processes* 41, no. 3 (1998): 390–404.

116 gambling on basketball: Ido Erev and Brent Cohen, "Verbal Versus Numerical Probabilities: Efficiency, Biases, and the Preference Paradox," *Organizational Behavior and Human Decision Processes* 45, no. 1 (1990): 1–18.

117 Research published in 2009: David Budescu, Stephen Broomell, and Han-Hui Por, "Improving Communication of Uncertainty in the Reports of the Intergovernmental Panel on Climate Change," *Psychological Science* 20, no. 3 (2009): 299–308.

117 an intelligence analyst: Scott Barclay, Rex Brown, Cameron Peterson, Lawrence Phillips and Judith Selvidge, *Handbook for Decision Analysis: Technical Report Tr-77-6-30 (DARPA)* (McLean, VA: Decisions and Designs, 1977), 66.

118 Kent was alarmed: Sherman Kent, "Words of Estimative Probability," in Donald P. Steury, ed., *Sherman Kent and the Board of National Estimates: Collected Essays* (Washington, DC: CIA Center for the Study of Intelligence, 1994), 151–166.

118 common occurrence: Richards Heuer, *Psychology of Intelligence Analysis* (Washington, DC: CIA Center for the Study of Intelligence, 1999), 154.

118 CRAs: I use "CRAs" as an abbreviation for "credit-rating agencies," but the regulatory term for those organizations is "nationally recognized statistical rating organizations," abbreviated NRSRO.

118 In order to make some sense: Michael Lewis, *The Big Short: Inside the Doomsday Machine* (Norton: New York, 2010), 51, fn.

119   TABLE 2: The table is taken from Donald MacKenzie, "The Credit Crisis as a Problem in the Sociology of Knowledge" (unpublished manuscript). MacKenzie attributes the data in this table to two papers. The first is Mark Adelson, "Bond Rating Confusion" (New York: Nomura Securities, 2006), available at www.securitization.net/pdf/Nomura/ Nomura_Bond_Rating_Confusion_Update.pdf. The second paper is by Erkan Erturk and Thoma Gillis, "Structured Finance Rating Transition and Default Update as of July 24, 2009" (New York: Standard & Poor's, 2009), available at www2.standardandpoors.com.

122   A 1971 study: Rita Simon and Linda Mahon, "Quantifying Burdens of Proof: A View from the Bench, the Jury, and the Classroom," *Law and Society Review* 5, no. 3 (1971): 319–330.

123   in the 1971 study: Ibid.

123   In a separate study: Rita Simon, "Judges' Translations of Burdens of Proof into Statements of Probability," *Trial Lawyers Guide* (1969): 103–114.

123   In a third study: Rita Simon, "'Beyond a Reasonable Doubt'— An Experimental Attempt at Quantification," *Journal of Applied Behavioral Science* 6 (1970): 203–209.

CHAPTER 6: THINKING BY NUMBERS

128   probabilistic revolution: Lorenz Krüger, Lorraine Daston, Michael Heidelberger, Gerd Gigerenzer, and Mary S. Morgan, eds., *The Probabilistic Revolution*, vols. 1 and 2 (Cambridge, Mass.: MIT Press, 1987).

128   *Super Crunchers*: Ian Ayres, *Super Crunchers: Why Thinking-by-Numbers Is the New Way to Be Smart* (New York: Bantam, 2007).

129   another paper on handicapping: Ruth Bolton and Randall Chapman, "Searching for Positive Returns at the Track: A Multinomial Logit Model for Handicapping Horse Races," *Management Science* 32, no. 8 (1986): 1040–1060.

132   Network analysis: "Untangling the Social Web," *The Economist*, September 2, 2010, http://www.economist.com/node/16910031.

132   Robert Shiller: Cited in "Data Birth," *The Economist*, November 18, 2010, http://www.economist.com/node/17519706.

133   unvalidated predictive models: Richard Paul Kitching, Michael Thrusfield, and Nick Taylor, "Use and Abuse of Mathematical Models: An Illustration from the 2001 Foot and Mouth Disease Epidemic in the

United Kingdom," *Revue Scientifique et Technique* 25, no. 1 (2006): 293–311.

133   was particularly critical: Interview with Richard Paul Kitching, Channel 4 News, broadcast at 7:00 p.m. on April 21, 2001. Transcript available at www.sovereignty.org.uk/features/footnmouth/pkinter.html.

134   "Every day, Fred": Karl Teigen and Gideon Keren, "Waiting for the Bus: When Base-Rates Refuse to Be Neglected," *Cognition* 103 (2007): 337–357.

135   such puzzles can be fun: For more probability puzzles, see Frederick Mosteller, *Fifty Challenging Problems in Probability: With Solutions* (Mineola, NY: Dover, 1988), 127–281

136   "In real life": Nassim Nicholas Taleb, *The Black Swan: The Impact of the Highly Improbable* (London: Allen Lane, 2007), 127–28.

137   Ronald de Sousa has noted: Ronald de Sousa, "Epistemic Feelings," in *Epistemology and Emotions*, ed. Georg Brun, Ulvi Doguoglu, and Dominique Kuenzle (Aldershot, England: Ashgate Publishing, 2008), 185–204.

138   Other such emotions: See also Michael Gruneberg and Joseph Monks, "Feeling of Knowing and Cued Recall," *Acta Psychologica* 38, no. 4 (1974): 257–265, and Robert Burton, *On Being Certain: Believing You Are Right Even When You're Not* (New York: St. Martin's Press, 2008).

138   depends on two factors: Asher Koriat, Sarah Lichtenstein, and Baruch Fischhoff, "Reasons for Confidence," *Journal of Experimental Psychology: Human Learning and Memory* 6, no. 2 (1980): 107–118. The same point is made in Gideon Keren, "Facing Uncertainty in the Game of Bridge: A Calibration Study," *Organizational Behavior and Human Decision Processes* 39 (1987): 98–114.

139   Paul Hoffman's biography: Paul Hoffman, *The Man Who Loved Only Numbers: The Story of Paul Erdős and the Search for Mathematical Truth* (New York: Hyperion, 1999).

140   "Every time a new set": David Boyle, *The Tyranny of Numbers: Why Counting Can't Make Us Happy* (London: HarperCollins, 2141), xix.

141   hazardous waste disposal: Lois Gibbs, *Love Canal: The Story Continues* (New York: New Society Publishers, 1998).

141   subjective numeracy test: Angela Fagerlin, Brian Zikmund-Fisher, Peter Ubel, Aleksandra Jankovic, Holly Derry, and Dylan Smith, "Measuring Numeracy Without a Math Test: Development of the Subjective Numeracy Scale (SNS)," *Medical Decision Making* 27, no. 5 (2007): 672–680.

142   People with poor numeracy: See Samantha Parsons and John

Bynner, *Does Numeracy Matter More?* (London: National Research and Development Centre for Adult Literacy and Numeracy, Institute of Education, University of London, 2006), www.nrdc.org.uk/publications_ details.asp?ID=16#.

CHAPTER 7: WEIGHING THE PROBABLE

145 flood warnings: Peter Webster, Jun Jian, Thomas Hopson, Carlos Hoyos, Paula Agudelo, Hai-ru Chang, Judith Curry, Robert Grossman, Timothy Palmer, and A. R. Subbiah, "Extended-Range Probabilistic Forecasts of Ganges and Brahmaputra Floods in Bangladesh," *Bulletin of the American Meteorological Society* 91, no. 11 (2010): 1493–1514.

147 exposed to probabilistic weather forecasts: Gerd Gigerenzer, Ralph Hertwig, Eva van den Broek, Barbara Fasolo, and Konstantinos V. Katsikopoulos, "A 30% Chance of Rain Tomorrow: How Does the Public Understand Probabilistic Weather Forecasts?," *Risk Analysis* 25, no. 3 (2005): 623–629.

147 Giacomo Casanova discovered: See Giacomo Casanova, *Histoire de ma vie*, ed. Francis Lacassin (Paris: Robert Laffont, 1993), Vol. 4, chaps. 4–11.

148 Kelly criterion: William Poundstone, *Fortune's Formula: The Untold Story of the Scientific Betting System That Beat the Casinos and Wall Street* (New York: Hill & Wang, 2005).

149 Jacob Pastor: personal communication.

151 upper and lower bounds: see Peter Walley, *Statistical Reasoning with Imprecise Probabilities* (London: Chapman and Hall, 1991).

151 a fundamental misunderstanding: My criticisms of imprecise probabilities are all predicated on a subjectivist approach to probabilities (see note to page 23, above).

512 A 2010 study: Nathan Dieckmann, Robert Mauro, and Paul Slovic, "The Effects of Presenting Imprecise Probabilities in Intelligence Forecasts," *Risk Analysis* 30, no. 6 (2010): 987–1001.

154 This oversensitivity: Other explanations of the favorite–long shot bias have been proposed that do not involve any bias in estimating probabilities. However, Erik Snowberg and Justin Wolfers have provided convincing evidence that probability estimation bias is the correct explanation. See their article "Explaining the Favourite–Long Shot Bias:

Is It Risk-Love or Misperceptions?," *Journal of Political Economy* 118, no. 4 (2010): 723–746.

154 first noted: Richard Griffith, "Odds Adjustments by American Horse-race Bettors," *American Journal of Psychology* 62 (1949): 290–294.

155 a murder mystery: Lori Robinson and Reid Hastie, "Revision of Beliefs When a Hypothesis Is Eliminated from Consideration," *Journal of Experimental Psychology: Human Perception and Performance* 11, no. 4 (1985): 443–456.

162 the opposite fallacy: For example, people tend to overweight base rates and ignore case information when solving the "bus problem" described in chapter 6.

162 the fallacy disappeared: Thomas Griffiths and Joshua Tenenbaum, "Optimal Predictions in Everyday Cognition," *Psychological Science* 17, no. 9 (2006): 767–773.

165 "planning bias": Daniel Kahneman and Amos Tversky, "Intuitive Prediction: Biases and Corrective Procedures," *TIMS Studies in the Management Sciences* 12 (1979): 313–327.

CHAPTER 8: HOW TO GAMBLE AND WIN

169 The most important book: John von Neumann and Oskar Morgenstern, *Theory of Games and Economic Behavior* (Princeton, N.J.: Princeton University Press, 1944).

169 expected value: Astute readers will notice that I have used the terms "expected value" and "expected utility" interchangeably. I did so because I judged that a discussion of the distinction between these concepts would have entailed a long digression that might not be of interest to the general reader.

173 hit the headlines: Patrick Barkham, "Hannah's Choice," *The Guardian*, November 12, 2008, www.guardian.co.uk/society/2008/nov/12/health-child-protection.

174 all the good things: In the previous example, which involved calculating the expected utility of asking a person out on a date, we only considered one potential benefit and one potential cost. The analysis of Hannah's choice is more complex because we explicitly consider multiple criteria. A whole field of research, known as multiple criteria decision analysis (MCDA), has developed to deal with the complexities that arise when considering more than one objective. The main problem is that different criteria may conflict, so we need to make trade-offs; the cheapest car may not be the most comfortable, nor the safest. See Ralph Keeney and Howard Raiffa, *Decisions with Multiple Objectives: Preferences and Value Tradeoffs* (New York: Wiley, 1976; reprinted, Cambridge: Cambridge University Press, 1993).

175   changed her mind: Matthew Weaver, "Right-to-Die Teenager Hannah Jones Changes Mind About Heart Transplant," *The Guardian*, July 21, 2009, www.guardian.co.uk/uk/2009/jul/21/hannah-jones-heart -transplant. See also Kirsty Jones and Hannah Jones, *Hannah's Choice* (London: HarperTrue, 2010).

176   "As the fighting wound down": James Fallows, *Blind into Baghdad: America's War in Iraq* (New York: Vintage, 2006), 128.

176   which one?: I have chosen to assume that a decision has already been to use military force against one—and just one—of the members of the axis of evil, so this decision is a choice between three alternatives. Of course, it was not obligatory to attack anyone at all, and one could represent this decision as a four-alternative choice. One could broaden the alternatives still further, to consider options like invading Iraq later, or sending the decision to some other group, or initiating some sort of limited campaign, or invading all countries in sequence. The first task for the decision analyst is to structure the choice in the most appropriate way.

176   memo by Donald Rumsfeld: Donald Rumsfeld, "Iraq: An Illustrative List of Potential Problems to Be Considered and Addressed," declassified memo, October 15, 2002, http://library.rumsfeld.com/doclib/ sp/310/Re%20Parade%20of%20Horribles%2010-15-2002.pdf.

178   we add up: It is not strictly necessary to make all the costs and benefits additive, but it certainly simplifies the math. This simplification is, however, bought at the price of ignoring potential interactions between the various objectives. For example, the value of access to Iraqi oil and military bases in Iraq is much greater if the invasion hurts US relations with neighboring countries than if it helps them. Aaron Brown (personal communication) thinks a more realistic analysis would be obtained by spelling out scenarios and assigning an overall probability and utility to each. In a best-case scenario, for example, the invasion is successful with minimal human and financial cost, Iraqis welcome the troops and quickly set up a prosperous, democratic, and liberal society that becomes a strong US ally and a force for positive change in the Islamic world. In a worst-case scenario, the invasion is a complete disaster with massive cost and casualties, resulting in a devastated Iraq split into violent fiefdoms, including one run by Saddam Hussein and another by Osama bin Laden; the United States is humiliated both militarily and by revelation of major scandals and atrocities, and many US troops are taken prisoner. We would also list a number of intermediate possibilities. One advantage of this approach is that the outcomes can be ranked in a linear scale (possibly with more than one dimension), so you're less likely to leave something out. In the additive approach described in the text, someone might forget to include a specific possibility such as, say, that a disaffected Iraqi commits a major terrorist act against the United States. But in the scenario approach, that would just get subsumed under general bad effects of a botched invasion. Another advantage is that the scenario approach forces you to consider the extreme possibilities. Something might have a positive expected value in the additive approach, but still have significant probability of unacceptably bad outcomes.

180   various assumptions: Among the assumptions I made when assigning utility points to the potential costs and benefits of invading Iraq in Tables 3 and 4 were the following: there would be between 2,000 and 3,000 US casualties; there would be between 20,000 and 30,000 Iraqi casualties; the cost of the war would be between \$121 billion and \$1.6 trillion; the statistical value of a US soldier's life is 10 million dollars; and the statistical value of an Iraqi life is 1 million dollars (from a US perspective). To arrive at a point value for ranges, I calculated the geometric mean of the upper and lower bounds, and assigned a probability of 80 percent. In arriving at these estimates, I attempted to do so on the basis of the information available in early 2002, and to avoid hindsight bias as far as possible. I converted these estimates into US utility points by using an "exchange rate" of 1 US utility point to 10 billion dollars. It may seem heartless to put a price on a human life, but it has the virtue of keeping us consistent; it is clearly irrational to say that each life is infinitely valuable when considering abortion, but worth only \$10 when considering capital punishment.

182   anticipate likely terrorist targets: See Heather Rossoff and Richard John, "Decision Analysis by Proxy for the Rational Terrorist," *Proceedings of the 21st International Joint Conference on Artificial Intelligence* (IJCAI-09), Workshop on Quantitative Risk Analysis for Security Applications (QRASA), Pasadena, Calif., July 11–17, 2009.

183   heated debate: Jason Burke, *The 9/11 Wars* (London: Allen Lane, 2011), 151.

183   "We want to bring": quoted in Abdel Bari Atwan, *The Secret History of Al Qaeda* (Berkeley: University of California Press, 2006), 179.

184   something like this: My example is based on that in Michael

Drummond, Mark Sculpher, George Torrance, Bernie O'Brien, and Greg Stoddart, *Methods for the Economic Evaluation of Health Care Programmes*, 3rd ed. (Oxford, England: Oxford University Press, 2005), 205.

186 variety of methods: Other methods of measuring QALY weights include the use of rating scales and the "time trade-off" (TTO). The QALY weights used by NICE are largely based on a survey of around three thousand people in the United Kingdom carried out by the EuroQoL group, a consortium of researchers in Western Europe. EuroQoL used the TTO technique in this survey rather than the standard gamble. Other systems, however, such as the Health Utilities Index, do base their scoring formulae on preferences measured by the standard gamble method.

188 badly wrong: Daniel Gilbert, Elizabeth Pinel, Timothy Wilson, Stephen Blumberg, and Thalia Wheatley, "Immune Neglect: A Source of Durability Bias in Affective Forecasting," *Journal of Personality and Social Psychology* 75, no. 3 (1998): 617–638.

188 One particularly dramatic example: Marie-Aurelie Bruno, Jan Bernheim, Didier Ledoux, Frederic Pellas, Athena Demertzi, and Steven Laureys, "A Survey on Self-Assessed Well-Being in a Cohort of Chronic Locked-in Syndrome Patients: Happy Majority, Miserable Minority," *BMJ Open* (2011), doi:10.1136/bmjopen-2010-000039.

188 his famous memoir: Jean-Dominique Bauby, *The Diving Bell and the Butterfly: A Memoir of Life in Death*, trans. Jeremy Leggatt (New York: Knopf, 1997).

CHAPTER 9: KNOWING WHAT YOU KNOW

192 "There are known knowns": Donald Rumsfeld, *Known and Unknown: A Memoir* (New York: Sentinel, 2011), xiii.

194 A good illustration: Iain M. Banks, *Excession* (New York: Spectra, 1998).

194 "black swans": Nassim Nicholas Taleb, *The Black Swan: The Impact of the Highly Improbable* (London: Allen Lane, 2007).

195 Dunning-Kruger effect: Justin Kruger and David Dunning, "Unskilled and Unaware of It: How Difficulties in Recognizing One's Own Incompetence Lead to Inflated Self-Assessments," *Journal of Personality and Social Psychology* 77, no. 6 (1999): 1121–1134.

196 "*The best lack all conviction*": William Butler Yeats, "The Second Coming" (1919), www.potw.org/archive/potw351.html.

198 there is a fourth category: Slavoj Žižek, "What Rumsfeld Doesn't Know That He Knows About Abu Ghraib," *In These Times*, May 21, 2004, www.inthesetimes.com/article/747/.

199 logical chains: Nick Bostrom, "In the Great Silence There Is Great Hope," commissioned for BBC Radio 3, *The Essay*, 2007, www .nickbostrom.com/papers/fermi.pdf.

199 "the Great Filter": Nick Bostrom, "Where Are They?," *Technology Review*, May–June 2008, www.technologyreview.com/Infotech/20569/. The idea of a Great Filter was first proposed by the American economist Robin Hanson in 1996 as a solution to the so-called Fermi paradox. In 1950, while discussing the possibility of intelligent aliens, the physicist Enrico Fermi asked, "Where are they?" He then made a series of rapid calculations using estimated figures and concluded that Earth should have been visited long ago and many times over. Hanson argued that the failure to find any extraterrestrial civilizations in the observable universe implies that something must be wrong with Fermi's reasoning. There must be, in other words, some Great Filter that acts to reduce the great number of sites where intelligent life might arise to the tiny number of intelligent species actually observed (currently just one: human).

201 "local thinking": Nicola Gennaioli and Andrei Shleifer, "What Comes to Mind," *The Quarterly Journal of Economics* 125, no. 4 (2010): 1399–1433.

202 how many piano tuners: See Lawrence Weinstein and John Adam, *Guesstimation: Solving the World's Problems on the Back of a Cocktail Napkin* (Princeton, N.J., and Oxford, England: Princeton University Press, 2008), 7–9. This book contains lots of Fermi questions to practice on, and guides you through the solutions.

203 How long a hot dog: This example is taken from ibid., 73–74.

204 Coronation Street: I owe this example to my friend Nic Wilson, whose skillful arguments helped me hone my thinking about the kind of estimation problems I discuss in this chapter.

205 "Before the war": James Fallows, *Blind into Baghdad: America's War in Iraq* (New York: Vintage, 2006), 64–65.

207 seemed to concur: Paul Krugman, "Listening to Mahathir," *New York Times*, October 21, 2003, www.nytimes.com/2003/10/21/ opinion/listening-to-mahathir.html.

207 When a harvest: Victor Niederhoffer, "The Speculator as Hero," *Wall Street Journal*, February 10, 1989, www.dailyspeculations .com/vic/spec_as_hero.html.

209   Niccolò Machiavelli claimed: Niccolò Machiavelli, *The Prince*, trans. W. K. Marriott and ed. Randy Dillon (Plano, Tex.: Veroglyphic Publishing, 2009), 78.

210   Ian Hacking argued: Ian Hacking, *The Taming of Chance* (Cambridge, England: Cambridge University Press, 1990).

210   this trend has now reached: Frank Furedi, *Paranoid Parenting: Why Ignoring the Experts May Be Best for Your Child* (Chicago: Chicago Review Press, 2002).

210   "The race is not": Damon Runyon, *More Than Somewhat* (London: Constable, 1937). The reference is to Ecclesiastes 9:11: "I returned, and saw under the sun, that the race is not to the swift, nor the battle to the strong, neither yet bread to the wise, nor yet riches to men of understanding, nor yet favour to men of skill; but time and chance happeneth to them all."

APPENDIX 1: RISK INTELLIGENCE TEST

219   Find the square: This final step has the effect of stretching out the upper end of the risk intelligence scale and compressing the lower end. This is useful because the lower range of values is rarely used, and by spreading out the higher scores it is easier to detect the smaller (but more difficult) gains in RQ among those who already have high levels of risk intelligence.

221   Brier score: Glenn Brier, "Verification of Forecasts Expressed in Terms of Probability," *Monthly Weather Review* 78, no. 1 (1950): 1–3.

APPENDIX 2: PERSONAL PREDICTION TEST

226   *vague concepts*: See Kees van Deemter, *Not Exactly: In Praise of Vagueness* (Oxford, England: Oxford University Press, 2010).

INDEX

Page numbers in *italics* refer to figures and tables.

NOTE ON THE AUTHOR

Dylan Evans is the author of several critically acclaimed books, including *Emotion: The Science of Sentiment* (Oxford University Press, 2001) and *Placebo: The Belief Effect* (Harper-Collins, 2003). He has a PhD in philosophy from the London School of Economics and is the founder of Projection Point, a company that designs risk intelligence training programs for corporate clients. He writes regularly for *The Huffington Post* and often appears on BBC Radio.